Colonialism and Social Theory

For the Uncle Rabbit Social Club

Colonialism and Modern Social Theory

Gurminder K. Bhambra
and John Holmwood

polity

First published in 2021 by Polity Press

Reprinted 2021, 2022

Polity Press
65 Bridge Street
Cambridge CB2 1UR, UK

Polity Press
101 Station Landing
Suite 300
Medford, MA 02155, USA

ISBN-13: 978-1-5095-4129-4
ISBN-13: 978-1-5095-4130-0(pb)

A catalogue record for this book is available from the British Library.

Typeset in 10.5 on 12pt Sabon
by Fakenham Prepress Solutions, Fakenham, Norfolk NR21 8NL
Printed and bound in Great Britain by TJ Books Limited, Padstow

The publisher has used its best endeavours to ensure that the URLs for external
websites referred to in this book are correct and active at the time of going to
press. However, the publisher has no responsibility for the websites and can make
no guarantee that a site will remain live or that the content is or will remain
appropriate.

Every effort has been made to trace all copyright holders, but if any have been
overlooked the publisher will be pleased to include any necessary credits in any
subsequent reprint or edition.

For further information on Polity, visit our website:
politybooks.com

Contents

Preface and Acknowledgements   vii

**Introduction: Colonialism, Historiography, and Modern
    Social Theory**   1
  The Idea of Modern Society   4
  Empires and European Colonialism   6
  Contemporary Sociology and the Construction of Its Canons   15
  Decolonizing European Social Theory   21

1. Hobbes to Hegel: Europe and Its Others   25
  Private Property and Possession in Early Liberal Thought   26
  Hobbes: The States of Nature and of Society   29
  Locke: Property and Self-Determination   32
  Stadial Theory and the Idea of Progress   38
  Hegel and the Master–Slave Relation   46
  Conclusion   50

2. Tocqueville: From America to Algeria   52
  Between Aristocratic and Democratic Rule   54
  The New (Settler Colonial) Nation and Its Three Races   65
  The Haitian Revolution   71
  Slavery and Abolition   75
  On Algeria   78
  Conclusion   80

3. Marx: Colonialism, Capitalism, and Class   82
  From Estates to Classes   84

Contents

The Critique of Modern Society 87
The Capitalist Mode of Production 95
The Real Subordination of Labour 102
Class Struggle and Politics 105
Conclusion 110

4. **Weber: Religion, Nation, and Empire** 112
Capitalism and Social Structure 115
The Spirit of Capitalism, the Spirit of Freedom .. 119
The Modern State 125
A Methodology for Social Science? 130
Conclusion 139

5. **Durkheim: Modernity and Community** 141
Milieu, Sociology, and Social Reform 145
Method 148
Types of Solidarity 155
Modern Community and Its Discontents 160
Moral Individualism, Nationalism, and the Question of
    Religion 168
Conclusion 175

6. **Du Bois: Addressing the Colour Line** 177
Colour Prejudice 179
Double Consciousness, Domination, and Equality .. 185
Black Reconstruction 191
The Colour Line and Colonialism 197
Race, Caste, and Class 202
Conclusion 205

Conclusion: The Fictions of Modern Social Theory .. 207

Notes 216
Bibliography 230
Index 251

Preface and Acknowledgements

In this book we discuss modern social theory in the context of the history of European colonialism and the construction of the United States as a nation with a 'manifest destiny' across the continent. The dominant accounts of modernity, which encompass ideas of liberty, democracy, and progress, are strongly determined by these events. Colonialism is largely absent from these understandings, yet it haunts everyday life in the self-defined centres of modernity. It forms the unacknowledged context of the 'migrant crisis' in Europe and of populist ressentiment and rejections of multiculturalism.

We came to write this book after a period of research leave in the United States in 2014–15. This coincided with celebrations of fifty years since the passing of the Voting Rights Act in the United States and an increasing recognition that, rather than having been built upon, many of the gains of this period were being dismantled. Black Lives Matter had recently emerged as a distinctive new protest movement – new, that is, to those unfamiliar with the facts of what Michelle Alexander calls 'the new Jim Crow' and resistance to it. Among our many conversations, and with the benefit of distance, we necessarily turned to the issue of how our own context in the United Kingdom was similar. The referendum on Scottish independence was under way and was making evident the fractures within Britain, fractures that would open more dramatically with the referendum to leave the European Union a couple of years later.

These events were part of everyday lived experience, yet seemed at odds with the dominant sociological sensibility. An overwhelming majority of academics supported remaining in the European Union and, in the aftermath of the vote, there was a call that they needed to reconnect with 'ordinary' citizens. A similar call was issued in the United States after the election of Donald Trump to the office of president. It is right that there should be introspection about such moments, reflection on sociology's broader failure to recognise the underlying currents and offer cogent analyses of the situation. Of course, it would have been better if these analyses had been available before the events – as the currents have been running over a long course. Just as the assumptions of economics came to be questioned after its failure to anticipate the financial crisis of 2008, so the assumptions of sociology and other social sciences are in question now.

One response is in favour of a realignment with the current flow. This is evident in calls by some in the United States and Europe to recognise the 'legitimate' claims of a white working class that has been 'left behind'. However, the apparent normalisation of these issues as being about 'class' and not about 'identity' reveals the strongest identity claim of all. After all, class issues could most easily have been addressed regardless of race and ethnicity, through inclusive social and economic policies. The focus on a special disadvantage to white workers, who were nonetheless relatively more advantaged than ethnic minority workers, indicated that the concern was less with economic disadvantage than with the inclusion of multicultural others.

Here we want to identify the social structural basis of this newly articulated identity politics and to understand how such a basis has been elided from contemporary sociology as a consequence of the conceptual frameworks bequeathed in the development of modern social theory. In none of the writers who make up the usual canon of modern social theory is there a discussion of race as central to the social structures of modernity. We trace this absence to a failure to account for the centrality of colonialism and empire within the modern world.

As we explain in the Introduction, our focus is self-consciously on European social theory and on European and US colonialism. In this sense, our book has a paradoxical quality. It answers recent appeals to 'decolonise' the curriculum by insisting on the need for a full acknowledgement of the nature of colonialism and its determining role in the construction of the modern world, including its 'metropolitan centres'. In doing so, our book does not claim that modern social theory has become irrelevant. While the concepts of sociology and social theory have been represented as universal, they embody particular experiences and epistemological claims. This limitation is an opportunity for reconstruction, to be achieved by taking the colonial context into account and by learning from others. This process is the same, both inside and outside the academy.

If, as Danielle Allen argues, you have always occupied the public space, then the demand by others to be part of that space too, and on equal terms, will seem a provocation and making room will be experienced as a loss. However, what is experienced in this way is the loss of an advantage over people who were previously excluded and dominated. In the circumstances, what needs to be done is not simply a matter of adding new voices, but one of transforming the public space so that it works for all. For example, from the perspective of Black Lives Matter, all lives do indeed matter. Yet those who argue 'all lives matter' fail to acknowledge the specific structures that maintain their own lives while damaging the lives of others. Black Lives Matter represents the self-organization of African American communities and the necessary protection of their lives. The injunction to others is to address the social structures that have made this movement necessary.

An equivalent issue in Europe is that of multicultural equality. All European empires were empirically multicultural and multireligious, but experienced no difficulty in managing the consequent differences from a position of hierarchical organization and domination. The current perception of a threat to European identity as a result of immigration fails to recognise that, in the course of colonial history, European populations moved in greater numbers and with greater effect on the populations they encountered than is the case in the course of migration *to* Europe. Those who argue that there is a national patrimony to which local citizens have a claim before any migrant others do suppress the fact that that patrimony was produced under colonial domination and extraction: it is the legacy of imperial subjects as much as of national citizens. Arguments that social rights of citizenship should be restricted do not understand how rights, when limited, become privileges. The threat to European values comes not from the outside or from multicultural others but from within, in the form of a failure to understand one's own history and its consequences for the configuration of the present.

Our approach to these issues has been shaped by conversations with colleagues and friends at the Institute for Advanced Study in Princeton. In particular, we would like to thank Danielle Allen and Didier Fassin as curators of seminars on these topics as well as our fellow participants. We would especially like to thank Sara Edenheim, Paul Gowder, Hugh Gusterson, Michael Hanchard, Gary Fine, Urs Linder, Charles M. Payne, Nicole Reinhardt, Valentin Seidler, Yuki Seidler, Cécile Stehrenberger, and Mara Viveros Vigoya. These conversations began much earlier in the United Kingdom, with Desmond King and Robbie Shilliam. They have continued and greatly enriched our understandings.

We have both taught modules on social and sociological theory over the years and thank our students, colleagues, and the institutions where we worked for the opportunity to think through these issues in a variety of contexts. Gurminder would like to thank her colleagues at the University of Sussex – in particular Buzz Harrison, Ali Kassem, Louiza Odysseos, and Anna Stavrianakis – and her colleagues in Sweden – in particular Gunlög Fur, Peo Hansen, Johan Höglund, and Stefan Jonsson. John would like to thank colleagues at the University of Nottingham – in particular Christian Karner, Roda Madziva, and James Pattison – and colleagues in Prague – Jan Balon, Radim Hladík, Jan Maršálek, and Marek Skovajsa. Thanks are also due to the Institute of Philosophy of the Czech Academy of Science and to the Czech Research Council for research funding associated with the history of sociology drawn on in the book.

We would like to thank Steve Kemp, Desmond King, Robbie Shilliam, and Andrew Wells for their close engagement with the manuscript at its various stages and for alerting us to errors and pitfalls for the removal of which we are really grateful. We would also like to thank Ipek Demir, Vicky Margree, Lucy Mayblin, William Outhwaite, and Mia Rodriguez-Salgado for their comments and suggestions for improving the manuscript. For conversations and collegial sustenance during the period of writing this manuscript, we owe a debt of gratitude to Bob Antonio, Michaela Benson, James Hampshire, Pauline von Hellerman, Zdenek Kavan, Julia McClure, Kathryn Medien, Karim Murji, Adam Seligman, and Heba Youssef.

Our editor at Polity Press, Jonathan Skerrett, has been especially supportive of the project, as has Karina Jákupsdóttir. We would also like to thank Manuela Tecusan for her close and thoughtful attention to the manuscript.

Introduction
Colonialism, Historiography, and Modern Social Theory

Modern social theory is a product of the very history it seeks to interpret and explain. Although some have presented theoretical concepts as standing outside history and, as such, as universal foundations for any understanding, this view is now significantly discredited by post-positivist philosophies of science. Theorising, like other human activities, is historically located and subject to change. It reflects its social circumstances, including the social relationships in which it is produced. Knowledge, where it is the product of privileged knowers, involves the exclusion of other knowers and marginalises their knowledges. These, then, exist as either alternative knowledges or oppositional, subaltern knowledges, outside the categories of what is presented as the mainstream. However, like Lynn Hankinson Nelson (1990), we do not see this as necessarily entailing a relativist argument. Expanding the range of knowers, we argue, is the basis for developing better understandings through dialogue and reconstruction. In this book we are seeking to address the categories that form mainstream sociology in order to reconstruct modern social theory through dialogue. We seek a more adequate account of modernity, inclusive of its otherwise disregarded legacies of colonialism, so that we can more effectively address pressing issues of the present. In this way we are seeking to reconstruct mainstream social theory rather than to dismiss it.

The argument that theoretical engagements with the world have a history applies across all disciplines, although our concerns are directed primarily at just three – sociology, politics, and history. The fact that history itself has a history is of profound significance to any understanding of social theory. The latter, as we shall see, is presented as being formed in the rise of modernity, that is, historically. Yet historical accounts of the processes attributed to modernity have themselves been subject to reinterpretation. One paradox of modern social theory as a historically formed enterprise is that it does not appear to be changed by changing historiographic accounts. Rather it relies upon a relatively unchanging view of the rise of the West, associated with the emergence of democracy, industry, and science. In this book, then, we draw upon newly understood histories associated with the recognition of colonialism and empire within the development of modern societies; and we do this with the aim of reconstructing social theory – in its European variant.

What we mean by reconstruction will become clear in the course of the book. But we should state at the outset that we are committed to criteria of coherence and explanatory rigour. One of the ways in which the categories of mainstream social theory are maintained is by arguing that there can be different orientations to social issues and that they derive from different value positions or definitions of the problem. These different orientations cannot be reconciled, but inquiries based upon them have common standards. As we shall see, these common standards are precisely what is at issue because they were formed in the course of the development of substantive theoretical claims that have been challenged. While the primary focus of this book is upon those substantive claims and how the colonial context bears upon them, we also address seemingly abstract methodological arguments, which have arisen in the context of denying the need for a more fundamental reconstruction of categories and concepts.

Theoretical development necessarily takes place through dialogue, and that dialogue is fundamentally altered by changes in the audience of social theory and its practitioners. Nelson powerfully demonstrates the significance of epistemological communities – and also their changing and overlapping natures, which are consequent upon the emergence of feminism and the inclusion of women in the academy. Feminism did not simply introduce new ways of knowing the world, it also transformed previously dominant ones, ways that had seemed secure. In this book we are arguing for a similar process with regard to colonialism and its legacy, both within modern social structures and within representations in modern European social theory.

While much postcolonial analysis is oriented towards the Middle East and South Asia (see Said 1995 [1978], Spivak 1988, Bhabha 1994) and decolonial studies focus on South America, the Caribbean, and, to a lesser extent, Africa (see Keita 2002, Mignolo 2007, Quijano 2007, Tageldin 2014, Ndlovu-Gatsheni 2015), the one part of the world most in need of such analysis is Europe itself. Europe is in urgent need of decolonisation and, paradoxically, this kind of process can happen only by taking seriously its colonial histories and by explicitly working through their contemporary manifestations. The world subjugated by Europe cannot examine issues in the present without taking into account that the past of having been colonised is central. Within Europe, however, there appears to be no recognition of a corresponding obligation (Césaire 2000 [1955]; for discussion, see Viveros-Vigoya 2020). Colonisation, it is assumed, was something that happened elsewhere – albeit at the hands of Europeans – and consequently has no perceived bearing on contemporary European politics. This is so both in terms of issues related to national polities in Europe and in terms of their relations to one another (as for example in the construction of the European Union) and to the rest of the world (Bhambra 2009).

In this book, then, we address how colonialism was the context for the particular forms and practices of knowledge associated with modern social theory as it is expressed within the 'western' academy and its canons. We draw on the understandings of scholars who write from postcolonial and decolonial perspectives, but we are not concerned here to set out the nature of their arguments. They have been discussed elsewhere (see Bhambra 2007, 2014). Rather we are concerned with the colonial entanglement of mainstream European social theory and, in particular, with those writers who have come to be regarded as figures central to it. In this sense we are engaging in a critique of the canon, but not with the purpose of either adding to it or denying it. Our purpose is to show how the canon – which we discuss below – has been used to develop concepts and categories for the understanding of modernity that elide its broader colonial context. By restoring that context, we seek to renew European social theory as an entity capable of learning from others and of contributing to general social theory, as one part of a global project.

At this point we should enter a caveat. Although European colonialism is more extensive than that exercised by Europe's northern powers, since Spain, Portugal, and Italy were colonial states too, European social theory came to be associated with northern Europe. Whereas this dominance is usually paired up with a particular sociological argument that connects Protestant Europe with capitalist modernity, we shall argue that it derives from the connection between colonialism and commercial enterprise. As already indicated, we are seeking to provide not a comprehensive account of European social thought but an account that pays heed to writers whose work is regarded as definitive for contemporary social theory.

The Idea of Modern Society

Contemporary sociology, in its Eurocentric mode, is formed around a straightforward historiography of modernity. This is a historiography that typically rests on ideas of the modern world as emerging out of processes of political and economic revolution – specifically, processes associated on the one hand with the eighteenth-century American Revolution and French Revolution and, on the other, with industrialisation, in Britain and elsewhere, in the subsequent century. These are what Robert Nisbet (1966) called 'the two revolutions'. The same historiography is seen as being underpinned by earlier cultural changes across Europe brought about by the Renaissance, the Reformation, and the scientific revolution (Bhambra 2007). Such understandings conflate Europe with modernity – and in this context the United States is treated as if it were coextensive with Europe, as one of its settler colonies. In this way they render the process of becoming modern, at least in the first instance, one of endogenous European development. At the same time, the rest of the world is regarded as external to these world-historical processes, and colonial connections are presented as insignificant to their development.

For many commentators, theoretical reflection on the processes in question takes place in two phases. The first phase would be the emergence of a distinctively European voice, associated with an eighteenth-century Enlightenment and involving reflection on religion, politics, and culture. This voice is taken to be philosophical in orientation and not to have yet developed a full sociological sensibility (Heilbron 1995). The second phase would be a development of the mid to late nineteenth century that culminates in the period of classical sociological theory associated with Weber and Durkheim.

Here a dominant sociological account of modernity comes to rest on two fundamental assumptions: *rupture* and *difference* (Bhambra 2007). A temporal rupture distinguishes a traditional, agrarian past from the modern, industrial present, and this distinction goes hand in hand with a fundamental cultural differentiation of Europe from the rest of the world – or, in the words of Stuart Hall (1992), with a separation of 'the West from the rest'. These paradigmatic assumptions have framed both the standard methodological problems raised by modern social inquiry and the explanations proposed in resolving them. It is these assumptions that we question.

While accounts of the Industrial Revolution and French Revolution – and, by implication, of modernity itself – have not remained unchanged over time, what has remained constant is the framing of the European origins and subsequent global diffusion within which these events are located. Whatever their other differences, the early sociologists believed themselves to be living through a (or perhaps *the*) great transformation in history; and they were concerned to understand how it had begun, as they wished to influence how it would be brought to the completion that, in their view, was inherent in it. Not only were others not recognised within accounts of the now canonical two revolutions, but the potential contribution of other events (and of the experiences of non-western others) to the socio-logical paradigm of modernity has rarely been considered. As Steven Seidman (1996: 314) remarks, sociology's self-conscious emergence coincided with the high point of western imperialism, and yet 'the dynamics of empire were not incorporated into the basic categories, models of explanation, and narratives of social development of the classical sociologists'.

Our argument is that modern social theory entails a *double displacement*. Empire has an earlier phase, namely colonialism. This phenomenon emerged from the fifteenth century onwards. It preceded the Enlightenment and was continuous with it. Colonialism was attributed to the European 'discovery' of new worlds and involved the appropriation of lands, their settlement, and the development of commercial trade in the resources extracted from them. The early period of colonialism, which involved the use of forced labour in mines and on plantations, is usually understood as a premodern phenomenon that is not essential to the development of modernity. This makes it easier to neglect the fact that European colonialism transformed into imperialism.

Identifying social theory with the period from 1830 onwards, then, makes it easier to normalise colonialism and to take for granted the overseas possessions of the national European states whose political structures of the rule of law, market exchange, bureaucratic administration, and political representation are proposed as part of the distinctive social and political configuration of modernity, independently of colonialism and imperialism. We shall argue instead that colonialism and imperialism are integral to modernity and not contingently related to it. Colonialism is not a manifestation of commercial enterprise in the last throes of feudalism, but is constitutive of the commercialism that would come to be seen as characteristic of modernity and integral to the development of the social and political institutions associated with it. By contrast, when empire is addressed, it is as a manifestation not of European modernity, but of the political organisation of earlier social formations. In this book we argue for the need to disentangle modern European empires from more general conceptions of empire (from before the existence of European colonial empires) and for the need to understand how modern European 'nation' states are shaped by their imperial and colonial past.

Empires and European Colonialism

For the most part, European social theory has been in denial of the colonial and imperial past of Europe and the significance of this past for how social theory has been configured. Such denial takes several forms. One is the absence of a discussion of European colonialism and imperialism and their legacies when reflecting on contemporary global social, economic, and political issues. Another, seemingly paradoxical form is the claim that we have spent too much time discussing the colonial past, that we should just move on from it and beyond any perceived need to make amends for it. A third form of denial is to argue that, in any case, empire and its typical forms of domination are by no means exclusive to Europe. By contrast, in this book we begin from a position that focuses explicitly on Europe, its colonial and imperial histories, and the ways in which these continue to shape the world. We also suggest that there was something distinctive about European empires by comparison with other forms of empire, something that does require redress. This redress would have two aspects. One concerns the policies that mitigate the inequalities that colonialism bequeathed. The other consists in a reconstruction of the categories and concepts through which modern inequalities are understood. In the present book we deal with this second aspect. While the first is materially the most important one, a major obstacle to its realisation is the failure to make the legacies of colonialism central to our understanding of modern society and its problems.

Standard histories of the emergence of the state within Europe usually regard the 1648 Treaty of Westphalia as central to the delineation and consolidation of the ideas of national sovereignty and political equality among states. In truth, the sovereignty in question was that of 'princes' and has come to be represented as national sovereignty retrospectively, once princely power was itself curtailed. The Treaty of Westphalia put an end to the Thirty Years' War between Protestant and Catholic powers in Europe – one of the many wars conducted among royal houses and their shifting alliances. It gave the contending princes sovereignty, that is, an authority that came to be associated with territorial boundaries. The key issue, however, is that, in subsequent centuries, European states did not simply exercise their sovereignty within the territorial boundaries of national states. They also exerted power and violence over territories and populations elsewhere. Sovereignty – more properly, mutual non-intervention – was to be respected, and then more in theory than in practice, only *in relation to other European powers*; it was not regarded as significant in encounters with peoples and lands beyond Europe. Indeed, as Antony Anghie (2006) argues, the doctrine of sovereignty was itself an explicit statement of the relationship between European powers and allowed the exercise of sovereignty over non-European others as an expression of that sovereignty. This explicitly legitimised, for Europeans, the terms of an imperialism that would incorporate the non-European world into the ambit of European powers – as a 'right to colonise' – at the same time as proclaiming these powers' own sovereignty and right to be inviolable.

Of course, there have been and are many different types of political system in world history. Perhaps the two dominant types associated with the state are *the empire* and *the nation* (Clemens 2016). Empires have a longer history than nations and are seen to have existed across many civilisations in a variety of forms – from the ancient Egyptian patrimonial empire to the Chinese feudal empire, passing through

Greek and Roman empires of the classical world based on city states and nomadic–sedentary empires such as the Mughal empire. There were also empires of conquest, which resulted specifically from European expansion and colonisation and included primarily the Spanish–American, Portuguese, Dutch, French, and British empires. In his comprehensive study of empires, Shmuel Eisenstadt (1963) compares a variety of empires and, although he notes differences between the political systems under consideration, suggests that there are general characteristics that are common to all of them. In truth, his discussion of European empires in the modern period is very limited, in part because he associates modernity with the development of the nation state, and not with empire. He relegates empires instead to earlier periods in history, despite the fact that the reach of empire is geographically far more extensive in the modern period than it was in antiquity or the Middle Ages.

We distinguish between empires of domination and empires of conquest and extraction and argue that, by assuming the latter form, European colonialism came to create a very different type of empire. Broadly, there is a type of empire that emerges out of pre-existing political formations and, in its expansion and socio-economic development, takes on the general features identified by Eisenstadt. This type includes the new political form that emerges as a consequence of (1) initiatives taken by rulers indigenous to the territory and (2) the development of centralised administrative and political organs designed to govern a defined, if expanding, territory. Incorporation may give rise to resistance, but it is also generally inclusive, being part of the order of rules and obligations that organise the claims to territory. By contrast, the type we refer to as the modern European empire of conquest and extraction operated at a distance and came to differ from this model in three significant ways. First, expansion involved the subjugation of populations who were subject to rule, but were not part of the order of rule. Second, this subjugation was organised on the assumption of the civilis-ational, religious, or racial superiority of the invading population. Third, the land and resources of the subjugated population were deemed to be available to the invading population to do with as it pleased. In our view, these elements suggest a qualitative difference between forms of empire. Not to recognise this difference is to perpetuate a false equivalence between political systems that ought to be understood as distinct.

The other aspect to keep in mind here is that the French, British, and Dutch empires (among others) were established during the same period when, it is claimed, they became *nation states*. The problem is the idea that these states *are* nation states that *have* empires – instead of more appropriately understanding what we call nation states as *being* imperial states, that is, empires organised around the core idea of a national project (one transferred from princes to parliaments). To collapse all varieties of empire into the same form and then to distinguish between empires and nations involves the same sleight of hand. It prevents us from examining what comes to be distinctive about European empires and their post-imperial claim of an under-lying essential nation to which empire itself was merely a contingent phenomenon. Within modern European social theory, then, the question of the legitimacy of political rule is primarily discussed in terms of the nation. Since colonisation and the establishment of imperial rule over others cannot be legitimised through such a discourse, it is usually evaded as a matter of relevant concern.

Indigenous peoples in Abya Yala or Turtle Island, territories that we call 'the Americas' today, were eliminated and dispossessed by European invaders, who claimed their land and resources in the name of European powers and with the authority of religion. Africans were removed from their own lands and forcibly transported across the ocean, to be coerced into labour on plantations in the New World. The wealth and resources of India were drained primarily by British traders, then by the British government, to the benefit of the 'mother country' and its 'settler offshoots'. After the much vaunted abolition of slavery in the mid-nineteenth century, millions of Indian and Chinese labourers were taken to work on the very same plantations, through systems of indenture (Thiara 1995, Allen 2017). African countries, depleted of their populations through the European trade in human beings, were then colonised for their land and other resources. The Belgian king, for example, appropriated the territory, resources, and population of the Congo (Nzongola-Ntalaja 2002). He extracted a personal fortune through enforced labour in the rubber industry that also led to the deaths of millions of people.

European colonialism was both a collective and an individual endeavour. It was carried out by states and heads of states, but also by European populations, through what has been called 'emigra-tionist colonialism' (Smith 1980). Included among these populations were those of the colonising powers, but also a wider variety of

Europeans, for example Poles, Hungarians, and Swedes. Those who were colonised and dispossessed in this process were incorporated into empires of domination and extraction, where the ruling polity understood itself as 'national'. Colonised others were not part of the national order, for which legitimacy was claimed. While in some cases they were recognised as subjects, they were not subjects insofar as legitimacy claims were concerned.

The modern world has been significantly shaped through historical processes and structures that have been in place since the late fifteenth century. These have formed our institutions and fashioned our understandings. Others were initially understood as 'non-believers', but by the mid to late eighteenth century they were considered 'ancestors'. As Locke wrote in the late seventeenth century and as will be further discussed in the next chapter, 'in the beginning all the World was America'. That is, in their discovery of the Americas, Europeans believed that they were encountering earlier versions of themselves. This laid the groundwork for particular understandings of hierarchies among populations across the world. If those peoples encountered by early European travellers were effectively understood as being – in sociological terms – their 'ancestors', then Europeans could both show them their predetermined future and be unconcerned about their passing away. The former was sanctioned by the belief in 'progress', the latter suggested that the disappearance of other cultures and peoples was not a consequence of European actions but a quasi-natural phenomenon. In this way Europeans justified to themselves their domination of others, and this justification was incorporated into modern social theory, as secular justifications replaced religious ones.

At its simplest, then, modern social theory is properly understood as a product of European societies from the fifteenth century onwards, embodied initially in philosophical reflections about social changes that were beginning to transform those societies. Looking back, it is straightforward to see these changes in terms of European exploration of new worlds in the Americas and in the Indian Ocean, together with the expansion of trade in precious metals and luxury commodities such as spices, exotic foodstuffs, and stimulants such as sugar, tobacco, and coffee. The forms of colonialism undertaken by European powers varied, but included the incorporation of territories into monarchic property to be governed by designated officials (in the case of English colonies, lord proprietors). A dominant form was the royal charter given to merchants for overseas trade. These ventures involved violent encounters with others, both to enforce trade and to require labour in mines and on plantations. Most European powers sanctioned trading companies – the English East India Company, the Royal African Company, the Dutch East India Company, the French East India Company, and so on – supported by wealthy speculators and frequently aligned with courts and more or less rudimentary parliaments (Phillips and Sharman 2020).

From the early 1600s, for example, royal charters were given to English merchants to explore opportunities for commerce and trade in Asia (e.g. the East India Company, chartered in 1600) and to travel westwards to colonise and convert the territories and populations of the Americas (e.g. the Virginia Company, chartered in 1606).[1] Jamestown was the first permanent settlement made by English colonists; it was established in 1607 and followed by others along the eastern seaboard, all of which led to the establishment of the Thirteen Colonies. These were based on the displacement, dispossession, and elimination of indigenous peoples in those territories and by the takeover, most notably, of the fur trade via the Hudson's Bay Company (chartered in 1670) (Dunbar-Ortiz 2014).

These companies were among what we would now think of as the first major capitalist corporations. As Thomas Macaulay (1848) set out, in 1676 every proprietor (or shareholder) in the East India Company received, as a bonus, a quantity of stock equal to that which was held, plus dividends amounting to an average of 20 per cent annually. He is reported to have stated: 'Treasure flowed to England in oceans.' The Dutch East India Company, for its part, was the first to come up with the ideas of transferable shares and separation of the role of management from ownership (Gelderblom, de Jong, and Jonker 2013). In truth, as Srinivas Aravamudan (2009) puts it, the true innovation was 'colonialism by corporation'. The companies employed militias to enforce their presence and maintain ports in foreign lands in order to facilitate their trade. Over the seventeenth century, corporate sovereignty over foreign lands was transferred to national sovereignty 'back home', as positions of rulership appointed by national governments replaced rule by the corporation and its officers on behalf of shareholders.

European overseas expansion occurred alongside a long century of brutal conflicts on the European land mass. These conflicts redrew boundaries, as conflicting religious loyalties among Catholics and

Protestants were mobilised in wars associated with the break-up of the main European political system, the Holy Roman Empire (an 'empire' in Eisenstadt's sense). Among these wars were the Eighty Years' War (1568–1648) between Habsburg Spain and its 'provinces' – which included Netherlands, Belgium, and Luxemburg – and the Thirty Years' War (1618–48) between Catholic and Protestant powers. These religious conflicts were expressed not only between states, nascent or otherwise, but within them; and they were manifest also in the English Civil War of 1642–52. The Peace of Westphalia in 1648 settled the Thirty Years' War and established the sovereignty of separate European states and the relations between them. This was, as we have seen, an iconic moment in the history of European self-understandings and understandings of the mutually binding nature of relations among states within an international order. However, as discussed earlier, nations outside Europe were not recognised and had no claim to sovereignty.

Competition between supposedly national powers was conducted via colonisation and military conflict designed to maintain a national interest in the domination of others. Thus all European powers – from Britain (with its separate nations of England and Scotland before union in 1707) to Portugal and Spain, France and the Netherlands, Sweden and Russia – were engaged in colonial expansion and competition. Warfare on the European landmass was transferred to the seas and to other lands. Indeed, during the eighteenth century European wars were frequently fought overseas, in competition for territory, such that they could be characterised as the first 'world wars' in history.

As we shall see in later chapters, imperial competition would also bring war back to the European continent. Weber and Durkheim, for example, would both confront a world war that neither of their theories was equipped to explain. Equally, techniques designed to quell resistance and rebellion in colonies would be used against domestic resistance – for example, events were more usually discussed only in terms of domestic class conflict, as happened in the 1848 revolutions across Europe.

The incorporation of other lands under European powers involved settlement and transfer of populations. This meant a massive movement of Europe's own populations, as well as the transfer of other populations through enslavement, indenture, and other forms of coerced labour, initially through plantations established by the trading corporations. This was not only a feature of early modernity but something integral to the development and mature phase of modernity. As colonialism expanded, it also came to be formalised into political institutions and cultural expressions. Thus the most obvious thing to be said about Britain (along with other European countries, such as France) throughout the nineteenth and indeed down to the mid-twentieth century is that it was an *empire*. In other words, its reach and self-definition went beyond its national boundaries.

While not all European countries succeeded in becoming empires, they all made an attempt at it: the last quarter of the nineteenth century was characterised as a 'scramble for Africa' in which European powers sought to divide up the African continent among themselves – that is, between the United Kingdom, France, Portugal, Germany, Belgium, Italy and Spain (see Brooke-Smith 1987). Further, as we have noted, European populations from across the continent were involved in 'emigrationist colonialism' (Smith 1980). Over four centuries, the population movements from Europe to the New World and beyond coalesced into a phenomenon that was markedly different from other, more quotidian movements and encounters. This is because European movement was linked to colonial settlement, which was central to the displacement, dispossession, and elimination of populations across the globe. While the idea of *Lebensraum* – 'living space' – was explicitly articulated in Germany in the late nineteenth century (Smith 1980), expansionist policies for land and territory for one's 'own' citizens had been central to the European colonial project since much earlier times.

Across the nineteenth century, around 60 million Europeans left their countries of origin to make new lives and livelihoods for themselves on lands inhabited by others (Miège 1993). Each new cohort of Europeans was allocated land at the edges of the territory that had already been settled. This was done in order to extend political control over contested border territories. In this way Europeans from across the continent participated in the elimination and dispossession of the populations that preceded them and were thus complicit in the settler colonial project. At least seven million Germans moved to these lands – to the United States in the north and to Brazil and Argentina in the south – becoming, by the late nineteenth century, one of the largest immigrant groups in the north of the Americas (Bade 1995). Large-scale Polish emigration started in the period after the Franco-Prussian War in the late nineteenth century; by the turn to the twentieth century nearly 2 million Polish people had moved to the Americas, while about 300,000 Polish colonists went to Brazil, another settler colony, by 1939 (Zubrzycki 1953). Two million subjects of the Dual Monarchy of Austria-Hungary travelled to the Americas (Zahra 2016), as did more than 8 million Irish people (Delaney 2000); 1 million of the latter left as a result of the mid-century famine caused by British colonial rule. By 1890 nearly 1 million Swedes, one fifth of the total Swedish population, were living in lands colonised by (and as) the United States. In addition, 13.5 million British people moved to white settler colonies across the globe (Fedorowich and Thompson 2013).

As already indicated, in this book we treat the United States as a European empire. Some have claimed, on the basis of the American Revolution and the Declaration of Independence, that the United States is the first new nation comparable with ones created after decolonisation in the twentieth century (Lipset 1963). However, it was white settler colonists in the Thirteen Colonies of the Eastern Seaboard that rebelled against the British government, demanding independence from what they regarded as illegitimate monarchic rule. In their terms, they were acting as free subjects empowered by the principles of Enlightenment. As Danielle Allen (2014) notes, the Declaration of Independence appealed 'to the Supreme Judge of the world for the rectitude of our intentions', which were 'to levy War, conclude Peace, contract Alliances, establish Commerce, and to do all other Acts and Things which Independent States may of right do'. The freedom of these colonies rested, however, on the appropriation of land from indigenous populations and on the creation of plantations worked by indigenous people, uprooted and enslaved Africans, as well as indentured servants from Europe; and the Declaration laid claim to the colonists' right to treat these people as they did. After independence they expanded to the south and to the west, creating what Steven Hahn (2016) has called an American empire rather than a nation (see also Byrd 2011 and Frymer 2017). We do not, then, regard white settler independence movements, whether in the Americas or elsewhere, as postcolonial but as the very expression of European colonialism.[2]

European empires – and the conflicts between them – grew during the period in which sociological theory was consolidated, yet empire itself was hardly mentioned. When they were at their height, the popular nineteenth-century sociologist and social philosopher Herbert Spencer drew up a typology in which a 'military' or 'militant' society based on force and coercion gave way to an 'industrial' society based on voluntary production and exchange (Hart 2018). The sleight of hand that portrays these categories as opposed was made possible by representing each as an 'ideal type' and by separating the nation ('industrial') from its empire ('militant'), notwithstanding that the nation represented itself and its institutions as imperial. Spencer was opposed to imperialism, but seemed unwilling to countenance that it was bound up with the systems of market exchange that he otherwise endorsed. A world once pacified into free trade could be represented separately from the mechanisms that created its conditions, and a moral sensibility oriented to peace and progress was left intact.

Spencer's device is not idiosyncratic but typical of the way in which European social theory, at one and the same time, both acknowledged and displaced colonialism and empire. Within modern social theory, overseas possessions are a contingent fact, something in addition to the core aspects of national states and their associated national societies and how those are to be understood. By contrast, drawing on postcolonial thought, our argument is that colonialism and empire are central to modern social theory through effects that last to the present. As Aravamudan (2009: 40) has argued, 'postcolonial interventions take aim at metropolitan etiologies that separate "domestic" from "overseas" political history'. Failure to recognise that the domestic and the overseas are coterminous is a severe weakness of contemporary social theory.

Contemporary Sociology and the Construction of Its Canons

What we propose, then, is a postcolonial intervention into the construction of modern social theory in its canonical form. Modern social theory represents a very particular kind of amnesia. Indeed, the significance of colonialism and empire is recognised in everyday culture – think, for example, of celebrations of 'discoverers' like Captain Cook and Christopher Columbus, of our knowledge of the Atlantic slave trade, or of the British empire itself; but it has no place within the system of theoretical categories that has developed in mainstream modern social theory. As might be expected, the expansive project of European colonialism could not go unremarked by writers who were living through it. This remains true even if they did not make it central to their reflections and were far from being critical of it. In part, the later amnesia is a consequence of developments within sociology itself, not least the construction of its own historical trajectory in the form of a canon.

As Raewyn Connell (1997) has argued, the idea of a set of founding figures who established a core conceptual framework or set of themes and thereby organised the discipline of sociology is relatively recent. According to her, this notion has two effects. One is to diminish the variety of voices of those who called themselves sociologists; the other is to amplify the voices of a few, who become the filter through which the history of the discipline is then viewed. In Connell's view, the sociologists of the nineteenth century and their public – broadly, an educated and professional public – were, by necessity, fully aware of empire as the context that provided them with both opportunities and subject matter.

Empire made other peoples and places available to the 'European gaze', which in turn presented them and their beliefs and practices as both 'other' and 'backward' from the perspective of the achievements of European peoples – more specifically, north European peoples and their kin, in settler colonies such as the United States, Canada, and Australia. For Connell, much sociology, especially in the late nineteenth century, operated by cataloguing various practices associated with kinship, religion, political organisation, and so forth. It was therefore a fragmentary discipline, associated with developing an 'encyclopaedic' grasp of a mosaic of cultural practices of different peoples. In the next chapter we address aspects of this 'gaze' and the role it played in the development of stadial theory – that is, a theory according to which societal development comes about in progressive stages.

We do not claim that the idea of a canon is problematic in itself. As Frank Kermode (1985) argued, a canon represents a shorthand, a way of focusing attention on a specific aspect of a tradition. For Randall Collins (1997), it is a simple truism that a conversation carried out in the past had at the time many more interlocutors than come to be recognised retrospectively, in accounts of that past that focus on selected contributions – which thereby become canonical. He argues that this should not be the reason for a 'guilt trip'. However, emphasising this rather misses Connell's point, which is about how a conversation of the past is edited and which topics are carried forward. For our purposes, what Connell very nicely sets out is a disjunction that arises in representations of the history of sociology when the latter comes to be understood as being about the self-understanding of modernity rather than about an external understanding of modernity's 'others'. While empire is the unselfconscious context for the former, it is elided in the latter. The idea that sociology's distinctive and specific topic is modern society emerges primarily in the post-Second World War period and is associated with the expansion of mass higher education. This produces a new audience for sociological writing, an audience of students rather than simply a wider public audience. A sociology that was fragmented around studies of global differences made available to western eyes by empire was in need of integration and a new jurisdiction. As Jeffrey Alexander (1987) has argued, the 'classics' – a canon of founding figures – became a means of integrating the discipline.

The expansion of mass higher education also coincided with ongoing anticolonial movements against imperial regimes across the world. European empires were largely dismantled in the postwar period. A new jurisdiction for sociology became associated with the idea of modernity and the development of national societies. This separated 'nations' from their erstwhile colonial and imperial engagements and turned the focus of sociology inwards. The problems of sociological concern were increasingly understood to be social divisions and exclusions internal to national societies and familiar to the new generations of students, who often were the first members of their family to attend university. In this context, issues of class and gender came to the fore, as would issues of sexuality a little later.

Most sociological accounts of European modernity begin with Nisbet's two revolutions as key formative events. However, it was not until the implications of these events became clearer that the main contours of modernity could properly be outlined – or at least so the story initiated by the new jurisdiction, or field for the application of sociology, went.

Robert Nisbet's (1966) acclaimed book *The Sociological Tradition* drew a distinction between the characteristics of traditional society and those of modern society according to which the French Revolution and the Industrial Revolution were decisive in creating a break with the past that ushered in the new society. This model involved the representation of earlier writers as precursors to the classical social theory that would consolidate in the mid to late nineteenth century, in the writings of Karl Marx, Émile Durkheim, and Max Weber.

Successive generations of social theorists from 1830 to 1920 were seen to provide the groundwork for the self-understanding of modern society – in particular the foundations of the modern social sciences and sociology. This was the core argument of Talcott Parsons's *The Structure of Social Action*. His book was first published in 1937, then reprinted in paperback in 1968, when its resurgence coincided with a growth in university programmes devoted to sociology.

Looking at these two books and their authors, in each case there was a paradox. Modernity was associated with historical changes that were evident from the sixteenth century onwards; but neither Nisbet nor Parsons began with the earlier formative events that produced the new society they analysed. Each one presented the core of modern social thought through writers that belonged to the late nineteenth century, which was the height of European imperialism. Yet neither author mentioned imperialism. Nor did they discuss the earlier period of colonial settlement, which both preceded it and was continuous with it.[3]

As sociology itself became consolidated, a canon of 'classical' theorists was formed. Their number was sometimes expanded to include Georg Simmel, Vilfredo Pareto, and the English economist Alfred Marshall (the latter two introduced by Parsons). But Marx, Weber, and Durkheim remained constant figures, even if the way in which they have been interpreted has differed. Our concern here is less with the expansion (or otherwise) of the canon as a set of writers than it is with the canon itself, as a set of categories. We are also interested in the correlative social and political conditions and in how these are involved in the construction of the idea of modernity.

In Marx, for example, we encounter a figure widely regarded as central to the consolidation of modern sociological thought. This description, however, is not straightforward. Talcott Parsons (1937) placed the true foundations of modern sociological thought among a generation of thinkers, primarily Durkheim and Weber, who wrote from 1890 to 1920.[4] This period coincides with the height of European empires and with the 'scramble for Africa', when European powers divided the continent between them after the Berlin Conference of 1884/5. European imperialism culminated in a world war, albeit the fact goes unremarked – as does the rise of fascism and the menace of the Second World War, which was looming at the time when Parsons wrote. Parsons's periodisation also had another effect. Marx was cast there as belonging in the prehistory of the founding of modern sociology (Holmwood 1996). It was not until the 1960s that dissatisfaction with Parsons's proposed synthesis began to be expressed. A new generation of sociologists argued that Parsons had displaced the specificity of *capitalist* economic relations from sociological understandings of modern society. Marx was brought into the canon, albeit without a great deal of consequence for its fundamental orientation towards the idea of a classical sociology.

The treatment of these writers was not substantially different in Anthony Giddens's (1971) influential *Capitalism and Modern Social Theory* from what it had been in Nisbet and Parsons; and this was a book that became the basis of most undergraduate courses in sociological theory in the United Kingdom. Unlike Parsons and Nisbet, Giddens did not focus primarily upon cultural values and issues of social integration; he concentrated instead on the social relations embedded in the modern, capitalist economy. Nonetheless, his temporal framing of modernity and the rise of modern social theory was much the same as that of Nisbet and Parsons, namely the period 1890–1920 and the writings of Marx, Weber, and Durkheim. Paradoxically, the canon was at once expanded and narrowed. Giddens (1971: vii) commented that 'the most striking characteristic of social thought over the hundred years from 1820 to 1920 is the very plethora of diverse forms of theory which were developed over that period'. However, he did not seek to engage with these forms. His purpose was different: it was to spell out the contemporary relevance of the three writers in terms of current problems in sociology. In the case of Marx, this relevance had two core aspects: the nature of critique and the class relations of the capitalist mode of production – aspects that will concern us throughout this book.

To some degree, the shift in sociological sensibility that Giddens represented was associated with the rise of new social movements such as feminism, which put gender firmly onto the sociological agenda. While approaches to class were accused of being gender-blind, Marx's approach to critique was nonetheless a source of inspiration for feminists – especially in Europe, where socialist feminism was more significant than in the United States. Equally, the civil rights movement in the United States was challenging racial inequality there. Indeed, Martin Luther King had been assassinated in 1968, which marked a new moment in that struggle. This also bore a relation to Marx. The great African American sociologist W. E. B. Du Bois had yet to be recognised as part of the canon, notwithstanding that his early writings fell within the supposedly foundational period of 1890–1920. He practised sociology in a racially segregated academy (a fact unremarked upon within white sociology), which was only beginning to be dismantled in the 1960s.[5]

Given this set of challenges, Parsons's sociological settlement appeared to be wanting. Sociologists grew more interested in the dynamics of class, and it did not immediately appear to be a problem that class was understood to be 'race-blind'. Du Bois, for example, especially in later life, was sympathetic to Marxism, and this attitude was to become common among many African American scholars after him. The reason is not too difficult to understand. In 1944 Gunnar Myrdal had published a commissioned report into race in the United States, *The American Dilemma*, using in it the terminology of caste – as had Du Bois himself earlier – to explain racialised hierarchies. Myrdal anticipated that American democratic values – the 'American creed' – would ultimately prevail and resolve these inequalities. In this respect, Myrdal represented an 'optimistic' interpretation, believing that the American creed was hostile to all status differences, including those of class (Myrdal 1962 [1944]: 671). However, among African American sociologists after Du Bois, the language of 'caste' used by Myrdal was criticised along with his idea that the American creed would enable the resolution of racialised hierarchies. 'Class', by contrast, could be understood as a universalisable term and concept, one that could appeal to a common condition across racialised differences (see Robinson 1983).

By the late 1960s, however, many African American writers were using the language of colonialism rather than that of class to understand local experience in the United States and to articulate a new Black Power movement (see Carmichael and Hamilton 1967). Yet, as Blauner (2001 [1971]) argued, the analysis of colonialism as integral to the construction of race relations in the United States and elsewhere was largely absent from sociology. When Giddens turned to a reinterpretation of Marx, Weber, and Durkheim, it was with the intention of reinvigorating 'the analysis of trends of development within the "advanced" societies' (Giddens 1971: 246) and of casting doubt on the 'implicit assumption that the main characteristics of the "developed societies" are *known*' (246). He wrote further that, 'paradoxically, in taking up again the problems with which they were primarily concerned, we may hope ultimately to liberate ourselves from our present heavy dependence on the ideas which they formulated' (247). As we will argue throughout the book, however, the 'problems' taken up in the past also cover topics that are neglected and misrepresented in the present more than they were in the past.[6]

Decolonising European Social Theory

Calls to decolonise the university in the 1960s were part of wider movements of decolonisation, especially in East Africa (Mamdani 2019). They involved challenges both to the western curriculum and to the nature of academic recruitment and training. Such initiatives were typically seen as 'anti-western', and it is only recently that a self-critical movement to decolonise the university has emerged in the western academy itself (Bhambra, Nişancioğlu, and Gebrial 2018). The impetus of this movement comes largely from Africa, via the examples of the Rhodes Must Fall and Fees Must Fall movements in South Africa. This book takes up one aspect of the wider discussion. It addresses the colonial context in which the contemporary European understanding of modern social theory has been formed. It takes seriously the histories that created the context for the development of these ideas and the ways in which these colonial histories were elided in subsequent discussions.

We place firmly within their times the theorists with whom we engage, and we discuss their writings in the light of the histories they were living through. Our purpose is to 'decolonise' the concepts and categories they have bequeathed to us. This is a process of contextual understanding and reconstruction. We do not claim to provide an exhaustive account of their writings on other topics. We are instead drawing attention to omissions in the secondary literature, and thus to the processes of 'purification' that have removed colonialism and empire from sociological understandings of modernity. In consequence, our purpose is to contribute to what Connell (1997: 1539) calls the 'genre of commentary and exposition', which constitutes the canon by reconstructing it from within.

Just as the enterprise of decolonising the curriculum would be purely scholastic if it did not address the inequalities and forms of domination that structure the wider society as well as the university, our concerns are also with the wider issues. The 'lead' societies of modernity (Parsons 1971) are currently beset by populism and xenophobic hostility to minorities and migrants. These social divisions are as urgent now as those of gender and class had appeared to be in the period of the postwar settlement. Indeed, they disrupt aspects of that settlement and the ways in which the categories associated with it have been understood. For much of the period of post-Second World War developments in European and US sociology, the Cold War and the ultimate demise of the Soviet system constituted the framing international issue. As Hansen (2002) argues, decolonisation was neglected and yet had a profound significance, even for those issues that were regarded as central. For example, a figure of the white working class has emerged across Europe and the United States and functions as a resonant category of analysis for the left behind, in explanations of both the 2016 UK referendum for leaving the EU and the election of Trump as president of the United States (Shilliam 2019). Yet the working class in these countries is not just white. Current sociology is implicated in these constructions precisely because it has neglected the roles of colonialism and empire. The tradition needs to be reconstructed and made to address current problems. The history of sociology and of its various self-understandings is bound up with wider histories that have produced our present moment.

Our book focuses on five key sociological figures of the nineteenth and early twentieth century: Tocqueville, Marx, Weber, Durkheim, and Du Bois. In the context of how European social theory is conventionally understood, our treatment of Marx, Weber, and Durkheim needs no further explanation. Tocqueville is not usually part of the sociological canon. Nevertheless, we argue that he is a major source for arguments about the significance of democracy to modernity, especially in the twin contexts of the 1776 US Declaration of Independence and 1789 French Revolution. More importantly, his less known discussion of slavery and of the treatment of indigenous people has serious implications for the development of that democracy and for how it is understood. For example, Tocqueville's arguments about the role of the movement of populations from Europe to the United States and its consequences for freed African Americans resonate with Du Bois's subsequent account of the colour line, in spite of their different sensibilities (see pp. 69–70 in this volume).

The inclusion of Du Bois has a different justification. Absence from the canon, as Toni Morrison (1989: 12) notes, does not imply an absence of processes associated with exclusion; rather it should cause us to interrogate the intellectual manoeuvres that are required to erase entire peoples from histories and societies that seethe with their presence. Morrison argues that, whereas canons can appear to be 'naturally' or 'inevitably' white, in fact they are 'studiously' so (14). As Francille Wilson (2006) and Aldon Morris (2015) have pointed out, Du Bois was actively excluded from the wider conversation of the academy in the United States. This was a consequence of the segregated nature of academic life there, as well as of the hostility that Du Bois received from community leaders such as Booker T. Washington. As a result, his contribution to the broader topics of sociology was not acknowledged at the time; only recently has his importance been more widely recognised. While Du Bois was extensively debated by intellectuals in his community, few white sociologists were citing scholars across the colour line, and not even his active political leadership gained him wider recognition. The partial desegregation of academic life has brought African American thought into the conversation, but the reason for including Du Bois is not simply to incorporate a once neglected voice. It is to pay attention to what the development of his thought can tell us about the nature of contemporary social problems.

In the introduction to his study of Durkheim's development of social realism, Robert Jones (1999) describes two possible approaches to the interpretation of ideas. Derived from Richard Rorty, the first one is a rational reconstruction that brings historical figures into dialogue with the present and its concerns. The second one is a historical interpretation that takes the writer back to the past and to the discussions that shaped his or her arguments and engagements. The latter approach is perhaps the one that is now most favoured; and it is also the one that informs our discussions throughout the book. It disrupts current conversations by replacing conventional understandings, which serve only to reproduce our current ways of thinking and doing sociology. As we indicated at the start of this introductory chapter, we are also addressing new historiographies that have substantially changed how histories of European modernity are understood. Placing authors in their context through new scholarship about their ideas and intellectual influences should also involve understanding that historical context differently as a consequence of new histories. As we have argued, much of the standard discussion of modern social theory depends on a standard historiography. We draw on these new histories as part of our engagement with that theory.

Our concerns, then, are also about the less fashionable mode of rational reconstruction, a reconstruction focused upon current issues of identity and difference and their relationship to histories of colonialism and empire. In this way we initiate a new dialogue between past and present, a dialogue largely absent from standard sociological understandings of modernity that are themselves represented as owing their first formulation to the authors we discuss. These writers *did* engage with colonialism and its associated practices of dispossession and forced labour, yet their discussions along such themes have largely been edited out in the process of canon formation. The fact that they could be edited out says something about the way they were initially set up. It also points to limitations in approaches that are carried forward into the present conceptual and methodological 'jurisdiction' of sociology and reinforce its problems.

We begin by placing the writings of the authors we discuss in a broader context of social and political thought, which ranges from Hobbes to Hegel. This situates social theory in the context of European liberalism (Seidman 1983) and demonstrates how that liberalism operates through a foundational exclusion of indigenous peoples, enabling their dispossession and subjection to forced labour. At the same time, modern social theory describes itself as embodying a project of freedom, albeit one that is deeply racialised. We look at this dialectic in each of the theorists examined in this book, to show how their constructions were entangled with colonialism. With Du Bois, we show a reverse process, whereby he begins from race – the colour line in the United States – and comes to understand it as a fundamental global division produced through histories of colonisation. Our purpose in this book is to expose the joint significance of colonialism and empire, as an organising principle, to the thought of these writers and thereby to the legacies they bequeath to social theory. Addressing colonial histories is a necessary preliminary to the reconstruction of social theory.

1
Hobbes to Hegel
Europe and Its Others

As we argued in the Introduction, colonialism was a precursor to empire. Each was part of the context in which European social theory developed; empire was the dominant political system of the western world in the period of classical social theory at the end of the nineteenth century. Our purpose in this chapter is to set out how this history came to be displaced from representations of modernity within European social theory. We argue that there are three steps in the displacement of colonialism from modern social theory. The first is to misrepresent arguments about sovereignty and private property as an early imagining of *capitalism*, instead of understanding them in their proper context of colonialism. In this way capitalism is erroneously separated from colonialism. The second is the misrepresentation of colonial encounters with others as encounters with people at different stages of social development. Here the possibility of 'universal' human progress is represented by European civilisation to which others are led. Finally, the stage of development of European societies – variously described as commercial society, capitalist society, or modern society – is taken to be the proper object of modern social theory. The conflicts believed to be internal to it will become the focus of subsequent developments in sociological thought. Together, these steps establish and explain social theory's emphasis on capitalist modernity and its divisions of class and gender. Racialised divisions – the product of colonial encounters – are made to look like external impingements on modern social and political structures rather than as features integral to them that derive from colonial domination.

In the present chapter we look at these steps in the writings of the English political theorists Hobbes and Locke and discuss the identification of stages of historical social development in the writers associated with the Scottish Enlightenment, before concluding with an examination of Hegel and his famous master–slave (or lord and bondsman) relationship. This relationship is particularly important in that it establishes the significance of 'recognition' for modern (inter)subjectivity. This is something of wide sociological import in terms of how ideas of a social self come to be configured – that is, as a modification of the liberal self and in alignment with an emerging sociological sensibility. Specifically, the master–slave relation plays a particular role in the development of Marx's thought and ideas of alienation. Yet the complex connections with colonialism are effaced and given in a formulation that is independent of colonialism and bears only a contingent relation to it. Slavery becomes a metaphor in the modern construction of freedom, but is separated from modernity and associated with premodern social conditions.

Private Property and Possession in Early Liberal Thought

A central feature of modern liberalism – classic liberalism, as it is frequently called – is the justification of private property and its expression in the rule of law. This identifies government with the maintenance of private property rights and with the free expression of those rights by individuals. At the same time, government places a constraint upon individuals in their self-determination and use of their property. They must acknowledge the similar rights of others and a framework in which those rights are protected. The crucial issue, then, is that of establishing the basis of government and the political obligations imposed on those subject to it, along with their corollary consent to be governed to each person's mutual benefit. It is this intellectual formation that comes to be understood as the beginning of capitalist modernity and modern liberal subjectivity.

In sixteenth- and seventeenth-century Europe (and earlier), government was typically identified with the powers associated with monarchic rule. This was widely understood to involve a God-given or divine right to rule (Bendix 1980). Such a doctrine also assigned God-given natural resources to the monarch, whose responsibility was to allocate their use to others as a manifestation of his or her powers. Taxation designed to pursue state interests – as for example in the financing of wars – was simply to be thought of as a reappropriation of resources previously distributed under the legitimate authority of the monarch. Of course, none of this meant that monarchical rule went unchallenged, or that monarchs did not have to negotiate their demands for taxes with the people from whom those taxes were being raised.

Conflicts were particularly acute in two kinds of context: the fiscal demands imposed by wars among European powers in the seventeenth century; and reinterpretations of religious authority, as happened in the Protestant Reformation in Europe. These issues were also central to the English Civil War of 1642–51, in which parliament was pitted against the monarch – a situation that led to the execution of King Charles I in 1649. Indeed, Charles's haughty response to being put on trial – 'I would know by what power I am called hither …' – is a vivid illustration of the prevailing view and of his self-understanding as the source of all powers (Kelsey 2004).

Charles I was invoking the political authority of monarchy, which he took to be both hierarchical and absolute. It was also patriarchal. Just as religious authority derived from God the father, so political authority modelled the monarch as father. Indeed, that conception of authority was mirrored in the household, which, in the relevant milieu, would have included both kin and servants. As the leading seventeenth-century English theorist of patriarchal rule Sir Robert Filmer put it,

> If God created only Adam, and out of a piece of him made the Woman, and if by Generation from them two, as parts of them, all Mankind be propagated: If also God gave to Adam not only dominion over the Woman and the Children that should Issue from them, but also over the whole earth to subdue it, and over all the Creatures on it, so long as Adam lived, no Man could claim or enjoy any thing but by Donation, Assignation or permission from him. (Quoted in Locke 1960 [1698]: 150)

It is this traditional, patriarchal view that early liberal political theory begins to overturn (while retaining its inscription in the household). In brief, it inverts the monarchy's claims to absolute rule and considers instead the justification of an order of government from the perspective of its subjects. The inversion necessarily has two requirements. The first is to establish how those subject to government can

cede authority to a power beyond or above themselves. The second
is to establish the resources of nature as a *commons* gifted by God to
all humankind – and not in the first instance to monarchs – in which
rights of possession and use derive from the activities of persons.
They then enter into a contract designed to found a government in
order to protect those rights.

Two seventeenth-century English political philosophers are particularly significant in the development of these ideas, which will be
central to political liberalism: Thomas Hobbes (1588–1679) and
John Locke (1632–1704). Their arguments represent a move to place
government under natural and positive law rather than to see law
simply as an expression of government. This new construction will
come to be regarded as the basis of European Enlightenment and as
something that, in principle, can be universalised beyond Europe.

An early qualification of this claim for universalism is provided
by C. B. Macpherson (1962), who contends that these propositions
derive from the experiences of a particular society, as it undergoes
significant social change. Macpherson is seeking to deny not the
narrative force of the constructions of Hobbes or Locke but rather
the universality of their claims about human nature. He argues that
what they treat as self-evident – to themselves and to their readers
– is in fact a human nature already 'socialised' through the relationships of seventeenth-century England. Specifically, for Macpherson,
'human nature' postulated by Hobbes and Locke is a form of
possessive individualism attuned to an emerging market society. In
other words, the human nature set out in liberal theory is a limited
bourgeois idea of the subject (or self), an idea integral to emergent
capitalism.

We do not want to challenge the broad substance of Macpherson's
claim that ideas of human nature bear the imprint of the society
in which they are developed. Rather we argue that the ideas he is
discussing develop more directly in relation to colonialism than in
relation to market society. They occur in the context of justifying
sovereign state power, the sovereignty of trading corporations, and
the nature of the political obligations of subjects to sovereign power.
This involves a commonwealth of individuals – understood as male
property owners and patriarchal heads of household – who enter into
covenants or contracts.[1] At the same time, there is an identification
of some as being outside the commonwealth but being subject to
its dread power. Colonial conquest was integral to the development

of these arguments and of claims not only about sovereignty over lands (potentially, territories occupied by others) but also over the seas (Treves 2015). Indeed, Hobbes and Locke were direct material beneficiaries of colonial activities; Locke in particular owned land in Carolina and served on bodies that administered the colonies. In Britain itself, similar forms of colonialism had occurred in the late sixteenth century with the conquest of Ireland, whose incorporation under monarchic rule involved population resettlement and chartered companies tasked with 'improving' agricultural productivity (Quinn 1966, Canny 2001).

Hobbes: The States of Nature and of Society

In articulating his universal account of human nature, Hobbes began by making a distinction between the 'state of nature' and the 'state of society'. The former meant attributing to human beings aggressive drives designed to fulfill their self-defined interests, potentially pitting each human against the other. This state was one in which self-interest was also potentially self-defeating. As Hobbes famously put it:

> In such condition, there is no place for Industry; because the fruit thereof is uncertain: and consequently no Culture of the Earth; no Navigation, nor use of the commodities that may be imported by Sea; no Commodious Building; no instruments of moving, and removing such things as require much force; no Knowledge of the Face of the Earth; no account of Time; no Arts; no Letters; no Society; and which is worst of all, continuall feare, and danger of violent death; And the life of man, solitary, poore, nasty, brutish, and short. (Hobbes 1991 [1651]: 89)

According to Hobbes, the state of nature was partly a theoretical construct, a 'fiction'. Indeed, he stated, 'it may peradventure be thought, there never was such a time, nor condition of warre as this' (89). As Macpherson suggests, the characterisation of the state of society gives us nonetheless an approximation of seventeenth-century England, including its engagements in trade and navigation. But it is apparent that at the forefront of Hobbes's mind, when thinking of the state of nature, were descriptions of encounters with indigenous people native to the lands of European 'discovery' – descriptions provided by priests, travellers, and settlers. Having declared that the state of nature was a fiction, Hobbes went on to say:

> but there are many places, where they live so now. For the savage people in many places of America, except the government of small Families, the concord whereof dependeth on naturall lust, have no government at all; and live at this day in that brutish manner. (89)

According to Aravamudan (2009: 45), Hobbes misrepresented contemporary accounts of indigenous societies, many of which describe them as 'highly organised, constituting a system of petty states in shifting alliances of mutual conflict and cooperation, war-making and trading'. We will return to the significance of such misrepresentations in the construction of different stages of the development of human society. However, the misrepresentation is not accidental. It is necessary for establishing European rights of possession and use against indigenous people already present on the land.[2] As we shall see with regard to Locke, were indigenous peoples to have been recognised as engaged in husbandry and trade, they would have established, through their activities, rights of their own. It is important to note that they *were* engaged in such activities and that the failure to acknowledge this fact was part of the process of legitimising the appropriation of their lands.[3]

For the moment, we are concerned to clarify the idea of government from the perspective of heads of households deemed to be selfish in the pursuit of their own desires yet capable of recognising their own interest in the formation of an agreement to be governed by an external power, that of the sovereign-state. Indigenous people assigned to the state of nature have the capacity to recognise the possible benefits of the state of society. This potential to see the significance of society was the very purpose of the fiction and the universality attributed to it. Indeed, from his (speculative) observations about the state of nature, Hobbes derived that it was in the interest of individuals to enter into a contract so as to constitute government – an entity designed to regulate their mutual engagements. This presupposed ceding sovereignty to an external entity, the sovereign or monarch, who was to be granted absolute power in the enforcement of laws. The sovereign provided protection to those under his (or her) rule and, importantly, against external actors.

For Hobbes, the contract to enter into society and establish sovereign power was not something that could be rescinded. It authorised the sovereign's absolute power and derived its legitimacy from the self-interest that initiated recognition of its need. The subsequent generations of a political society – that is, those born into the commonwealth – were also bound by it. However, this power could be dissolved as a result of the actions of the sovereign him- or herself. The sovereign was granted the authority to conduct war, but loss to another sovereign created conditions of obedience to the new power, by virtue of the need to maintain life after defeat.[4] Consequently, in Hobbes's judgement, indigenous peoples should acknowledge their obligation to the commonwealth, which sought to absorb them on the basis of this very reason, or, if they resisted and failed, they must recognise its compelling power. Indeed, Hobbes admitted that most 'empirical' commonwealths were formed by conquest. As Mehta (1999) points out, liberal thought does not ground the state in the traditions and practices of a territorially delimited people, but in an agreement that is in principle arbitrary in its geographical range.

Hobbes's justification of sovereign power may strike modern readers as authoritarian rather than liberal. However, his account contained elements that would prove attractive to later thinkers. While his deductive approach was based upon an idea of egoistic individualism, it was one where the capacity for reason allowed individuals to see the advantages of association.[5] The latter was understood to provide benefits beyond the state of nature – for example, those of trade, 'commodious building' (or 'convenient Seat', i.e. dwelling), and 'knowledge, arts and letters'. In other words, it was 'society' that provided what would come to be understood as civilisation. Should others not wish to be part of it, they could be compelled, on the grounds that otherwise they must, by virtue of their selfish natures, threaten to dispossess it. As Macpherson (1962: 24) puts it, '[i]t is the man who would "plant, sow, build, or possess a convenient Seat" who must expect to be invaded and dispossessed by others seeking to enjoy the fruits of his labour (which invasion is the substance of the "competition" Hobbes sees in the state of nature)'. This construction is one of the ways in which indigenous people come to be represented as 'savages' who pose a threat that warrants the use of extreme, and exemplary, force against them.[6]

Hobbes, then, does not regard the occupation of the Americas and other colonised lands as an 'invasion', precisely because indigenous people had not, in his view, set up their possession and use of the land. The reason why indigenous people had no rights of possession and use was a topic that received a fuller treatment in Locke. The latter, like Hobbes, wrote in a natural law tradition in which the laws enjoined upon human beings derived from God. Implicitly, of course, this was a Christian god, or perhaps an Abrahamic god – that is, the god of a creed where different interpretations could create schisms and religious wars. But these did not call into question the basic precept of natural law, namely that God had given human beings dominion over the natural world. In addition, the nature of this dominion and the principles according to which it should be exercised were discoverable through human reason, itself understood as God-given. Indeed, it was the common relationship with God that created a kind of equality, even as it included a warrant for the inhuman treatment of others.

Locke: Property and Self-Determination

Locke's arguments were set out in his *Two Treatises of Government*, first published anonymously in 1689, then revised by him in subsequent editions. The first treatise was directed at Filmer's patriarchal theory of government, while the second set out Locke's own version of social contract theory. Here Locke sought to create the basis on which the common patrimony can be taken into private use. For him, natural resources such as land or minerals were given to all humankind, as part of the commons. They were not assigned to a monarch, they were not for him to distribute, but were available to everyone: 'The Earth, and all inferior Creatures be common to all Men' (Locke 1960 [1698]: 287).

While Hobbes began from the natural selfishness of human beings, Locke argued that each human being has a right to self-determination and to enjoying the benefits of exercising that right.[7] As Hampsher-Monk (1992: 88) puts it, 'for Locke, human beings are primarily centres of rights and duties (rather than, as with Hobbes, centres of appetites)'. Since rights were God-given, it followed that they were given to everyone and must be respected in others. The basic right to self-determination was formulated by Locke (1960 [1698]: 287) as a right to *self*-possession, by virtue of which 'every Man has a *Property* in his own *Person*'. Thus, 'whatsoever that he removes out of the state that Nature hath provided, and left it in, he hath mixed his Labour with, and joyned to it something that is his own, and thereby makes it his property' (288). The exercise of this right, however, was constrained by what was due to others. Specifically, Locke set out two constraints. The first was that 'enough and as good' must be left for others; the second, that there should be no spoilage or waste. We shall return to Locke's discussion of these two constraints.

On this basis, Locke proposed a contract theory of government and political obligation similar to that of Hobbes. Property and its protection were the purpose of government, and people entered into society in order to set up a government to protect property: 'For the preservation of Property being the end of Government, and that for which Men enter into Society, it necessarily supposes and requires, that the People should have Property, without which they must be suppos'd to lose that by entring into Society, which was the end for which they entered into it' (360).

Locke was writing at a time of extensive reorganisation of property and customary rights to use the land, in England and elsewhere. For example, peasants were bound by complex obligations to work the lands of their landowners (lords), for which they received small plots of land that they could use for their own subsistence; and they also had rights to graze livestock on common pasture, to take fish from common ponds and rivers, and to forage in the woods for food, fallen branches, and sticks for firewood. However, a process of enclosure through the fencing off of land was removing these common rights, commuting labour obligations into wages, and excluding rural workers from grazing their livestock or entering woods, streams, and forests.

The 'commons' in popular parlance was not the commons of the state of nature in Locke (or Hobbes), since it already embodied a complex negotiation of differential rights and obligations assigned to different categories of owner (lords, church officials, etc.), to different categories of tradespeople, and to servants (agricultural and domestic). Indeed, as Williamson (1987) argues, since the medieval period, what was called 'common land' in England was privately owned, usually by the lord of the manor. This was the basis on which it could be fenced and enclosed, and those with customary access to it could be excluded. Just such an assertion of narrow private property rights was under way, displacing the rural population from the land and creating a new kind of rural poor.

At the same time, as we shall see when discussing Marx, the enclosure movement created new categories of crime and punitive sanctions in support of private property rights. Some of Marx's (1975 [1842b]) early articles, for example, were about the introduction, by the provincial Rhine Assembly, of laws against the theft of wood. In England, the sanctions against theft also contributed to the settlement of colonies – for example, they involved the penal transportation of convicted felons to the colonies, for forced labour, a practice that began in the early seventeenth century, with transportation to the American colonies, and was carried on most famously through transportation to Australia, down to the mid-nineteenth century (Ekirch 1987). These were practices contiguous with the slave trade, albeit differently justified.

How did Locke defend this state of affairs? Herman Lebovics (1986: 579) puts the question starkly: '[What] permitted him to justify the actions of rapacious and rebellious men of wealth of his and later ages and at the same time hold forth a promise of unprecedented political participation for the many?' The answer lies in Locke's treatment of 'spoilage' and in the function he finds for 'money', but also in his recognition of the role of the colonies in providing opportunities for those displaced by enclosure at home.

Locke was clear that the fact that the commons were God-given imposed a duty upon humans. God's expectation was that the commons should be put to use. As Locke stated, 'it cannot be supposed he meant it should remain common and uncultivated. He gave it to the use of the Industrious and Rational, (and Labour was his title to it)' (Locke 1960 [1698]: 291). The obligation to put the land to use was necessarily expressed through possession and the possible displacement of others. It took place among people who were perceived to occupy the land without mixing their labour with it. In the case of indigenous people who occupied land subject to European colonialism, we can see that it was important that they be represented as living *off* the land, not *through* the land. In other words, they were represented as hunting and gathering, and not as engaging in practices of husbandry, which involved the cultivation of land. This argument was reinforced by the claim that allowing land to be unused and permitting an abundance of fruit beyond what was gathered for daily consumption represented a form of spoilage. Thus indigenous people were also in conflict with the command that '[n]othing was made by God for Man to spoil or destroy' (290).

But did the accumulation of wealth not risk being itself a form of spoilage? And how could it be reconciled with 'enough, and as good left in common for others' (288)? It would be spoilage if stocks of food were accumulated and left to rot. However, money had developed as a store of value. Goods were produced and distributed on a market, and what was accumulated was money.[8] In turn, money could be put to other productive ventures, and thus the accumulation of money expanded possession into what was, for Locke, a virtuous circle. One of its uses was colonial expansion through ventures that absorbed the labour of the domestic population displaced by enclosure. Thus, for Locke, the commonwealth need not involve the creation of a surplus population pushed outside the contract that brought the commonwealth into being. Instead, the commonwealth potentially extended its boundaries into colonies, where the land 'unused' by the indigenous inhabitants was seen to be available to settlers. The commonwealth, then, was not simply a 'national' patrimony, but one that incorporated colonial territories. Indeed, for those commenting on the dilemmas of national government, colonialism potentially diminished the domestic labour supply and needed to be balanced by the way in which the colonies might expand the market for domestic products or provide the raw material for domestic manufacture.[9]

The demand for labour to create settler colonies was served not only through the movement of an English – and in fact European – peasantry displaced by enclosure, or by people who sought the freedom to pursue their dissenter religious beliefs (as in the case of early Puritan settlers). As we have already commented, this demand was also met by the forced labour of those transported as a punishment for transgressions against new laws of private property. In addition, colonial settlers imposed labour on native populations through enslavement, as well as through the transportation of captured Africans into slavery. This was a trade that began in the mid-sixteenth century and encompassed the enslavement practised on the Indian sub-continent and the transportation of indentured labourers through Asia and the East Indies (Allen 2010, 2017). These impositions of labour were justified by Enlightenment thinkers through references to the virtues of labour, *including for those who did not will it for themselves*.

Enforced labour from people deemed to be criminals was straight-forwardly justified according to Locke's ideas of natural rights.

These people had transgressed against the property rights of others; therefore their claims for possessing their own selves could be forfeited. In that respect, theft had entailed a recognition of the rights of property, by making one's own that which belonged to another. But what of the enslavement of Africans as part of the transatlantic slave trade, and what of the enslavement of indigenous populations elsewhere? After all, Locke condemned slavery, writing that it was 'so vile and miserable an Estate of Man, and so directly opposite to the generous Temper and Courage of our Nation; that 'tis hardly to be conceived, that an Englishman, much less a Gentleman, should plead for't' (Locke 1960 [1698]: 141). Some have argued that Locke was focused on the local issue of enslavement after conquest and, specifically, after the Norman Conquest (Farr 1986). However, as Jennifer Welchman (1995) argues, it is implausible that Locke was unaware either of the enslavement of Africans or of slavery in the English colonies in North America – after all, he was one of the nine Lords Protector of the Carolinas charged with the promotion of colonial settlement and a shareholder in the Royal African Company, which was engaged in the trade in human beings.

According to Welchman, the answer is found in Locke's arguments about political (civil) society and the state of nature. In his eyes, Africans and indigenous peoples existed in the state of nature, and the strife attributed to that condition meant that their warlike transgressions – among themselves or against settlers – placed them in breach of natural rights. One consequence was that they could become the property of others – including other tribes – and, as such, traded as property by their owners.[10] As Welchman (1995: 79) puts it, 'it would be sufficient cause to enslave a man in sub-Saharan Africa if he was known to have threatened at least one person or if he had tolerated or concurred in one such assault. It would not be necessary that the captor be the person attacked, nor would it be necessary that the captive remain in his captor's hands. Being property, the captive might be sold, bartered, or given to whomever his captor pleased – even Europeans.' Yet Locke (1960 [1698]: 269) also argued that '[c]reatures of the same species and rank ... should also be equal one amongst the another'. The point is that Locke did not deny that human beings were of one species, but he claimed that justified enslavement created two ranks, of which only one enjoys equality. Enslavement was a 'vile and miserable' condition only among those with the *rank of equals*.

Locke argued that 'servants' created property for their masters: 'the Grass my horse has bit; the turfs my servant has cut; and the Ore I have digg'd in any place where I have a right to them in common with others, become my *Property*, without the assignation or consent of any body. The *labour* that was mine, removing them out of that common state they were in hath *fixed* my *Property* in them' (289). In Macpherson's (1962) account, this passage is indicative of Locke's elision of a wage contract, which would come to be central to Marx's understanding of capitalism and to his critique of liberalism's justifications of it. However, for Locke, the servant was under the patriarchal authority of the master, whose right to property is being described. Everything with which that labour was mixed – including any surplus generated and converted into monetary profit – became the property of the master and expressed the labour right of the master, since property was justified on the grounds that it followed from labour. And it was clear that having property in the labour of others rendered the property created through that labour the property of the master. As James Tully (1980: 136) suggests, Locke was operating within a conventional understanding of a 'master–servant' relation, which, as Robbie Shilliam (2020) argues, was otherwise a constraint on the development of 'free labour'. Indeed, for Shilliam, the 'master–servant' relation was akin to a 'master–slave' relation, begging the question of a distinction in status between 'service' and 'enslavement' in a context where the latter was deemed appropriate for some, but not others.

It is easy to see why Macpherson should treat such passages as indicative of a nascent capitalist understanding. However, the arguments about the labour contract appear in a context of justifications of forced labour and colonialism. The Marxist metaphor of the labour contract as 'wage slavery' on account of the extraction of an 'unpaid' surplus has to be set against the *real slavery* endured by other populations. In Lebovics's view, Locke bound liberalism and colonialism together: 'he made the colonial empire a vital bond between Britain's new elite and those they governed. He thereby strengthened the nascent liberalism of British society by building into it the promise of growth, of more for all, of social peace through empire' (Lebovics 1986: 580–1).

What was true of the British empire was also true of other European empires and their justifications of themselves qua empires. The emergence of capitalist modernity was continuous with colonialism, and the existence of colonial opportunities helped to manage domestic discontent engendered by the displacement of populations through enclosure. Specifically, colonialism itself can be seen as an integral part of the enclosure movement of Europeans (including those who were themselves dispossessed within Europe) on a global scale. The very corporations set up in the early modern period – the East India Company, the Virginia Company, the Royal African Company in England, and corporations operating under other royal charters – existed not simply for the purpose of trade, but to facilitate the possession of land, the development of plantations, and the use of forced labour (Aravamudan 2009).

Stadial Theory and the Idea of Progress

Hobbes and Locke, as we have seen, each relied upon a distinction between a state of nature and a state of society. Locke (1960 [1698]: 301), for example, famously announced: 'in the beginning all the World was *America*, and more so than it is now'. Each referred to reports of indigenous peoples and their customs as evidence that these populations approximated to the fictional state of nature, occupying a relatively empty land.[11] The purpose, for both of them, was to set out a theory of government and to establish the role of private property in the understanding of the (modern) self. It was left to later social theorists to distinguish between different types of society, to articulate them in relation to its earliest manifestation – what was called 'hunter-gatherers' – and to differentiate them from an emerging form of modern society, with its own distinct and defining features. Just as Hobbes and Locke constructed a fictional state of nature, so later writers constructed modernity as a fiction, specifically by producing a theory of 'commercial society' in which the colonialism that is integral to it was elided.

   In these respects, the writers of the mid to late eighteenth century continued the process of (mis)representing their society to its members – the very process that Macpherson had discerned in Hobbes and Locke. Primary among these writers were the French *philosophes*, Montesquieu (1689–1755) and Anne Robert Jacques Turgot (1727–81), and the writers of what came to be known as the Scottish Enlightenment – for example David Hume (1711–76), Adam Smith (1723–90), William Robertson (1721–93), John Millar

(1735–1801), and Adam Ferguson (1723–1816). Montesquieu (1965 [1748]), in *The Spirit of Laws*, was perhaps exemplary in his wish to demonstrate that individuals were products of their society and that societies varied across time and space. He was less concerned with the condition of humanity in abstraction, but rather focused on the particularity of nations and cultures as constituted through their geography, climate, traditions, and practices. This was evidently a 'sociological' approach, albeit one that emphasised the discrete character of human societies and communities without also recognising their interconnections.

While colonial encounters were not specifically addressed, it is not difficult to see that in many cases they provided social theorists with their data. Such encounters also contributed to the growing belief that 'travelling in space also meant travelling in time; the Others they encountered [there] were earlier versions of themselves' (Fox 1995: 16). One potentially positive aspect of such arguments was that it relativised European self-understandings and found a common humanity across cultural differences. Montesquieu (2008 [1721]), for example, in his *Persian Letters*, imagined travellers to Europe describing to a credulous domestic audience the customs and practices they had come across, and thereby disrupting his own readers' unselfconscious adherence to their customs.[12]

It is in this development that Johan Heilbron (1995) and others have seen the emergence of a proto-sociological theory where, as Christopher Berry puts it, different social practices are described as something more than a set of exotic travellers' tales; and the attempt is 'to place this diversity in some sort of order' (Berry 1997: 88). The different thinkers of the Scottish Enlightenment developed their understandings of progress in relation to a variety of ideas as to what the stages of this process were. But, for all the variety, they all pictured them as successive steps in an historical development. Further, each stage was believed to generate particular ways of being and behaving and to generate distinct personalities and character traits – that is, forms of subjectivity. The superiority of these thinkers' own society was believed to be demonstrated through association with traits such as civility, good manners, refinement, the cultivation of the arts, and so forth.

It was in 1767, with the publication of Ferguson's *Essay on the History of Civil Society*, that the *progress* of a people came to be attributed to the subdivision of the tasks distributed in it and historical stages were regarded as consecutive, evolutionary, and culminating in 'modern' society. While Ferguson, like Montesquieu, believed that physical factors of geography and climate played a part in enabling distinctions to be made between societies, the variables that he took to be fundamental were explicitly social ones, namely the nature of economic activities and the character of social relations. The latter he associated with issues of 'national defence, the distribution of justice, [and] the preservation and internal prosperity of the state' (Ferguson 1966 [1767]: 135). These were the key domains in which distinctions had developed between societies.

Even the physical factors under discussion were addressed from the perspective of the meeting of human needs and the possibilities for social progress in other respects that this entailed. When Ferguson discussed the climate or the existence of fertile land, for example, his remarks were directed to what these conditions would enable people to do and produce. Land that required the investment of labour and skill was seen to condition a people to 'retain their frugality, increase their industry, and improve their arts' (Ferguson 1966 [1767]: 142). This, in turn, would have the potential consequence of transforming the mode of subsistence, moving it from agriculture to commerce through the accumulation of wealth generated through increased industriousness and consolidated by the institution of private property.

In effect, social theory began to coalesce around a representation of different types of society, their structures, and specific moral constitutions (as Durkheim would later come to term them). Essentially, four types of society came to be identified, each one characterised by its typical mode of subsistence: hunting and gathering; pastoral (i.e. the nomadic tending of herds); settled agriculture; and commercial society. The essential idea of this stadial theory of history – one that was picked up and developed subsequently in sociology – was that 'societies undergo *development* through successive *stages* based on different *modes of subsistence*' (Meek 1976: 6). This was an idea that would be developed further by Marx in his conception of different modes of production, leading to a redescription of commercial society itself in terms of its *capitalist mode of production*.

While the stages were seen as progressive, each stage marking an advance on the previous ones, the ultimate stage, that of commercial society, was treated both as distinct from and as potentially contemporaneous with other modes of subsistence, from which it had emerged or with which it had been juxtaposed (albeit the process by which the latter happened was not explicitly discussed). Ferguson (1966 [1767]), for example, argued that it was only by studying contemporary 'savage' and 'barbarian' societies that it was possible to draw conclusions about the influence of different situations on 'our' ancestors: 'the inhabitants of Britain, at the time of the first Roman invasion', he wrote, 'resembled, in many things, the present natives of North America' (75). It is in their present condition, then, 'that we are to behold, as in a mirrour, the features of our own progenitors; and from thence we are to draw our conclusions with respect to the influence of situations, in which, we have reason to believe, our fathers were placed' (80). Even while dismissing the possibility of knowing the exact origins of the inhabitants of the Americas, Robertson (1818 [1777]: 49) similarly made the point that studying them should complete the history of the human mind. Such a history, he suggested, was possible only by getting to know people as they existed in all different stages of society; and the inhabitants of the Americas were to be regarded as 'the rudest form in which we can conceive him [the human being] to exist' (50).

There were fears about the negative character traits potentially generated by this new, commercial mode of subsistence. The move away from personal dealings and relations in commercial transactions to impersonal ones, regulated not by benevolence and kindness but by concern for one's own advantage and interest, was believed to increase the distance between individuals and to loosen the ties of mutual dependence. For some, and for Ferguson in particular, the rise of commercial society was bound to entail a loss in spirit, solidarity, and courage and to signify the end of virtue itself, 'as formerly free arms-bearing citizens had become content to pay mercenaries to defend them' (Pocock 1977: 292). Such concerns would form the basis of claims that the emergent modern sensibility contained within it an analytical component, capable of immanent critique and of reforming the very order it sought to justify.

The vindication of commercial society rested on the accumulation and distribution of wealth across classes, such that all members of society were able to enjoy a better standard of living than had previously been possible (Smith 1970 [1776]). Alongside wealth, freedom was the other key characteristic ascribed to commercial society. Smith believed that members of commercial society enjoyed a liberty that was denied to subjects who lived in societies characterised by other modes of subsistence, as the surplus generated by commerce 'bought' the freedom of individuals. So circumscribed, freedom consisted in part in the ability to choose and change one's occupation and to improve one's conditions through the accumulation of wealth. What was paramount for the thinkers of the Scottish Enlightenment was to specify the nature of the effects of particular social arrangements and to attempt to understand how these could be enhanced or, conversely, how their disruption could be prevented. An example of this attitude is Adam Smith's (1970 [1776]) pronouncement, in his *Wealth of Nations*, about the significance of market exchange relations within commercial society and about the dangers of disrupting their operation and damaging their beneficial effects. This was a concern also shared by Hume.

A civilised society, according to Hume (1898 [1752]), was one in which property was secure, industry was encouraged, and the arts were able to flourish. The dissipation of extended kinship ties and of ties of ascriptive and exclusive loyalty was further believed to open up space for the development of natural sympathies, sociability, and friendship (Silver 1990). Civilisation was seen to require commerce, and commerce, since it rested on a set of expectations and beliefs, was deemed to require stability and security. As Berry (1997: 125) notes, exchange entails specialisation and necessitates giving up a self-sufficient life in favour of one that is interdependent. This interdependence then requires forms of organisation and the establishment of rules and regulations to protect individuals from the unpredictability inherent in freely constituted social relations. The development of cities was also seen as fundamental to the loosening of individual ties of economic dependence and social subservience.

Even though people were still subject to the constraints of economic self-provisioning, the introduction of industry was generally believed to generate degrees of social freedom that had previously not been possible. As Hume wrote on the relationship between the refinement of the arts and the impetus to sociability,

> They flock into the cities; love to receive and communicate knowledge; to show their wit or their breeding; their taste in conversation or living, in clothes or furniture. Curiosity allures the wise; vanity the foolish; and pleasure both. Particular clubs and societies are everywhere formed: both sexes meet in an easy and sociable manner; and the tempers of men, as well as their behaviour, refine apace. So that ... it

is impossible but they must feel an increase of humanity, from the very habit of conversing together, and contributing to each other's pleasure and entertainment. Thus *industry*, *knowledge* and *humanity* are linked together by an indissoluble chain, and are found, from experience as well as reason, to be peculiar to the more polished, and ... the more luxurious ages. (Hume 1898 [1752]: 271)

This sociability extended to relations between the sexes. For example, Millar's *Origin of the Distinction of Ranks*, published in 1779, is frequently identified as the first sociological treatment of social stratification, and hence a precursor to concerns with issues of social class. However, the bulk of his discussion of different stages of society was concerned with relations between men, women, and children. According to him, patriarchal power – 'the power of the husband, the father and the civil magistrate' (Millar 1990 [1779]: 243) – was reduced in polished nations by comparison with what it had been in pastoral and 'savage' ages.

The tendency to associate the increase in wealth with the progress of a society was most apparent in the work of Smith (1970 [1776]) and Turgot (1973 [1766]). Both these thinkers pointed to the division of labour as fundamental to the 'turning of land to account' and to the subsequent growth of commodity exchange and accumulation of 'movable wealth', that is, money – and, for Turgot (1973 [1766]: 134, 145), also enslaved people. Once it was possible to generate a surplus of 'movable wealth' and thus establish a reserve or 'a capital', Turgot suggested that that reserve could be safeguarded as insurance against an uncertain future or could be used to advance manufacturing and industrial enterprises (150, 151). Turgot and Smith differed in the emphasis they placed respectively on land and labour as being generative of wealth; but in both cases the primary explanation was an endogenous one. The implication was that the use of labour applied to land arose initially in the form of serfdom, which could then be transmuted to waged labour.[13]

The rise of commerce, then, was generally attributed to the way in which, after the institution of agriculture, a surplus was realised and the division of labour extended. In these circumstances, a society based on commerce was not seen to be 'the product of external forces like the pressure of population on resources' (Berry 1997: 97); it was rather considered to emerge through an internal reorganisation of productive social relations and the accumulation of movable wealth.

As the wealth of (some) nations increased and countries began to develop economically, it was suggested that this occurred 'because *within the framework of these changing modes of subsistence* there was a gradual increase over time in the division of labour, commodity exchange, and the accumulation of capital' (Meek 1976: 222).

While it was tacitly accepted that the definition of 'movable wealth' and capital included enslaved people as well as money, discussion of the former was limited, both in the work of the theorists of the time and in that of subsequent commentators. Turgot (1973 [1766]) referred briefly to the aspect of owning enslaved people as one element of wealth generation, but this aspect was not expanded upon, nor were its implications for subsequent analysis drawn. When writers of this period discussed slavery, they treated it primarily as a feature of militaristic societies based on settled agriculture. For the most part, they took their examples from classical antiquity, especially the Greeks, and not from the active enslavement that they may have witnessed during the period of emergence of the new form of commercial society, which they believed would supersede the one based on settled agriculture. While most social theorists recognised the condition of slavery, they did so primarily while pointing out that this practice had existed in earlier stages of society, or by way of finding an analogy for contemporary practices that were radically different in other respects; thus Marx referred to free labour as having the form of 'wage slavery'.

Yet such activities were not marginal to the modern society on which they were reflecting; nor were they outside the direct experience of social theorists. By the middle of the eighteenth century, a substantial proportion of the European bourgeoisie generated and accumulated its wealth on the basis of commercial activities connected to the slave trade and other trades of 'dispossession', such as the fur trade.[14] It was not uncommon for people to invest in these commercial activities even as they argued for the abolition of slavery (Sala-Molins 2006).

The focus on classical slavery served two related purposes. First, it located the practice of slavery in the ancient world, where it was associated with the settled agricultural mode of production in the extended household that was the Greek *oikos* (or the Roman *domus*). This comparison enabled slavery in contemporary society to be seen as a residual form associated with the agricultural mode of subsistence, along with other kinds of unfree labour such as serfdom and bonded labour. With this, contemporary forms of slavery did not have to be addressed in the context of *the emergence of commercial society*, but simply as a practice left over from previous societies, and one that would diminish as commerce extended its domain. This was further reinforced once commercial society came to be understood as industrial capitalist society founded on waged labour.

Millar, for example, regarded slavery as a consequence of warlike relations among tribes in the 'savage' stage of society, where captives were either put to death or put to use. He acknowledged the encounter between Europeans and African tribes on the coast of Guinea, but attributed the barbarity of the trade to the latter and not to the demand for enslaved people generated by the market, notwithstanding that the market was the primary institution of the 'polished' age. This was an echo of Locke's justification of the enslavement of people whose lives were assigned to the state of nature. Thus, Millar wrote,

> the negroes upon the coast of Guinea ... from their intercourse with the nations of Europe, derive yet greater advantages from sparing the lives of their enemies. At the same time, it cannot be doubted, that, as the encounters of those barbarians have upon this account become less bloody, their wars have been rendered more frequent. From the great demand for slaves to supply the European market, they have the same motives to seize the person of their neighbours, which may excite the inhabitants of other countries to rob one another of their property. (1991: 248–9)

Even as Millar recognised the deep involvement of European commercial society in slavery, he absolved the two of any necessary interconnection – 'By what happy concurrence of events has the practice of slavery been so generally abolished in Europe?' (1991: 261) – aligning slavery with serfdom and observing that liberty secured a more productive workforce.

In fact, as Peter Kolchin (1987) has shown, slavery in Europe grew commensurately with enslavement in the Americas. From the sixteenth and seventeenth centuries to the 1860s, systems of unfree labour were put in place at Europe's eastern and western edges (the latter being the Americas), and the numbers of people made unfree expanded with the growth of commercial society itself, as colonial plantation systems supported economic growth in Europe. Peasants in Russia, for example, were not 'always already' unfree, but were *actively enserfed* in this period; and their bonds were tightened rather than loosened. While slavery was a racialised system and serfdom was not, a presumed innate 'inferiority' of serfs was socially established and reinforced. We will argue that the significance of slavery is that it instituted the lasting significance of race to modern social structures. However, racialised difference itself depended on the wider significance of unfree labour in the development of modernity. Far from being the backward hangover of a traditional society in the process of modernisation, unfree labour was an integral part of modernity – the very modernity that was praised for its inauguration of freedom (Robinson 1983).

None of the social theorists of the eighteenth century saw slavery (or other predations) as generative of commercial society or integral to its functioning, and thus in need of being explained and integrated into the *understanding of commercial society itself*. This was so, as we have already commented, in spite of the economic significance of the types of trade associated with slavery and other forms of dispossession. Any contradictions between thought and behaviour – between considering oneself civilised and living in a society that perpetrated chattel slavery – could be placed outside the theoretical framework under discussion and did not require resolution within it. To the extent that the mode of subsistence was taken to be a heuristic device, these thinkers were able to acknowledge the existence of differences between their schemas and the observable phenomena of slavery and dispossession, but these differences did not call into question the integrity of the framework or their own self-image as civilised and polite. 'Savagery' or 'barbarity' was presented as the prior condition of those subject to violent dispossession, and not as the reality produced under the 'polish' of commercial society.[15]

Hegel and the Master–Slave Relation

The further development of commercial society brought in its wake more fundamental transformations than those initially identified within the theory of stages. While colonial relations receive some recognition in initial discussions of commercial society, they become attenuated to the point of disappearance as the idea of commercial society and its distinctive institutional forms become more elaborate and are understood as an embodiment of reason and liberty that takes on universal historical significance. In the writings of the German philosopher Georg Friedrich Wilhelm Hegel (1770–1831), the stadial account of history was presented as a developmental process. As Perez-Diaz succinctly puts it, Hegel was concerned to develop, 'a theory of the rational society or ethical community of modern times, a definition of the present situation as approaching that model, and a statement about the historical tasks for this time' (Perez-Diaz 1978: 15, see also Taylor 1975).

In these respects, Hegel offered a theory of human history as a rational reconstruction from the perspective of the modern present, outlining different historical developments and their contribution to the current realisation of freedom. One consequence of Hegel's rational reconstruction of history was a specific form of Eurocentrism, in which the history of European development and self-realisation was presented as 'universal history': 'world history travels from east to west; for Europe is the absolute end of history, just as Asia is the beginning' (Hegel 1975 [1830]: 197), he argued. This was a dialectical development whereby contradictory manifestations were overcome and transformed until freedom was universalised. It is hard to overestimate the significance of this formulation to modern social theory. It lies at the heart of Marx's own critique of capitalism and is central to the critical theory of the Frankfurt School. But in this way a deeply problematic Eurocentrism was embedded in modern social theory, in both its liberal and its critical manifestations.

For critical theorists, however, Hegel's claim that the social institutions of Europe emergent in his day represented the end of history contained the possibility of self-criticism.[16] The institutions embraced and validated by Hegel might themselves come to be found wanting in relation to the very standards of justification he set out. For Marx, these standards animated the idea of a different future, for example, and the reconstruction of institutions in the light of the possibilities that they contained. Thus, where Hegel largely endorsed present institutions, Marx would reveal their contradictory character and the need for further social transformation in order to fulfil human possibilities. It was precisely this idea of reason as 'dialectical' that allowed an understanding of modern social theory as capable of 'self-repair'. Modernity's 'darker' sides (enslavement, colonialism, and empire) are facts that require little conceptual pause because, as Mehta (1999: 162) very nicely says, there 'is a promissory note of future release conditional on following a specific trajectory of development'.

Two sets of arguments by Hegel are relevant here. Put very simply, the first concerns the development of human self-understanding and the dialectical relation between freedom and unfreedom, while the second concerns the ethical character of the institutions of modern society – family, civil society, and state. We will address the latter in a subsequent chapter, in the context of Marx's criticisms and how these institutions help to establish his alternative account. In the first set of arguments, Hegel countered liberal understandings of subjectivity with a philosophy of recognition, and did so through the figure of the master–slave relation.

Hegel began with the idea of the consciousness of a 'self' that developed in relation to an 'other'. At least initially, this consciousness was of a being potentially thwarted by the other. The two selves appeared to each other as the same in their immediate identity as selves, but as opposed – or in contradiction – to each other. Human history was understood as a dialectics of recognition, as exemplified in the master–slave relation; but it was presented by Hegel separately from the concrete reality of slavery as it existed at the time, which he explicitly endorsed. In his highly influential discussion of Hegel's *Phenomenology of Spirit*, Kojève (1969: 8) sets out the nature of this dialectic in stark terms: 'Man is never simply man. He is always, necessarily, and essentially, either master or slave.' In effect, Kojève suggests that Hegel is conceptualising the relation between the state of nature and the state of society. He describes the master–slave relation as a life-and-death struggle, but it is a struggle in which each self, conscious of itself, necessarily entails engagement with another self, equally conscious. This is what sets up conflict, but also the possibility of mutual 'recognition'.

The encounter can be understood initially in terms of domination, of one self exerting its will over the other – that is, of mastery and servitude. However, Hegel was concerned to show that this situation was untenable from each side. The master seeks recognition from the other, but cannot accept a recognition that is coerced rather than freely given. On the other hand, the one who is enslaved is bound to work on behalf of the master, but in labour discovers the possibility of independence from the master. At the same time, the master is made dependent on the slave through the latter's labour for the master. As Hegel put it, 'it is only with the release and liberation of the slave that the master also becomes fully free' (cited in Williams 1997: 79). The point of Hegel's argument, then, was not to claim that a life-and-death struggle was at the heart of all institutions, as Kojève (1969) claimed, but rather its opposite (Williams 1997). The master–slave relation was self-defeating when considered from either of its sides. Outside the state of nature, reciprocal recognition was the condition of freedom.

As we have argued, slavery was very real in Hegel's own time. Notwithstanding his arguments about recognition, Hegel endorsed it in highly racialised terms. This was possible because, in his treatment of recognition, Hegel provided a philosophical account of freedom and coercion that was independent of any specific institutional expressions of human relationships. His demonstration of the contradictory nature of the master–slave relation was, for him, consistent with a practical endorsement of slavery. The concrete development of human freedom passed through different incomplete historical manifestations before it culminated in European modernity and the end of history. Indeed, in common with other Enlightenment writers, Hegel saw freedom from domination as the specific condition and achievement of European modernity. Human beings in a state of nature were 'free in themselves', in that they had the capacity for freedom; but they were not 'free for themselves'. It was through this distinction that Hegel justified the enslavement of those who did not yet express the freedom attributed to them (Bernasconi 2000, Stone 2017).

Like other theorists, Hegel represented early human society, for him exemplified in the Americas or in sub-Saharan Africa, as savage and barbaric, with its people barely human. In a religion based upon magic and fetishes, there was little conception of the divine through which humanity imagined itself, and therefore little self-respect and respect for others (Hegel 1975 [1830]: 218).[17] Lacking respect for humanity, this type of society practised both cannibalism and slavery. Although Hegel condemned slavery, he represented the enslavement of Africans by Europeans as positive for them. 'Negroes are enslaved by Europeans and sold to America', he wrote. However, 'bad as this may be, their lot in their own land is even worse, since there a slavery quite as absolute exists: for it is the essential principle of slavery, that man has not yet attained a conception of his freedom, and consequently sinks down to a mere Thing, an object of no value' (183).

Hegel proceeded, in anachronistic fashion, with a characterisation of the social relations of what he believed to be early society: there the consequence of European contact fashioned a trade in human beings that was then represented as the essence of the societies it despoiled. Hegel wrote that 'parents sell their children, and children their parents, as either has the opportunity' (183). The reports of European traders and missionaries, who left out of their account the hospitality offered to Europeans on first contact, were used by Hegel to depict the 'savagery' of indigenous people in their opposition to being displaced from their land and taken into possession as commodities. Their resistance to this fate was not a mark of their humanity and of the corresponding inhumanity of Europeans, but a further indication that indigenous people lacked humanity. Thus Hegel wrote that their resistance was a further example of their 'want of regard for life', which in his view characterised their local practices of enslavement. Their courage in the face of Europeans derived from this inhumanity and from a wanton disregard for life. Thus Hegel wrote 'of the great courage, supported by enormous bodily strength, exhibited by the Negroes, who allow themselves to be shot down by thousands in war with Europeans' (183).

Overcoming domination – the master–slave relation – was the historical achievement of Europe, and it did not seem to Hegel to be a contradiction that it should occur in the circumstances of an extensive commodification of servitude. Indeed, the section on the master–slave relation in *The Phenomenology of Mind* was written shortly after the Haitian Revolution, which was widely reported in the press at the time (Buck-Morss 2000). On this topic Hegel was silent. We will return to it in the next chapter.

Conclusion

In this chapter we have set out the ways in which the reality of colonialism was displaced from accounts of the development of a distinctive modern society, which was to be understood separately from its colonial context. Insofar as the development of modern society was associated with the accumulation of wealth from colonial endeavours, the significance of that wealth was represented independently of how the wealth itself was appropriated by European political communities. With the development of stadial theory, modern social theory created representations of modernity and other types of society. To the extent that slavery was acknowledged, it was attributed to earlier societal forms and justified as a method of ameliorating the intrinsic 'savagery' of others; the availability of enslavement promised a better alternative to existence in 'barbarous' conditions. Chattel slavery – the commodification of other humans, which is specific to the modern form of enslavement – was either justified as necessary to bestowing the benefits of civilisation upon benighted others or represented as following from their savagery. In this way Europeans projected their own savagery upon others, presenting their ways of life as intrinsically warlike and their resistance as aggressive rather than defensive. The barbarity of incorporating forced labour into market exchange relations was ignored. Once this displacement had been made and the stadial theory of society had been represented as a truthful account of human development, modernity could appear to its members as the achievement of universal – and universalisable – freedom.

In the next chapter we will show how these representations shaped the understandings of democracy and of the political community of equals, since these are presented as among the major achievements of European modernity.

2

Tocqueville

From America to Algeria

This chapter addresses Alexis de Tocqueville's classic studies *Democracy in America*, and *The Ancien Régime and the Revolution*. Along with the revolution in France in 1789, the US Declaration of Independence in 1776 is widely regarded as a world historical moment that helped to define the political institutions of the modern world. Tocqueville discussed both countries as providing exemplary material for understanding political democracy. His claim was that the rebellion of colonists in America emerged in a society relatively free from the constraints of feudalism and thereby represented a purer form of democracy. He contrasted its achievements with the problems that continued to beset France after its revolution. In particular, he suggested that the key difference between the two was that, while the United States had established healthier associational forms of democracy, albeit with a new risk of the 'tyranny of the majority', in France there was a problematic centralisation of power that the revolution exacerbated. This brought the risk of despotism.

Some today might question whether these revolutions in America and France were actually democratic; among other concerns, the denial of franchise to all but propertied white men, the dispossession and genocide of indigenous peoples (a consequence acknowledged and described in some detail by Tocqueville), and the institution of slavery within the United States and the colonies claimed by France can be cited. Few, however, go on to re-examine the claims made in the context of taking these apparent historical 'anomalies' seriously. What Danielle Allen (2014) describes as the performative work of the US Declaration of Independence – that '[w]e hold these truths to be self-evident, that all men are created equal, that they are endowed by their Creator with certain unalienable Rights, that among these are Life, Liberty and the pursuit of Happiness' (cited in Allen 2014: 27) – is typically taken to be a normative commitment to democratic government that can wash away what the former president of the United States, Barack Obama, called the stains of the original sin of enslavement, to achieve a more perfect union (Obama 2009).[1]

The apparent universalism of the declaration and of the tradition of natural rights that underpins it is not something that is merely besmirched by a contingent particularism against which its cleansing principles can ultimately be turned. As we saw in the previous chapter, there are deeper structures – both material and intellectual – associated with colonialism that are at work. These structures were integral to the very principles being articulated. What Tocqueville passed over, in both the United States and France, was the broader colonial conditions of the political institutions and processes he was analysing and how they were associated with the centralisation of power he otherwise deplored.

France, like England (Great Britain after 1707), had begun a process of colonisation in the sixteenth century and was consolidating its incursions into Africa with the invasion of Algeria in 1830, around the time of Tocqueville's visit to the United States. Equally, the United States was beginning its process of territorial expansion out of the original thirteen colonies on the Eastern Seaboard that had been involved in the declaration of independence. This process included the Louisiana Purchase in 1803 – that is, the purchase, from France, of lands stretching from the Gulf of Mexico to Canada and to the Rocky Mountains in the west; and East and West Florida ceded from Spain in 1819 (Frymer 2017).[2] Indeed, Tocqueville anticipated US expansion to the Western Seaboard,[3] in other words, the creation of an 'empire' and not simply a 'nation': 'I cannot help thinking that they will someday become the world's leading maritime power. They are driven to rule the seas, just as the Romans were driven to conquer the world' (Tocqueville 2004 [1835]: 470).

Tocqueville wrote extensively about colonialism, but until very recently this was rarely acknowledged in secondary literature and was not seen as central to the evaluation of his claims about democracy. In this chapter we take issue with the silencing of colonialism and race within narratives of political modernity by locating the work of Tocqueville squarely within the context of its time. In addition, we draw attention to the arguments made by Tocqueville that did deal with such issues but that have often been neglected by scholars of Tocqueville. In *Democracy in America* he did address the racial limits of American democracy: he discussed the two races excluded from it – 'Indians and Negroes' – in the concluding chapter of the first volume, titled 'The Future Condition of the Three Races in the United States' (Tocqueville 2004 [1835]: 365). His analysis was not taken up in social theory, where its significance for thinking on democracy more generally is disregarded. Significantly, as Colwell states, 'this chapter is either omitted from most of the popular one-volume editions of *Democracy in America* or is abridged to leave out all mention of the Negro' (Colwell 1967: 95, footnote 15). The excision of this chapter – which makes up around a quarter of the first volume – reinforces the celebratory narrative in which democracy is presented as foundational to the self-identity of the United States in its role as modernity's 'first new nation' (Lipset 1963).

In the present chapter we set out Tocqueville's understanding of democracy on its own terms before going on to re-examine his claims in the context of his discussion of indigenous peoples and the relations between the races that inhabit the United States. This is followed by a discussion of two other sites of political conflict and their place – or rather their absence, both relative and absolute – from Tocqueville's deliberations on political modernity. These sites are Algeria, a country colonised by France in pursuit of the imperial ambitions that it believed would consolidate its national status, and Haiti, the French colony that liberated itself from colonial rule and enslavement in the years of the French Revolution and on which Tocqueville appears not to have made any significant public comment.

Between Aristocratic and Democratic Rule

Alexis Charles Henri Maurice Clérel, Comte de Tocqueville, was born in 1805, into nobility, on a family estate in Normandy. He died in 1859. His wider family took part in the conservative reaction to the changes brought about by the French Revolution in 1789, but Tocqueville himself looked forward. He participated in public office, initially as a magistrate and subsequently as a deputy of the Constituent Assembly, rising briefly to minister of foreign affairs in

1849. Throughout his career he commented assiduously on contemporary politics and public affairs. However, the politics of the period was frequently in turmoil. His early years were spent under the First Empire of Napoleon I. This had replaced the First Republic established in 1792 and was followed by the restoration of the Bourbon monarchy in 1814 under the rule of Louis XIII and Charles X. In 1830 this regime was in its turn replaced by the 'July monarchy' of Louis-Philippe d'Orléans, which gave way to the Second Republic between 1848 and 1852. Then, after a *coup d'état* engineered by the president, Louis Napoleon, the Second Empire was established and continued until 1870.[4] This instability was a motivating concern of Tocqueville in his search for the conditions of a more stable order.

Tocqueville was what was known as a 'legitimist', a supporter of the Bourbon monarchy, and after its demise in 1830 he judiciously took 'leave of absence' from France. Together with his friend, collaborator, and fellow aristocrat Gustave de Beaumont, he travelled to the fledgling United States, ostensibly to study its penitentiary system. For nine months spanning the period May 1831–February 1832, the two travelled across areas of recent settlement and into the contested territory of the frontier and witnessed the forced expulsion of the Choctaw people from their lands. On their return to Paris, they published, both jointly and separately, works that covered the topics of the US penitentiary system, democracy, slavery in both the French colonies and the United States, and French colonialism in Algeria (Bhambra and Margree 2010).

Best known among these works is Tocqueville's *Democracy in America*, which provided a comparative sociology of the institutions of democracy and freedom in America and Europe, in the context of the problems faced by republican democracy in France. Although Tocqueville is widely seen as liberal, his orientation was broadly conservative and his attitude to property and to the institutions through which it is expressed (e.g. the rights embodied in the landed estates of the aristocracy) was positive. Democracy was to be understood as the spirit of the age, but needed to be tempered by moderating and stabilising influences that, in Europe, found expression in the role of an aristocracy that served in particular as the basis of the orderly relations of the multiple geographies that made up the nation.

Democracy in America was published in two volumes, the first appearing in 1835 and the second in 1840. After the publication of the latter, Tocqueville travelled to Algeria with Beaumont in 1841; it was one of his first visits there. He was interested in purchasing an estate in Algeria, but that ambition did not come to fruition (Jardin 1988). In 1856, shortly before his death, Tocqueville produced another major study on the problem of democracy in France: *The Ancien Régime and the Revolution*. This work set out the continuities of the old feudal political regime of absolutist monarchy – which, despite the disruption of political revolution, facilitated a form of authoritarian democratic absolutism, thereby underscoring the lessons to be derived from both the American and the French Revolutions presented in *Democracy in America*. There was also a third country that served as a term of comparison – a *tertium comparationis* – and is less remarked in the secondary literature in this capacity: Great Britain (although see Drescher 1964 and Spring 1980). It experienced the loss of its American colonies even as it consolidated its colonial domination elsewhere. Unlike France, however, it avoided political revolution and experienced adaptations of its aristocracy to new sources of wealth. This consolidated the role of landed wealth in the political order, an outcome that Tocqueville strongly advocated (Spring 1980).

Tocqueville did not produce treatises or systematic theoretical studies on the objects of his interest, but rather an accumulation of observations on contemporary social and political events and historical developments, organised through a series of sharp analytical distinctions. Gianfranco Poggi (1972) has usefully suggested that this approach can be understood in the light of a later sociological development: Max Weber's idea of 'ideal types', where a theoretical construct is held to clarify conceptual connections that are exemplified by multiple empirical observations.[5] As Weber put it, the ideal type has a heuristic purpose, and its validity is not called into question by empirical instances that deviate from it (see ch. 4, pp. 130–9 in this volume). The purpose was to clarify an otherwise messier social reality by accentuating specific features in it. Tocqueville's specification of two types did not imply that one would fully replace the other; he favoured the moderating influence of 'aristocracy' on 'democracy'.

Of course, this manner of proceeding is particularly prone to bias by excluding issues regarded as not pertinent to the purpose of clarifying the nature of a connection. For example, is Tocqueville's 'tolerance' of slavery and advocacy for French settler colonialism in Algeria to be treated as irrelevant when we consider the validity of his arguments about the institutions of US political democracy? Once such a judgement is made, the very substance of Tocqueville's observations about those other matters can be left aside. This setting aside takes its most egregious form, as we have suggested, in the abridgement of the standard single volume edition of *Democracy in America* to a version that omits the chapter on the enslavement of Africans and the dispossession of indigenous peoples.

Poggi (1972) has nothing to say about these topics directly, but his interpretation is a faithful rendering of the standard sociological view of Tocqueville's contribution (in fairness, Poggi represents one of the first texts to present Tocqueville as a sociological classic, on a par with Marx, Weber, and Durkheim). According to him, Tocqueville can be understood as providing an account of two ideal types of political order and their sociological conditions. One is an *aristocratic order*, the other a *democratic order*. The former is an order based on hierarchy, while in the latter equality is central. There is a developmental process that connects them but, although Tocqueville was interested in the consequences of social change, he was less interested in what produced it. He preferred to live in the present and amid its problems.

The nature of the aristocratic order provided a point of contrast that would be familiar to Tocqueville's readers. As Poggi suggests, for contemporary readers, the opposite is the case. To us it is the aristocratic order that appears unfamiliar, so we will spend some time setting out its salient characteristics. In general, Tocqueville was setting out the positive legacy of an aristocratic order (as well as some of its problematic consequences) for modern society. This is where his third case, relatively unstudied – that of Britain – is significant. There the adaptation of the aristocracy to commercial society had a moderating influence on the possible excesses of democracy. It was in the United States and France, however, that, for Tocqueville, the nature of modern democracy, its positive substance, and its intrinsic problems could be discovered more easily. The United States was relatively without an aristocratic order, as a consequence of its being established *de novo* by English colonists. After independence, the colonists set up a political system separate from the relations of rule organised through a monarchy. In France, aristocracy was displaced by a political revolution. The United States represented the pure 'spirit' of democracy and its attendant risks, whereas France provided the example of a political democracy that developed as despotism. As Rajshree Chandra (2013: 32) neatly puts it, the former is where 'equality becomes a condition for democracy and the latter (less enduring than the former) where democracy becomes the condition for equality'. In other words, in the United States democracy followed from pre-existing social equality, whereas in France political equality (democracy) confronted social inequality and rank in the wider society.

Essentially, Tocqueville characterised an aristocratic order as a political system divided between the mass of the population and what he called a privileged caste. The latter was organised hierarchically through the privileges, immunities, and duties of a nobility. It operated as a network through which power was exercised by the monarch. The nobility did not owe its position directly to the monarch, but it was part of a system of patronage that was exercised from the centre and emanated from the court. The monarch appointed the members of the court, his ministers, and was advised by a Constituent Assembly made up of the aristocracy, the clergy, and the third estate – namely commoners such as peasants, merchants, and tradespeople from the towns. The nobility's privileges were based on landed estates, and the mass of the population owed duties to its local nobles. Thus, as Tocqueville (2004 [1835]: 686) put it, 'in countries that are organised aristocratically and hierarchi-cally, power never addresses the totality of the governed directly'. Indeed, from the perspective of the 'people', 'since one man is tied to another, the ruler may confine himself to controlling those at the top of the hierarchy. The rest will follow' (686). The 'top' of each hierarchy was the local member of the nobility. The Roman Catholic Church represented a separate basis of power, one that transcended the 'nation', but was organised regionally and locally and was under the patronage of local nobles. It had privileges similar to those of the nobility, both in the use of the land and in the raising of tithes (or church taxes). There were, thus, different sources of tension, and conflicts could well emerge in what Tocqueville presented as a stable political order.

Peasants were not yet 'Frenchmen' (Weber 1976): they did not possess a common national identity as French. It was the monarch who expressed the 'national will', through a class of nobles who owed him allegiance while they ruled locally. Membership of this class engendered a common sentiment of belonging to a caste, a status group, or an estate. The nobility derived its status from claims to land and from inheritance, as daughters were required to make alliances through marriage and younger sons by acquiring positions in the church, in the army, or in various offices. This status was expressed in social distance from the population below, which, according to Tocqueville, understood itself locally. In this context, then, there was no 'public sphere', but an agglomeration of local arrangements governed through aristocratic privileges and local assemblies, magistracies and courts. These were united 'nationally' through the political arrangements of monarchic rule.

It was this system of political rule that came to be at issue in the Revolution of 1789. In part, this happened because a series of monarchs had sought to increase their power and wealth through a process of selling appointments and disrupting the system of privileges by birth. As Tocqueville described in *The Ancien Régime*, this weakened local orderly relations. However, part of what was disruptive was the growth of commercial society in towns and, more generally, the growth of commercial wealth. As we shall see, this commercial wealth derived in very significant part from colonialism and the charters given by the monarch to trading companies, factors absent from Tocqueville's account (despite his own willingness to take advantage of the opportunities created in this way through his intended purchase of an estate in Algeria).

In Tocqueville's view, the basis of aristocratic wealth was the landed estate and the traditional modes of husbandry, which together provide a stable income for displays of taste and manners. Land could be accumulated through marriage or through conquest and incorporation (armies were organised around aristocrats, who were the leaders of their divisions). It was the stability of its wealth, as well as its definition of place, that gave the aristocracy, according to Tocqueville, a stable and 'disinterested' presence in the political order. He wrote:

> the masses can be seduced by their ignorance or their passions. A king, caught off guard, can be induced to vacillate in his designs, and in any case no king is immortal. But an aristocratic body is too numerous to be ensnared yet not numerous enough to yield readily to the intoxication of mindless passion. An aristocratic body is a man of resolve and enlightenment who never dies. (Tocqueville 2004 [1835]: 263)

In England, the enclosure movement – or 'agricultural improvement' – provided a means by which landowners could increase their wealth. In France, by contrast, the particularity of feudal arrangements slowed a similar movement (Rozental 1956). To be sure, there were calls for agricultural improvements there as well, especially from the physiocrats, and in Tocqueville's view these contributed to a ferment of public commentary that criticised the backwardness of the nobility. In this context, the commercial interests that were developing in towns separated themselves from the interests of the nobility in the same locality. This was represented by Tocqueville in *The Ancien Régime* as a form of fragmentation of the binding relationships of the old order.

At the same time, public opinion associated with commercial interests was becoming increasingly hostile to the influence of the church and its hierarchies. In effect, Tocqueville's argument was that there was centralisation of power at the court and in the person of the king, who ruled through a bureaucratic administrative machine, and that this machine was operated by a cadre of officials and was increasingly independent of the old aristocratic order. The situation created the possibility of political revolution as a consequence of the weakening of intermediate constraints: 'the central power in eighteenth-century France ... had already succeeded in destroying all the intermediate authorities and, since nothing but a huge and empty space had emerged, from a distance central government appeared to each citizen to be the only means of maintaining the social machine, the single necessary agent of public life' (Tocqueville 2008 [1856]: 77). In these circumstances, centralised power was more easily seized and then wielded.

Moreover, the fragmentation of the old system meant that the country was increasingly socially divided – town against countryside, commercial interests against landed interests, amid rising anticlericalism. As Tocqueville put it,

> I am astonished at the surprising ease with which the Constituent Assembly was able to destroy at a stroke all the former French provinces, several of which were more ancient than the monarchy and then to divide methodically the kingdom into eighty-three distinct districts as if it were dealing with the virgin soil of the New World ... In fact, while they seem to be dismembering living bodies, they were only butchering dead flesh. (83)

In effect, 'social divisions' between classes (in the Tocquevillean sense of distinct social groups with different privileges, obligations, and interests) were sharpening and, although the growth of commercial wealth and the increased monetisation of privileges and obligations were rendering actual differences less pronounced, there was no basis for solidarity. Social order was replaced by a political order imposed from above by 'leaders'. The revolution was predicated on claims for liberty, but the reality was recurrent 'despotic' rule.

The situation in the United States presented different characteristics from those in France. The social distinctions typical of the aristocratic order were breaking down in France and elsewhere in Europe and a new balance that favoured commercial interests was emerging. But those pre-existing distinctions had not passed on to the European colonies in the United States: the English and other settlers and colonists had equality of rank. True, the various 'companies' and 'societies' responsible for settlement acted under charters and monopolies that had been granted by their respective crowns, and the land that was appropriated, divided, and distributed frequently had various of the old privileges and entitlements attached to it. However, the populations that constituted the early voluntary settlement – what Tocqueville called 'the Anglo-Americans' – did not themselves labour under such privileges, but as equals.

Of course, where land was brought into large-scale agricultural use for the production of cash crops such as tobacco, cotton, or sugar, a plantation system of forced labour was put into place across the Americas. In that respect, the phenomenon observed in Europe that some described as a re-entrenchment of serfdom in the East (Kolchin 1987) was mirrored in the West by the introduction of enslavement. However, here we will follow Tocqueville's own primary device of subsuming democracy in America under the narrative of one race – that of the English colonists. We will return to the significance of this construction, not least because it becomes part of the designation of the southern states or colonies of the United States as 'the old South'. This label indicated aspects of an aristocratic status or order that was represented by 'gentlemanly' plantation owners and is made to appear already anachronistic from birth, notwithstanding that it was integral to colonialism. In this way, when Tocqueville treated the expulsion of indigenous peoples from the land and the imposition of forced labour on transported Africans as if they were issues separate from his primary narrative, he also elided problems of stratification by rank in 'white' society that were associated with the plantation system.[6] There are 'some relics of aristocratic institutions amid the most complete democracy', as Tocqueville (2004 [1835]) put it.

As already remarked, for Tocqueville it was the equality of status among Anglo-Americans that made democracy not only possible, but necessary. Volume 1 of *Democracy in America* set out the social conditions for democracy, while volume 2 explained how political democracy had a reciprocal influence on social conditions. To be sure, there were differences in wealth and other circumstances of individuals, but not in their standing as equal members of society. Even their differences in wealth and income were less great than elsewhere. Tocqueville argued that the abolition, after independence, of laws of entailment associated with heritable property meant that wealth would be divided among children. The abolition of those laws also had an equalising effect by comparison with the rules of primo-geniture (the favouring of first-born sons) that applied within the aristocratic order. Those rules contributed to a sense of rootedness to place typical of the nobility, whereas among Anglo-Americans there was no orientation to 'lineage' expressed through 'place', but only an aim of doing the best for oneself and setting up one's children.

It was a particular kind of ethos that Tocqueville sought to draw out:

> not that there are no wealthy people in the United States, just as there are everywhere. Indeed, I know of no other country where the love of money occupies as great a place in the hearts of men or where people are more deeply contemptuous of the theory of permanent equality of wealth. But wealth circulates there with incredible rapidity, and experience teaches that it is rare for two successive generations to garner its favors. (Tocqueville 2004 [1835]: 57)

The consequence was that all were required to undertake an occupation, and this frequently required apprenticeship, such that the level of general education was high. At the same time, the relative absence of large inherited wealth meant there was no rentier income to support a leisured (and learned) class: 'I do not think that there is any other country in the world where, as a proportion of the population, the ignorant are so few and the learned still fewer. Primary education is within the reach of everyone; higher education is within the reach of virtually no one' (58).

What Tocqueville was keen to set out was the immediacy of social relationships. The markers of status typical of European society, whether wealth or family, were absent, and geographical mobility meant that reputation had to be built in the present. What Tocqueville was describing was a social state of equality, in contrast to the social state of a society of rank. A society of equals, he argued, faced with the construction of political institutions, will necessarily turn to democracy (or despotism): 'I know of only two ways to achieve the reign of equality in the world of politics: rights must be given either to each citizen or to none. For nations that have achieved the same social state as the Anglo-Americans, it is therefore quite difficult to perceive a middle term between the sovereignty of all and the absolute power of a single individual' (60). The rest of the two volumes was designed to show why the former prevailed, while indicating some of the risks of the latter.[7]

According to Tocqueville, the spirit of equality prevailed through all aspects of social life, from township through to county and state. As he put it,

> it is at the local level that the strength of a free people lies. Local institutions are to liberty what elementary schools are to knowledge; they bring it within reach of the people, allow them to savor its peaceful use, and accustom them to rely on it. Without local institutions, a nation may give itself a free government, but it will not have a free spirit. (68)

This everyday engagement with public affairs was the ground that nurtured more remote forms of representation at the level of the state. Meetings could be called to settle issues, and different functions of governance and public provision were submitted to their scrutiny.

Just as he appreciated France's 'localism' under the *ancien régime*, Tocqueville recognised the same quality in New England townships in the United States. However, in the latter, this quality of localism was integrated within wider systems of representation and operated on the basis of similarity. At the level of the state, there was a recognition that popular sovereignty was not an abstract thing but was grounded in concrete particularity, albeit one where different townships were mostly similar in their populations and practices. As he put it, 'Europeans believe that they establish a foundation for liberty when they deprive the social power of some of its rights; Americans, when they divide the exercise of that power' (78). It would not be correct to present this localism as merely a counterweight to centralisation. The division of the social power was embedded in each of the levels, and so the federal authority of the union of states was balanced horizontally and vertically. Unlike in France, here this division operated in an orderly fashion as a result of the underlying similarity of a society of equals.

To some degree, this similarity was bequeathed by the happenstance of the religious belief of the Puritan settlers, whose antagonism to religious hierarchy involved a form of Christianity that Tocqueville described as republican and democratic. Again, unlike in France, where religion was a source of division, in the United States religion reinforced the general character of the society. Indeed, according to Tocqueville, the migration of Irish Catholics, notwithstanding their 'religious zeal and ardor', did not mitigate their republican and democratic commitments. Tocqueville reversed the normal anticlerical sentiments of European proponents of liberty and argued that he regarded religion as positive for democracy in that it was a source of meanings that went beyond self-interest, to which a society of equals might otherwise be prone. 'Despotism', he wrote,

> can do without faith, but liberty cannot. Religion is much more necessary in the republic ... [that French proponents of liberty] advocate than in the monarchy they attack, and most necessary of all in a democratic republic. How can society fail to perish if, as political bonds are loosened, moral bonds are not tightened? And what is to be done with a people that is its own master, if it is not obedient to God? (340)

In many respects, then, while Tocqueville took social equality to facilitate political democracy, the two were not fully commensurate for him. Because there are fewer differences among people in the absence of social rank, it is possible for them to be swayed and for electoral 'majorities' to overrule 'minorities' in much the same way in which intermediary checks had dissolved in the *ancien régime*. Religion constituted an 'inner voice' that could guide individuals independently of the sway of opinion. But there were also protections offered by the different levels of government. Significantly, however, religion did not serve to moderate the treatment of those placed outside the constitution, while the expansion south and west heightened an underlying conflict with Africans and indigenous people.

The New (Settler Colonial) Nation and Its Three Races

Given the emancipatory moment conventionally attributed to modernity, it is significant that the new American republic depended upon colonisation, dispossession, and enslavement, while reflections upon these processes tend to be absent in most scholars' accounts. The sole historical reference to the circumstances of the founding of the American republic in Peter Wagner's (2001) sociological interpretation of modernity, for example, is about the extermination of the native population and the destruction of its societies. This reference fits in with the European historiographical tradition of a stadial development of societies – 'in the beginning, all the world was America': in this way indigenous peoples could be at once placed within that project and *dis*placed, as no longer part of its *telos*.

However, Africans, whose migration was continuous with that of white settlers but was forced, and whose labour was also coerced and appropriated by those settlers, are represented as having no place in this new world. In part, this was because the Thirteen Colonies presented two faces, one of enslavement, the other of free labour – conventionally associated with southern and northern states and with the latter's victory over the former in the Civil War of 1861–5. Tocqueville wrote a quarter of a century before these events, but the war was prefigured in his writings. Significantly, he did not believe that the end of slavery in the southern states would bring an end to racism; he thought that it would rather serve to *generalise* throughout the union the racism that enslavement was bound up with. This is an argument that resonates with that of Du Bois, as we will see in a later chapter.

Tocqueville's position was clear in the arguments he adduced in the extensive chapter 'The Future Condition of the Three Races in the United States', which concluded volume 1 of his *Democracy in America* and without which, as he himself suggested, it was impossible to understand the future possibilities for democracy in America. Tocqueville clearly stated that the land of the United States was occupied by three races and that his account of democracy was about only one of them. This was because the history of the other two was one of their subjugation by the very institutions and practices that were otherwise being praised. He wrote that the positions of these two groups 'were tangential to my subject: they are American but not democratic' (Tocqueville 2004 [1835]: 365). Both groups, he continued, 'suffer the effects of tyranny, and while their miseries are different, both can blame those miseries on the same tyrant' (366).

Tocqueville, then, was acutely aware of the contradiction that was generated in the social and political community of modern democratic America by the enslavement of Africans and by the dispossession of indigenous peoples, on which the new society was founded. He regarded such treatment both as an infringement of the rights he ascribed to Anglo-Americans and as one of the most serious dangers that confronted the new society. He observed that, 'between the extreme inequality created by slavery and the complete equality to which independence naturally leads, there is no durable interme- diate state. Europeans ... with respect to the black man they violated all the rights of humanity, and then schooled him in the value and inviolability of those rights' (418).

The displacement of indigenous peoples, according to Tocqueville, was a process continuous with the development of the colonies and their expansion after independence. Indigenous people were present only 'in anticipation' of what the New World was to become. It was, for Tocqueville, 'an empty cradle awaiting the birth of a great nation' (29). While acknowledging that the territory to which the Europeans came 'was inhabited by numerous tribes of native peoples', Tocqueville went on to claim that 'at the time of its discovery it was still no more than a wilderness'. This was so because, in his words, 'Indians occupied it but did not possess it. It is through agriculture that man takes possession of the soil, and the first inhabitants of north America lived by hunting.' In consequence they delivered themselves to 'inevitable destruction'. Tocqueville wrote that 'the ruin of these tribes began the day the Europeans landed on their shores. It has continued ever since and is even now being carried through to completion.' The initial processes of this destruction were the dispos- session of indigenous nations from the territories consolidated as the Thirteen Colonies, the Louisiana Purchase in 1803, which more than doubled the territory claimed by European settlers, and the further expansion westward authorised by the 1830 Indian Removal Act. This Act, issued under the Presidency of Andrew Jackson, provided the ostensibly legal basis for the forced removal of the Five Civilized Tribes – the Cherokees, the Creeks, the Choctaws, the Chickasaws, and the Seminoles – and their replacement by European settlers over the subsequent two decades.

As Tocqueville noted, 'nowadays the dispossession of the Indians is often accomplished in a routine and – one might say – perfectly legal manner' (375).[8] In this way the consolidation of European rule over indigenous territories occurred through the making and breaking of treaties as much as through direct conquest and dispossession (Belmessous 2015).[9] The Louisiana Purchase, for example, represented an agreement between the governments of the United States and France, but excluded from that agreement the indigenous nations, which had already signed agreements with France. The treaties signed by these nations with the British government were similarly broken.

The treaties that the United States made continued to be broken and remade, such that in the early nineteenth century the Cherokee nation had had over half of its lands taken from them. As increasing numbers of Europeans were moving to the lands claimed by the United States, there was pressure for yet more land for the new arrivals. The Georgia state government petitioned the federal government for the forced removal of the Cherokees in the 1820s; this was ratified by Andrew Jackson when he became president in 1828. He did it by overruling the US Supreme Court's decision in favour of the Cherokee nation's right of sovereignty to that territory. The forced removal of the Cherokees, which occurred in the late 1830s, is known as the Trail of Tears – a series of relocations in which more than a quarter of the Cherokee population died or was killed in the process. The land from which the Cherokees were removed was then allocated, through the Georgia land lottery, to European settlers who had three years of established residency in the state (Smithers 2015).

This episode was just one in a long line of such removals; and the earlier displacement of the Choctaw people had been witnessed by Beaumont and Tocqueville. It was precisely what occasioned Tocqueville's reflections, in *Democracy in America*, on the tyranny visited upon indigenous peoples. The tyranny elicited sympathy, but Tocqueville did not call for a rectification of the injustice. This paradoxical situation will be further highlighted when we come to consider his writings on the French colonisation of Algeria and his failure, in that context, to express much sympathy for the people who were suffering French tyranny; worse still, Tocqueville justified it. For now, though, we continue with his reflections on witnessing forced removal:

Toward the end of 1831, I found myself on the east bank of the Mississippi, at the place the Europeans called Memphis. During the time I was there, a large band of Choctaws arrived ... These savages had left their native land and were trying to make their way across to the west bank of the Mississippi, where they hoped to find the refuge promised them by the American government. It was then the heart of winter, and the cold that year was unusually bitter. The snow on the ground had frozen, and enormous chunks of ice floated on the river ... I watched them embark for the voyage across the great river, and the memory of that solemn spectacle will stay with me forever. Not a sob or a cry was to be heard despite the large number of people; all were silent. Their misfortunes were old, and they sensed that there was nothing to be done about them. (Tocqueville 2004 [1835]: 374–5)

We can already see, in Tocqueville's description, the idea – derived from stadial theory – of the 'nobility' of a 'savage' people consigned to the past by its 'pride' (not a negative trait for Tocqueville, given his own aristocratic temperament). Such nobility would be contrasted by him to what he represented as the 'abjection' of the enslaved Africans, who were part of the future but could not be accommodated within it, except by coercion. Tocqueville accepted that the tyrannies he described were extreme; African and indigenous peoples alike have been torn from their homelands and from their 'chains of memories'. But they represent opposite outcomes: 'the Negro exists at the ultimate extreme of servitude, the Indian at the outer limits of freedom. The effects of slavery on the former are scarcely more disastrous than those of independence on the latter' (368). The only prediction he offered as to the fate of indigenous populations pointed bleakly to their extermination: 'I believe that the Indian race in north America is doomed, and I cannot help thinking that by the time Europeans have settled the Pacific coast, it will have ceased to exist' (376).[10]

For African Americans, the situation was also bleak. Tocqueville's text was ambiguous and included a deep racial prejudice about the African capacity for liberty – a prejudice similar to the one found in Hegel and discussed in the previous chapter.[11] However, unlike Hegel and other writers, Tocqueville did not suggest that enslavement could have an improving effect. Rather he ventured that the institution of slavery itself may produce a learned incapacity, which he described as an evil. But the difference between slavery in the ancient world and slavery under modern colonialism was that in the former the masters and those enslaved were of the same race. Slavery, he claimed, was abolished under Christianity but reintroduced for what he called 'one of the races of man' (393).[12] Modern enslavement, then, derived from racial prejudice and entrenched it. In consequence Tocqueville stated: 'you can make the Negro free, but you cannot make him anything other than an alien vis-à-vis the European' (394). This was because, even in the North, in the absence of slavery, racial prejudice organised social relations to the severe detriment of African Americans.

To some degree, Tocqueville dealt with the issue of enslavement by indicating that it was not in the interests of white society. He did not give an account of the economic system of the South – the plantations for sugar, tobacco, and cotton and their requirement for large-scale labour – but he indicated its consequences for the development of free labour and its significance both to prosperity and to American mores. In the southern states, labour was associated with the condition of enslavement and was consequently avoided by whites, who sought out leisure. By contrast, where there was no enslavement, there was a whole range of employments undertaken by industrious white settlers. Tocqueville noted that, in the century since the establishment of the colonies, 'in provinces where people owned virtually no slaves, population, wealth, and prosperity were increasing more rapidly than in provinces where people did own slaves' (397).

However, where slavery was abolished, abolition was, as Tocqueville noted, 'not in the interest of the Negro but in that of the white man' (397). Moreover, 'the prejudice against Negroes seems to increase in proportion to their emancipation, and inequality is enshrined in mores as it disappears from laws' (397). The population growth in provinces without the plantation system brought in migrants from Europe; and they, in turn, displaced freed Africans while reproducing the same racial prejudice. This was as true of those states that abolished slavery before the Civil War. Thus Tocqueville argued:

> freed Negroes, as well as those born after slavery has been abolished, do not move from north to south but rather find themselves in a position vis-à-vis Europeans analogous to that of native Americans. They remain half-civilised and deprived of rights amid a population infinitely superior to them in wealth and enlightenment. They are exposed to the tyranny of laws and the intolerance of mores. (404–5)

It should be recalled from the last section that Tocqueville began his account of the United States by evoking the spirit of equality – 'the mores' – that characterised social relationships and its consequences for democracy. Enslaved Africans were subject to tyranny, but free Africans were also excluded from the 'society of equals', and thus from participation in political democracy. According to Tocqueville, social segregation was complete:

> In nearly all the states that have abolished slavery, voting rights have been granted to the Negro, but if he goes to the polls, he puts his life at risk. He can complain that he is oppressed, but all his judges will be white. The law grants him access to the jury box, but prejudice keeps him out. His son is excluded from the school where the child of European ancestry goes to study. No amount of money can buy him the right to sit next to his former master in a theater. In the hospital he lies apart. The Black is permitted to implore the same God as the Whites but not to pray at the same altar. He has his own priests and his own temples. The gates of Heaven are not closed to him, but it is scarcely as if inequality ends where the other world begins. When the Negro is no more, his bones are tossed aside, and the difference in his condition manifests itself even in the equality of death. Thus the Negro is free, but he cannot share the rights, pleasures, labors, or sorrows – not even the tomb – of the person whose equal he has been declared to be. (396)

For the most part, Tocqueville adopted a dispassionate tone in his description of the rights and wrongs of democracy in America. Yet his language, when describing Africans, was at best neutral but frequently veered towards endorsing the attitudes and mores of white Europeans in America. Thus he commented that 'this man, who was born in degradation, this alien placed in our midst by servitude – we scarcely recognise him as possessing the common features of humanity' (394). Other descriptions of the abjection of enslaved Africans were equally extreme and disturbing. At their root, we suggest, lies the association he made between liberty and property. Having described slavery as an 'evil', Tocqueville inverted the problem: 'the most redoubtable of all the ills that threaten the future of the United States stems from the presence of Blacks on its soil' (392). Blacks were a threat to the system of possession instituted by white settlers. They rebuked its ideas of liberty, and yet it seems that Tocqueville could not contemplate their inclusion in that system as free and equal human beings. At the same time, by virtue of their repudiation of that system, indigenous peoples are assigned a dignity in their defeat.

The Haitian Revolution

One of the surprising aspects of Tocqueville's treatment of democracy and the institution of slavery was his failure to mention the French colony of Saint Domingue – Haiti, as it came to be known – and to make any but the most cryptic references to it in his texts. Colonialism was directly relevant to the comparison between France and the United States, and this was one of Tocqueville's core concerns. It was integral to the weakening of local political relations in France and contributed to the centralisation of power by the monarch. Throughout the period addressed in *The Ancien Régime*, France was in competition with other European powers for colonial possessions that could provide treasure from mining, plantations, and trade in human beings. As with the Dutch and the English, this competition involved setting up trading monopolies under royal charter. By the end of the seventeenth century, French companies had established territory in 'New France' (Canada), 'Louisiana' (the land from the Mississippi Basin up towards Canada), and in the Caribbean ('French Guiana', Saint Lucia, Guadeloupe, Martinique, and Saint Domingue). A French East India Company was also established in 1664. Britain had been forced to cede its US colonies by 1783, while Louisiana was sold by the French to the United States in 1803 (as already mentioned). This purchase was occasioned by the Haitian Revolution. And this conjunction of events gives us perhaps the key to understanding Tocqueville's views of Africans in the United States: far from being abject, they posed a threat of revolt. Notwithstanding that even in his terms that should be a revolt against tyranny, he took the threat to be one of existential violence towards Europeans.

Revolts by enslaved people in Saint Domingue in the early 1790s forced the French to send two commissioners, Sonthonax and Polverel, to the colony to quell the rebellions. Instead, upon surveying the situation on the ground, they decreed the abolition of slavery in 1793. This decree was ratified in Paris, the metropole, at the National Convention in February 1794, and extended to all French overseas colonies. As C. L. R. James (1989 [1938]) recounts in his classic *The Black Jacobins*, three deputies from Saint Domingue arrived in Paris in January 1794 to participate in the Constituent Assembly: Bellay, a formerly enslaved person who had bought his own liberty through labour carried out in his own time; Mills, who was of mixed ancestry; and Dufay, a white man. Their entrance, James states, caused much excitement among the other assembled deputies, as it signalled the last gasp of the 'aristocracy of the skin' and a move towards the consecration of full equality.

The three deputies were welcomed as representing the free citizens of Saint Domingue. Bellay addressed the Assembly, 'pledging the blacks to the cause of the revolution and asking the Convention to declare slavery abolished' (James (1989 [1938]: 140). This was followed by a motion by Levasseur, who represented the department of Sarthe: 'When drawing up the constitution of the French people we paid no attention to the unhappy Negroes. Posterity will bear us a great reproach for that. Let us repair the wrong – let us proclaim the liberty of the Negroes. Mr. President, do not suffer the Convention to dishonor itself by a discussion' (James (1989 [1938]: 140). The Assembly, James notes, rose in acclamation and Lacroix proposed the draft of the decree, which was to be despatched immediately to the colonies as follows: 'The National Convention declares slavery abolished in all the colonies. In consequence it declares that all men, without distinction of colour, domiciled in the colonies, are French citizens, and enjoying all the rights assured under the Constitution' (140–1).

In light of these events, Napoleon's mission to restore slavery in the French colonies in 1802 was *an active attempt to enslave citizens*. This stirred understandable outrage in Saint Domingue. James reports Toussaint L'Ouverture stating: 'I took up arms for the freedom of my colour, which France alone proclaimed, but which she has no right to nullify. Our liberty is no longer in her hands: it is in our own. We will defend it or perish' (281). Defend it they did, as the war instigated by France led to France's defeat.[13] Saint Domingue, now to be known as Haiti, restated its commitment to the abolition of slavery and in its constitution of 1804 asserted its complete independence from France. In renaming Saint Domingue as Haiti, the revolutionaries honoured the name that had been given to the island by the Taino people, their predecessors on the land who had been wiped out by the Spanish and French colonisations (Geggus 2002: 207–20). Sibylle Fischer (2004: 266) argues that, by making freedom from enslavement and racial discrimination the bedrock of political understandings and by unlinking citizenship from race, the Haitian constitution radicalised and universalised the idea of equality far in advance of the other revolutions of the time. Despite this, or perhaps because of it, the French state refused to recognise Haiti and enforced a global economic blockade on the island, pushing it to bankruptcy within twenty years.

In April 1825 the French monarch, Charles X, who numbered Tocqueville among his supporters, conceded Haiti its independence in exchange for an indemnity of 150 million francs. The abolition of slavery, followed as it was by the declaration of independence, had deprived French owners of their property in all forms – land, estates, and human beings, that is, people they had enslaved, who were consequently regarded as property. Once France had formally recognised Haiti's independence, it was argued, there was no way for the former French settlers and colonists to 'reclaim' their property unless an indemnity was paid. This was in line with other actions taken by Charles X for restoring the wealth of those who had lost land and property as a consequence of the abolition of feudalism in France. Indeed, the law of indemnity, which set out the 'reparations' to be paid to the nobles who had fled in the aftermath of the revolution (the *emigrés*), was passed just ten days after the one relating to Haiti. Hence the year 1825 saw compensation paid for the 'violations' of property rights that had taken place three decades earlier, both in the metropole and in the French empire more broadly. However, the first was to be paid by the French government, while in the case of the Saint Domingue indemnity it was the formerly enslaved who were to 'reimburse' their former enslavers (Beauvois 2010, 2017).

As Frédérique Beauvois explains, what was exceptional about the indemnity coerced from Haiti, by comparison to other such forms of compensation in relation to abolition, 'was the fact that it was not an internal governmental decision, but the fruit of transactions from one state to another' (Beauvois 2009: 109). Further, it was not just the loss of those who had been enslaved that was part of the calculations, but all the immovable property that had been relinquished when the French settlers had fled the new state of Haiti. In the decades prior to the 1825 ordinance, there had been many discussions about what form the concessions required by France would take. Henri Christophe, who ruled the north of Haiti during this period, fiercely opposed any compensation to be paid to the French, arguing:

What rights, what arguments can the ex-colonists then allege to justify their claim for an indemnity? Is it possible that they wish to be recompensed for the loss of our persons? It is inconceivable that Haitians who have escaped torture and massacre at the hands of these men, Haitians who have conquered their own country by the force of their arms and at the cost of their blood, that these same free Haitians should now purchase their property and persons once again with money paid to their former oppressors? (Quoted in Beauvois 2010: 112)

It was not until after his death that any transaction was made possible between Haiti and France.

The compensation that was determined was equivalent to 'a sixth of the total income of France in 1825 and five years of income of Haiti' (Beauvois 2010: 634) and was to be paid in five annual instalments. This proved impossible and Haiti was required from the outset to take out loans from French banks in order to pay the French government. In 1838 the total was reduced to 90 million francs. This was remitted to France in full by 1883. However, the amount that this cost Haiti was far in excess of this figure. Plummer (1988) suggests that Haiti borrowed over 166 million francs towards the end of the nineteenth century in order to clear its coerced debts and that more than a half of that money went towards paying off commission, fees, and interest payments. It is not clear quite how much of the money paid in compensation to the French state was ever disbursed to the French colonists and settlers. As Beauvois (2010) argues, given the derisory figures returned to the French colonists and planters, it appears that the significance of the indemnity was more to provide income for the French state and to punish a rebel colony that had had the temerity to become sovereign.

In this context, it is clear that the relationship between Haiti and France was entangled and protracted and did not end with Haiti's declaration of independence from France in 1804. Rather there were continuous negotiations regarding the nature of the future relationship between the two states and, after the ordinance of 1825, Haiti contributed a significant revenue stream into French accounts. Given that Tocqueville was active in French politics during the period in which the indemnity from Haiti was being negotiated, and in view of his own concerns about abolition and how it was to be financed, it appears unlikely that he was unaware of the history of the island or of the alternative it symbolised. And yet, as Nesbitt (2013: 76) argues, 'Tocqueville completely suppresses the events of the Haitian Revolution from his narrative'. However, it is a plausible conclusion for us to draw that this movement contributed to his judgement that African Americans posed a threat to the future of democracy in America, rather than making him look at their freedom as integral to democracy. An equivalent representation of slavery as a threat to French interests explains Tocqueville's more general arguments on abolition.

Slavery and Abolition

On his return to France from America, Tocqueville sought to establish his political career by standing for election to the Chamber of Deputies. He succeeded in 1839, on a second attempt, as a representative of the Norman district of Valognes. He represented Valognes until the 1851 coup of Louis Napoleon Bonaparte, after which he left political life. After completing the second volume of *Democracy in America* in 1840, Tocqueville turned his attention more directly to France's foreign and colonial policy and wrote reports on slavery in the French colonies and on the new colonial project in Algeria (Stone and Mennell 1980; Pitts 2001). The glory of France was intimately tied, in his eyes, to its colonies. Further, as in his argument that slavery would be abolished in the United States as a consequence of the interests of white settlers, he approached abolition in the French context from the perspective of the coloniser.

Tocqueville believed that France would not be able to hold onto its colonies if abolition was not implemented, especially as Britain had abolished slavery in all its colonies in 1833. At the same time he argued that slave owners ought to be compensated for the loss of 'property' that this would entail. There was much discussion about who should bear the costs of emancipation. Tocqueville's solution was to request the state to compensate all slave owners; then the state would be reimbursed through a tax on the wages of the freed slaves, who would be apprenticed to the state for a transition period. In this way those who had been enslaved would be paying reparations to those who had enslaved them for the latter's loss of property. There was no suggestion that the former might be compensated for their loss of liberty. Tocqueville's primary concern was to manage an orderly process of emancipation that would not adversely affect colonial economies or their beneficiaries.

Tocqueville's stance seemingly stands in stark contrast to his refusal to acknowledge the magnitude of the events of the Haitian revolution and what they might mean for debates on emancipation within France. Instead, his public writings on the matter referred primarily to the British debates on abolition. As Strong (1987) notes, in August 1833 Tocqueville had travelled to Britain and witnessed discussions in the House of Commons on the Slavery Abolition Act – or, to give it its full title, 'An Act for the Abolition of Slavery throughout the *British* Colonies; for promoting the Industry of the manumitted Slaves; and for compensating the Persons hitherto entitled to the Services of such Slaves'. Abolition, with all the provisos set out in this document, was enacted from the following year across the British empire, with the exception of any territories in the possession of the East India Company (these covered much of the Indian subcontinent) and the islands of Ceylon and Saint Helena. In return for abolition, the planters were given 'an indemnity of £20 million in exchange for one-quarter of the slaves' time and "full wages in lodging, clothing, food and other allowances" for the former slaves during the apprenticeship period' (Beauvois 2017: 203). France, meanwhile, proposed a number of commissions that each deferred the question of abolition and with it that of compensation.

In 1835 Tocqueville became a member of the abolitionist *Société française pour l'abolition de l'esclavage* and, over the subsequent decade, as Nesbitt (2013) highlights, wrote two important texts on the problems facing French abolition. The first, produced in July 1839, 'The Report Made to the Chamber of Deputies on the Abolition of Slavery in the French Colonies', was the culmination of a government commission headed by Tocqueville. It proposed the general and simultaneous abolition of slavery in the French colonies and an indemnification to be paid to those who had owned enslaved people. The recommendations made here 'were designed to correct the defects of British emancipation' (Strong 1987: 208), namely that its move to gradual abolition through an apprenticeship period too closely resembled the system of slavery that had preceded it. But this report was not debated and instead, in March 1840, another commission was organised by the government. This commission was led by de Broglie, and Tocqueville participated as a member in it. As Strong states, 'the de Broglie commission report was widely praised when it appeared in 1843'; however, 'it met the same fate as the earlier legislative studies' (209).

This was the occasion for Tocqueville's second major contribution to the debate on abolition, through the publication of his essay 'The Emancipation of Slaves' in the journal *Le Siècle*. In his public writings Tocqueville was uncompromising in his condemnation of slavery, which he saw as contrary to the 'principles of justice, humanity, and reason' that are central to universal natural rights (quoted in Nesbitt 2013: 71). However, he was also concerned not to be unjust towards 'those of her children who live in the colonies, nor lose sight of her greatness, which demands that these colonies progress' (Tocqueville 2001 [1843]: 221). Tocqueville argued that, if those who have been enslaved by France have the right to be free, then 'it is incontestable that the colonists have the right not to be ruined by the freedom of the Negroes' (221). This, he argued, was because, while the colonists may have taken advantage of the situation of slavery, they did not establish it, and therefore ought not to be held accountable for it. As in his 1839 report, Tocqueville made the point that the interests of the colonists needed to be protected through the payment of 'an indemnity representing the monetary value of the freed slaves' (223). The costs of this indemnity would be shared between the state and those who had been enslaved; that is, 'half the indemnity is furnished by the metropole, the other half by the labor of the blacks' (224).

Central to this essay was Tocqueville's statement that '[w]e have seen something unprecedented in history, slavery abolished, not by the desperate effort of the slave, but by the enlightened will of the master' (199). The 'desperate effort' referred to here indirectly points to the Haitian Revolution. The 'enlightened will' is that of the British and their abolition of slavery. However, Tocqueville urged his fellow countrymen not to forget that the 'notions of freedom and equality that are weakening or destroying servitude everywhere' were reawakened by them, the French, during the Revolution of 1789. We were the ones, he stated, 'to give a determined and practical meaning to this Christian idea that all men are born equal ... and to guarantee each man an equal right to liberty'. The English were simply 'applying *our* principles in their colonies ... Are they to be more French than ourselves?' (207). Slavery in French colonies was eventually abolished in 1848, but the project of colonisation remained intact.

On Algeria

The 'French' principles of equality that Tocqueville espoused were consistent, at least in his mind, with colonial domination as an expression of French national interests. Moreover, this domination extended to the subjection of local populations in colonial settlements, even where enslavement was not practised. This was evident in Tocqueville's 'Letters to Algeria' published in 1837. The first letter was based on documentary research on the indigenous peoples of Algeria and an account of earlier Ottoman rule; the second consisted of an analysis of French colonial policy there (Pitts 2001). In the second letter Tocqueville presented a vision of colonial society in which the indigenous population would voluntarily assimilate into French culture and laws and, together with the settlers, would establish a French-dominated civilisation across North Africa (Pitts 2000).[14]

In 1840, one year after his election as deputy, Tocqueville visited Algeria and reversed his belief in the possibilities of the indigenous population assimilating into French culture. France initially invaded Algiers in 1830, which led to a decade of restricted occupation; then, in the 1840s, it embarked on the total conquest and colonisation of the area under the command of General Bugeaud. Bugeaud advocated and implemented razzias, which meant that 'villages were razed, harvests burned, livestock confiscated or slaughtered, and … certain resisting tribes which sought refuge in caves were smoked to death' (Richter 1963: 370). The actions of the French army in Algeria were criticised by many in the Chamber of Deputies. As Richter observes, opinions across the range were expressed – from full approval to qualified criticism and to Deputy Lamartine denouncing the razzia 'as a system of extermination' (389). Tocqueville's response was more ambivalent and cannot be understood separately from his commitment to the French nation and his belief in the signal importance of French imperialism to its stability and future flourishing. As Pitts (2000: 297) writes, 'nineteenth-century France's unstable and unsettling domestic regime led many liberals to embrace imperialism as a kind of national salvation'. Empire, then, was Tocqueville's solution to the travails of building a stable national community.

It was only after travelling to Algeria that Tocqueville came to understand the extent to which Algerians were opposed to colonisation. At this point he revised his vision of an amalgamated society and moved on to one of 'a colony composed exclusively of European immigrants' (Welch 2003: 243). From ideas of assimilation and amalgamation, Tocqueville transited seamlessly to ideas of pacification and domination. In his 'Essay on Algeria', written after this visit, Tocqueville developed the argument that domination and colonisation ought not to be separated. In this essay domination is understood as French governance over the indigenous population, and colonisation is the transplantation of French settlers to the territory and the dispossession of the local populations. Domination without colonisation, he argued, 'would not be worth the time, the money, or the men that it would cost us' (Tocqueville 2001 [1841]: 62). Conversely, colonisation without domination would 'always be an incomplete and precarious work' (63). Further, it was the dispossession associated with colonisation that, Tocqueville acknowledged, was opposed by the local population more than the issue of governance.[15]

Tocqueville visited Algeria for a second time in 1846 and was appointed by a parliamentary commission to draft two reports on 'military requests for additional funds for their operations in Algeria, and for evaluating the military colonies proposed by General Bugeaud' (Pitts 2001: xxv). Pitts suggests that these reports indicate a shift in Tocqueville's thinking, from being a clear advocate of the necessity of colonial violence to making a more cautious examination of the moral problems of empire; at the same time, he remained firmly committed to the idea of Algeria being a French colony for the benefit of the French nation. As Tocqueville wrote in his 'First Report on Algeria', 'the final goal we ought to have in view ... [is] not a colony properly speaking in Algeria, but rather the extension of France itself across the Mediterranean' (Tocqueville 2001 [1847]: 161). Given Tocqueville's knowledge of the ways in which racial inequality structured the democracy of America, together with the hostility expressed by French slave owners towards his proposals for gradual abolition, Richter (1963: 396) states: 'Tocqueville had few reasons to support the position central to his report: that the colonisation of Algeria by Frenchmen was fully compatible with justice to its native inhabitants.'

After 1847, Tocqueville 'did not comment on Algerian affairs again, either publicly or in his correspondence' (Welch 2003: 238). This is a fact that scholars on this aspect of his writings regard as 'astonishing'. Reading Tocqueville's work on Algeria sheds further light on his understandings of democracy, and in particular of its limits. As Richter (1963: 363) argues, 'Tocqueville conspicuously failed to apply to the French action in North Africa the sociological insight and ethical awareness he had demonstrated in his study of the United States'. While Tocqueville can be seen at least to have been sympathetic to the claims of indigenous peoples in the Americas and of those who had been transported there and coerced into labour on plantations, he seemed unable to apply those insights, limited as they were, to aspects of European – and particularly French – colonialism beyond the new world.

However, as we have suggested, Tocqueville's arguments about the United States might be better understood if they were reinterpreted in the light of his comments on Algeria. The democracy he found in America and was sympathetic to was racialised. Tocqueville was willing to restrict the functioning of democracy along these lines, in service of French colonial interests, just as he recognised similar interests at play in other European powers and endorsed them as reflecting European superiority. As Curtis Stokes (1990) writes, Tocqueville celebrated the British defeat of the Indian Mutiny, claiming it to be a triumph of both 'Christianity and civilisation' and reaffirming Britain's status as a great nation. He also rejoiced when China was defeated by European powers in the Opium Wars, and 'concluded that he was pleased that Europeans "are successively submitting all other races" to their empire or influence' (Stokes 1990: 6).

Conclusion

Scholars have long sought to reconcile the Tocqueville who was sympathetic to increasing equality between the races in America with the Tocqueville who rejoiced at the colonial victories of Europeans and their submission of other races. Or, as Cheryl Welch (2011: 53) puts it, 'scholars have increasingly puzzled over the apparent dissonance between Tocqueville's liberal and imperial voices'. However, as Stokes (1990: 6) argues, the problem with this idea of there being two Tocquevilles, or two separate voices, is that 'it fails to recognise that the unifying racial theme in Tocqueville's writings is the marginalising of the cultures of people of color'. If we separate out the two strands, there can be little reflection on the ways in which liberalism and imperialism are mutually constituted (Mehta 1999). For all of Tocqueville's anguish at the violence meted out to indigenous peoples and enslaved Africans, he made no concomitant critique of the colonial processes of expansion and conquest by European nations.

3

Marx
Colonialism, Capitalism, and Class

In Marx we encounter a figure widely understood as central to the consolidation of modern sociological thought and as one of its 'founding fathers'. That designation, however, is not straightforward. As we have seen, Talcott Parsons (1937) – whose construction of the classical canon was to be so influential during the 1960s, when sociology expanded and consolidated – placed the foundations of the discipline in 1890–1920 and related it primarily to Durkheim and Weber. He regarded Marx as a figure from the prehistory of social theory, whose valuable insights were better expressed by Weber (Holmwood 1996). The turn to Marx that took place in the 1960s and 1970s was due to dissatisfaction with Parsons's seeming over-emphasis on processes associated with the maintenance of social order. For Parsons's critics, Marx provided two missing elements: a concern with critique; and a concern with the class relations of the capitalist mode of production. The fact that Marx's early writings were not well known at least until the 1950s meant that earlier interpretations could seem to have been based on an overly positivistic version of his thought that had made him seem outdated. His true significance could now be restored. The renewed interest in Marx represented by these sociological recuperations was primarily organised around the concepts of practical criticism (dialectics), class, and social change. Yet, as we shall argue in this chapter, colonialism disrupts each of these domains.

The previous two chapters have shown how European colonialism was central to the development of modern society, which would become the primary focus of social theory. Yet colonialism and its processes and institutions – private possession and displacement of populations, settlement, enslavement, and forced labour on plantations and in mines – have not been central topics of inquiry. Moreover, they have receded as concerns, even as colonies developed into empires. Hegel, for example, articulated a dialectics of recognition in terms of the master–slave relationship, but neglected the commodification of forced labour – chattel slavery – although this feature was integral to modern society. Equally, although he wrote at the same time as the Haitian Revolution, he was silent on its implications (Buck-Morss 2000). Freedom was not on the march, it would seem, in the Haitian resistance to the system of slavery and in the implementation of a constitution free of racial domination. Tocqueville, for his part, described the distinctive features of Anglo-American democracy separately from the circumstances of indigenous people and African Americans. When he did write about them, he acknowledged the racialised character of Anglo-American democracy; but, sharply pertinent though his analysis may be in many respects, it did not stop him from extolling that democracy. One could hardly say that he was troubled by the tyranny against African Americans and indigenous people, except to indicate the possibility of violence towards Anglo-American democracy. While Marx's sensibility was very different – he was a fierce critic of colonialism – the structure of his thought was similar. He understood colonialism primarily as one of the forms of primitive accumulation, and imperialism followed from the logic of a capital–labour relation that was defined independently of it.

In this chapter we are concerned with the structure of Marx's argument and not with the many comments he wrote on colonialism. Indeed, their detailed analysis and expectations of future developments were subordinated to that overall structure. In the discussion on class, for example, colonialism played a central part in explaining how 'free labour' came to be understood as the defining feature of capitalist class relations. Yet, as Cedric Robinson (1983) powerfully argued, racialised hierarchies explain to some extent why Marx's expectations (immiserisation, proletarianisation, and social polarisation), which are based on the logic of capitalism, are confounded by the subsequent developments of national welfare states, which modify these outcomes for some citizens and not others. National welfare states incorporate a colonial patrimony that functions to the advantage of domestic populations and at the same time facilitates conventional social distinctions of status and gender that Marx had understood as subordinate to the dominant class relation. We pay particular attention to the early development of his thought; but our aim is not to provide a more nuanced account of his conception of class analysis. We suggest that his later thought is problematic just insofar as the concept of class is difficult to reconcile with the require-ments of a postcolonial sociology, to which his earlier writings were intrinsically more open. In other words Marx was most open to colonialism *before* he discovered class and worked out the conceptual apparatus of the capitalist mode of production, in which this new category was embedded.

From Estates to Classes

Karl Heinrich Marx was born in 1818 in Trier, which was then part of the Prussian Rhineland (it became part of the unified German empire in 1871), and died in London in 1881. He was forced to move in response to political persecution, first to Paris in 1843, then to Brussels and Cologne, before finally settling in London in 1849 after the 1848 Revolutions in mainland Europe. These political movements reflected the social dislocations brought about by the transformation of agriculture and the early development of industrial production. They also reflected the political upheavals of the breakdown of old absolutist regimes and the rise of new political institutions that embodied elements of popular sovereignty, especially after the French Revolution (Hobsbawm 1962, 1977).

In his discussion of the social and political significance of this disorder, Marx drew on the intellectual resources of German idealism in philosophy, on French radicalism and socialism in politics, and on British political economy (McLellan 1973). At least initially, however, his critical reflections on contemporary society derived from Hegel's engagement with liberal thought and its implications for putatively modern social structures. Hegel's mode of argument shaped Marx's dialectical approach, even though it was the material conditions rather than 'spirit' that engaged Marx. Marx was deeply interested in how societies represented themselves to themselves through their philosophers, policymakers, and practical 'men of the world'. He started by taking Hegel's arguments on their own terms, in order to establish their limits and the need to develop a more radical criticism.

That criticism had to engage with the task of *changing the world* in order to realise human freedom (or emancipation from unjust domination), as Marx (1975 [1845]) declared in his eleventh thesis on Feuerbach. By contrast, Hegel had understood the present to be an approximation of freedom as already realised in the world.

Up to a point there are also parallels to be drawn with Tocqueville, who was a near contemporary of Marx, though they did not directly engage with each other (Edwards 2007).[1] All three were concerned with the breakdown of the old feudal order and the delineation of the new society that would take its place. Hegel and Tocqueville were both concerned to reconcile aspects of the status hierarchies and social order of the old society with the commercial relations of the new. As we have seen, Tocqueville understood modernity, in ideal typical form, as headed in the direction of a 'society of equals' and its accompanying political institutions. Hegel, for his part, was much more committed to maintaining a hierarchical order of estates (i.e. status groups) – specifically, agricultural and commercial estates – and understanding their social and political expression under a revised liberal constitution.

Marx was scathing about both positions. The necessary condition for the truth of Hegel's reconciliation was the stability and inclusivity of the order he was seeking to justify. In his 'Critique of Hegel's Doctrine of the State', Marx (1975 [1843a]) regarded this condition as contradicted by the emergence of what might be called an 'estate of no estate' (Lubasz 1976) – that is, a growing population of poor people that fell outside the duties and obligations of the estate system, and therefore outside Hegel's conceptual scheme. In the course of Marx's development, this estate of no estate would be reinterpreted as a *proletariat*; in other words it would be represented not as a group outside society – and hence an external limit to Hegel's theory – but as a group integral to the new society. The proletariat would be the real and contradictory foundation of this new society and, beyond it, the agent of another, transformed society.

Further, according to Marx, hierarchy was not going to be replaced by equality, as Tocqueville supposed, though this might happen in a future communist society.[2] As market exchange relations progressed, Tocqueville's 'society of equals' would reveal itself to be a society of divided classes. Indeed, as Marx (1973 [1852]) put it in 'The Eighteenth Brumaire', emerging here was not only a political despotism of the kind seen in France, on Tocqueville's admission, but a social despotism of the bourgeoisie as a class over and above other classes.[3] 'The Eighteenth Brumaire' was an essay about fragmentary social classes, and the moment in French politics that Marx described in it was the *coup d'état* by Napoleon's nephew, Louis-Phillipe, that had followed the suppression of revolutionary uprisings in 1848.

The bourgeoisie, which according to Marx was in the ascendant in the new republic, had allied itself with 'the financial aristocracy, the industrial bourgeoisie, the middle class, the petty bourgeoisie, the army, the Mobile Guard (i.e. the organised lumpenproletariat), the intellectual celebrities, the priests and the rural population'.[4] Marx argued that a defeated proletariat had not yet learned how to express its interests. Its demands, he thought, were 'utopian "humbug", which must be finished with'. Yet, even at this intensely focused moment, in Paris, colonialism was present. The insurrection was put down; 'over 3,000 insurgents [were] butchered after the victory, and a further 15,000 ... transported without having been convicted' (Marx 1973 [1852]: 154). But he does not mention that it was the French African army that was used to suppress the insurrection, by razzia methods developed in colonial Algeria (Sessions 2015). Further, the insurgents were transported to Algeria to be used as colonial labour force (Delnore 2015).

Marx developed his critical approach, at least in the first instance, in the absence of a rigorous sociological account of class. Nevertheless, by the time of 'The Eighteenth Brumaire' we can see contours of such an account developing, namely those associated with the ideas of social learning through struggle and of the proletariat as the agent of future social change. This development of class analysis has consequences for the nature and kind of criticism that would follow, including the foreclosure of specific possibilities of understanding modernity differently. Put very simply, if we interpret the estate of no estate as consisting of all those dispossessed and impoverished through the development of modern commercial society, then the category would be populated much more variously than when it is understood as a nascent proletariat formed within the capital–labour relation. It would include all those dispossessed and coerced by colonialism (Robinson 1983). This is the space for reinterpreting critique in terms of anticolonial and postcolonial theory, but that would require a reconstruction of the concept of class.

As we shall see, the trajectory of Marx's thought was different. Furthermore, it was taken and reinforced by later writers in a yet more explicitly Eurocentric direction. The societies whose social structures and forms of representation through estates were under review were already empires with significant subject populations. These populations, however, had no place in these theories, except as representatives of earlier stages of history, destined to be either eliminated or made part of a 'civilising' process. So far as Marx is concerned, they would be incorporated through a process of proletarianisation in which the European proletariat would be their vanguard – indeed, given the emphasis on learning, we might call it a socialising rather than civilising process. But first we will present the development of the idea of critique in Marx's early writings.

The Critique of Modern Society

As we saw in chapter 1, Hegel accepted a key aspect of the liberal conception of freedom and its association with private property – namely that freedom partly resides in the rational self-reflection and personal responsibility of a *person capable of property*. This was an idea that Marx would reject, but initially he followed the lines set out by Hegel's dismissal of the conclusions drawn by liberal theorists. For Hegel, the liberal self-understanding was *alienated*, founded upon the very denial of common membership in society that alone could give meaning to the idea of individual rights, and in particular to their mutual recognition. This theme, of a contradictory theoretical development, would form the basis of Marx's own critique of Hegel and would provide contemporary social theory, especially the Frankfurt School, with a major model of critique.

Hegel argued that the standard liberal individualist account misunderstood the interdependence between individuals that was integral to an advanced division of labour. He wrote:

> when men are thus dependent on one another and reciprocally related to one another in their work and the satisfaction of their needs, subjective self-seeking turns into a contribution to the satisfaction of the needs of everyone else. That is to say, by a dialectical advance, subjective self-seeking turns into the mediation of the particular through the universal, with the result that each man in earning, producing, and enjoying on his own account is *eo ipso* producing and earning for the enjoyment of everyone else. (Hegel 1952 [1821]: 129–30)

For Hegel as for Durkheim later, the advanced division of labour created the differentiation between individuals and their mutual dependence. This circumstance explained both the claims made for a theory of individualism – that is, claims to individual independence – and their deficient character. Ultimately this deficiency came from lack of awareness of the grounding of such claims in a prior social interdependence. In contrast to liberal theorists, then, Hegel emphasised that, against appearances, the modern social order was a community of ends and not a mere set of individuals externally connected through contracts.[5] In doing so, he also identified the separate institutional spheres of family, civil society (with its associated order of 'estates', commercial and agricultural), and state that contributed to a complex set of distinct but interrelated forms of ethical life.

We need not dwell too much on the details of Hegel's scheme or of Marx's criticism of it, which he worked out in his early writings. For our purposes, we can concentrate on Marx's analysis of the structure of estates in modern civil society and the relation between state and civil society. His critique was *internal* or immanent in the sense that he took Hegel's own criteria for theoretical adequacy and applied them back to his theory. It is customary to regard this as a form of philosophical critique, as opposed to a scientific critique concerned with *external* standards of adequacy. However, as we suggested in the Introduction, this is a false distinction, and one that has been undermined by post-positivist accounts of science (Outhwaite 1987). Although these stress an irreducibly interpretive moment in science (and thus affirm the need for theoretical or philosophical critique as an aspect of scientific argument), their corollary, not so frequently formulated, is that there is also an irreducibly evidential moment in interpretation.

What we show is that Marx's analysis linked Hegel's ethical aim of reconciliation with the institutions of modern social life to explanatory claims about the nature of those institutions and the processes of change intrinsic to them – that is, the relative stability or instability of their arrangements. Making this link involved the identification of what was necessary and what was contingent. In other words, Marx's philosophical writings were centrally concerned with the underlying explanatory claims of Hegel's theory. Most importantly for our purposes, in both Hegel and Marx the designation of what was necessary and what was contingent cannot be handled by claiming the 'ideal typical' nature of the theoretical constructs, precisely because that which is necessary is also designated as being *real* (Rose 1981).

At the core of Marx's critique of Hegel were the major problems raised for Hegel's scheme by an increasingly impoverished population that fell outside the categories of his theory (Lubasz 1976). This was a special category of poor, not encompassed by the moral ties that bound the master and the journeyman in craft guilds, or the landed proprietor and the agricultural servant. Agricultural servants may have been poor, but they were incorporated through reciprocal obligations and could be represented in the internal differentiations of the system of estates. What was striking to most social commentators by the late eighteenth century was the increasingly large population of day labourers outside such ties. This population formed a new class: the unincorporated poor. They were an estate – that is, a *group* – without property and without recognised claims; at the same time they were not an estate, because they lacked recognition and were living as day labourers. Their only security was their own capacity to work and someone else's need for their labour – which, in the circumstances (a rising population and the transformation of agriculture), expressed itself in an abundant supply of available labour. In Marx's view, the unincorporated poor were left outside Hegel's scheme, and therefore put a limit to the universality of its ethical claims.

In his early writings, Marx did not directly identify this group as a 'proletariat' that held the key to the nature of capitalist political economy. Nor was this omission crucial to his critique of Hegel and of modern society, since at issue here was the nature of social changes and their developmental tendencies, together with Hegel's success at representing them. Nonetheless, Marx did not present the property-less poor as a mere external limit upon Hegel's scheme – in Hegel's language, as a mere contingency – but as a group whose fate was bound up with the processes that Hegel analysed. The propertyless, Marx (1975 [1842b]) argued, were not propertyless by nature but were rendered such through a historical process whereby their 'property', which consisted in traditional rights to common goods – for example, the right to collect fallen wood or to graze their animals on common land – had been taken away from them in the formation of individualised private property rights.

Compulsory labour under feudal arrangements was, to Marx, an obvious expropriation of the labour of the peasant, but the privatising of rights previously held in common was also a form of expropriation. Marx saw that peasants had had the means to generate their own petty property, since they were able to generate a surplus above their subsistence needs. But as that surplus had been generated from their own designated plots within feudal arrangements, it was now lost to them with the privatisation of land. The condition of being 'free labourers' appeared now to be governed by impersonal, 'natural' exchange relations. However, Marx argued that the violence of the past – the processes by which workers were brought to the condition of day labourers – was central to their present condition. The stultifying, degrading, and alienating conditions in which they laboured showed the forced character of apparently free labour (Marx 1975 [1844]). The 'freedom' to labour, far from constituting independence and liberty for workers, as liberal theorists supposed and Hegel accepted, was in fact a form of dependence, namely the workers' dependence on the owner of the means to purchase their labour.

For Marx, then, work in an advanced division of labour and during the free development of commercial relations did not provide the mutual satisfaction of needs identified by Hegel as the condition of the rationality of the division of labour. For example, according to Hegel (1952 [1821]: 133), the specialisation associated with the advanced division of labour was positive because 'a man actualises himself only in becoming something definite, i.e. something specifi- cally particularised; this means restricting himself exclusively to one of the particular spheres of need'. For Marx, on the contrary, the actual circumstances of labour were a substantive denial of the 'concrete particularity' and individuation that Hegel identified as positive attributes of the advanced division of labour.

The worker's labour was 'external' in the sense that it did not validate the worker and satisfy a need, but was a means to an end, and that end was subsistence. In such circumstances, Marx wrote,

> the worker denies himself, feels miserable and not happy, does not develop free mental and physical energy but mortifies his flesh and ruins his mind ... His labour is therefore not voluntary but forced, it is *forced labour*. It is therefore not the satisfaction of a need but a mere *means* to satisfy needs outside itself. Its alien character is clearly demonstrated by the fact that as soon as no physical or other compulsion exists it is shunned like the plague. (Marx 1975 [1844]: 326)

The requirement to discipline workers for work preoccupied bourgeois agitators for the repeal of supposedly overgenerous schemes of granting relief from poverty. But this requirement was not to do with the absence of an ethic of personal responsibility in workers. Rather it was a consequence of the *character of work*; and that consequence ensued when the labour of some was purchased by others as a means, without regard for the conditions in which that labour must be delivered. The labour contract placed no obligation on the purchaser outside very narrow terms. There was thus an absence of social responsibility among members of the commercial estate; but this was systemic, in that employers were constrained by market requirements to ensure that they do not deviate from others in the terms they offered to workers.

Hegel intended for this social responsibility to be expressed within the institutions of civil government, but Marx argued that this was not possible. His comments on the proceedings of the Rhenish parliament – for example, concerning the distress of the Mosel wine growers – showed the impotence of the legislators when it came to addressing the 'contingencies' of the market, as they feared disturbing the market mechanism itself and thus the basis of good governance. Marx wrote:

> The *distressed state of the Mosel region* is at the same time a *distressed state of the administration*. The *constant* state of distress of part of the country (and a state of distress, which, beginning almost unnoticed more than a decade ago, at first gradually and then irresistibly develops to a climax and assumes ever more threatening dimensions, can well be called *constant*) signifies a *contradiction between reality and administrative principles*. (Marx 1975 [1843b]: 347)

Marx was indicating the unwillingness of the civil administration to take on the role that Hegel had assigned to it. As his theory developed, he reinforced his criticism by arguing that reform alongside capitalist market exchange was impossible. He further stated that any recognition of the need for reform must push forward, towards transformation and the abolition of the social relationships of private property.

For Marx, then, impoverishment and alienation were a consequence of the specific form of private property relations in bourgeois commercial society. Modern commercial society revolutionised production and created unprecedented riches, but at the same time degraded the worker and *created a specific problem of poverty*. The self-understandings of capitalism reflected this process, but in an inverted form. For example, bourgeois political philosophy recognised that, were goods to be abundant, there would be no need for the restrictions on access to them that private ownership represented. Hume, when evoking hunter-gatherer societies, wrote: 'why give rise to property, where there cannot possibly be any injury? Why call this object *mine*, when upon the seizing of it by another, I need but stretch out my hand to possess myself to what is equally valuable?' (Hume 1898 [1752]: 180).[6] Commercial society was characterised by unprecedented wealth and abundance, yet also by endemic poverty, which it could not resolve. Reform was not possible unless it tackled the underlying cause, which rested in the system of bourgeois private property.

It should be clear that the processes that Marx described with reference to 'enclosure' movements and 'agricultural improvement' in Europe were also characteristic of colonialism. The problem of poverty that Marx discerned in Europe was generalised through its colonies and empires. However, the dispossession of indigenous populations in the colonies was not accompanied by free labour, but by unfree labour in the form of enslavement and indenture (Greer 2012; Nichols 2018); moreover such labour was transported from Africa and from the Indian Ocean world to serve the various colonies.

Marx was vehement in his opposition to colonialism, but it is hard to avoid the conclusion that his greater concern was for the European peasantry and its dispossession (see Hobsbawm 1964). In part, this is a consequence of how he had imbibed a stadial theory of development in which the populations that fell victim to colonial dispossession were presented as having modes of production different from that of European feudalism. He set out his views on this topic in his Notebooks, in the section on 'precapitalist economic formations' that was subsequently published as the *Grundrisse* (Marx 1973 [1857/8]). This involved differentiating 'ancient', 'Asiatic' or 'oriental' formations from a 'Germanic' type associated with the developmental tendencies that led to the transformation of feudalism. According to this model, the primitive accumulation that preceded the development of capitalism (as Marx would later characterise it) took off within European feudalism and was then exported to other territories through colonisation. But the idea of free labour was not exported there too. Within Marx's version of the stadial account, the trajectory of social development towards a society beyond capitalism passes through the social forms produced by European capitalism.

More importantly, any comments that Marx made on colonialism quickly returned to the theme of capitalism's developmental tendencies and central mechanism of the capital–labour relation, which he predicted would absorb all 'aberrant' forms of labour. While Marx did acknowledge that those subject to colonial domination were capable of political resistance, that did not alter the underlying developmental account, which was grounded in his theory of the capital–labour relation and its Eurocentric trajectory. For example, he wrote that 'the Indians will not reap the fruits of the new elements of society scattered among them by the British bourgeoisie, till in Great Britain itself the now ruling classes shall have been supplanted by the industrial proletariat, or till the Hindoos themselves shall have grown strong enough to throw off the English yoke altogether' (Marx 1973 [1853]: 221). He further elaborated on the rapacious consequences of British rule as the true rule of capital (222):

> we must not forget that they are only the organic results of the whole system of production as it is now constituted. That production rests on the supreme rule of capital. The centralisation of capital is essential to the existence of capital as an independent power. The destructive influence of that centralisation upon the markets of the world does but reveal, in the most gigantic dimensions, the inherent organic laws of political economy now at work in every civilized town.

However, those 'inherent organic laws' seemed to work otherwise than Marx anticipated. Forced labour was not generally replaced by free labour. As we saw in our discussion of Tocqueville, the United Kingdom abolished the slave trade across the Atlantic in 1807 and slavery itself in its colonies in the West in 1833, while France abolished it in 1848. Marx makes little of these events, except to absorb abolition into his own nascent theory of class. While he acknowledged slavery as a source of commercial wealth or 'primitive accumulation', he took it that an industry based on free labour was more efficient (Federici 2004). Thus, in a review written together with Engels, the two commented that, 'as soon as the free labour of other countries can deliver sufficient supplies of cotton more cheaply than the slave labour of the United States, then American slavery will be broken together with the American cotton monopoly and the slaves will be emancipated, because they will have become useless as slaves' (Marx and Engels 1973 [1850]: 297). However, enslaved labour was not replaced by free labour but by other forms of forced and indentured labour (in France these were subsumed under the term *engagement*), where labourers were transported through imperial circuits from one place to another, the better to secure compliance within the regimes of colonial plantations (Allen 2017).

The very spaces where Marx and Engels imagined the American cotton monopoly would be broken were those of empire: 'not only in the East Indies, but also in Natal, the northern region of Australia and all parts of the world where climate and conditions allow cotton to be grown' (Marx and Engels 1973 [1850]: 296). Just ten years later, in 1860 and continuing until 1910, the British transported 152,000 indentured labourers from the Indian subcontinent to Natal, as part of the replacement of enslaved labour, which was supposed to be abolished (Thiara 1995). As we shall see in greater detail later, in the 1890s the journal of the German Verein für Sozialpolitik (German Economic Association, lit. 'Society for Social Politics') was discussing the adoption of plantation labour processes from Alabama to be implemented in Germany's African colonies (Zimmerman 2010). The adoption of the wage labour system on plantations was negligible, as the Chicago School sociologist Edgar Thompson (2010 [1932]), himself the son of a southern plantation owner, would argue in his account, unique in mainstream sociology, of the racialised plantation system as a global phenomenon.

Yet nothing in Marx's immanent critique of Hegel and of his treatment of alienated labour foreclosed the inclusion of colonial forms of labour, of chattel slavery alongside wage slavery, of forced labour alongside free labour. The problem arose precisely because of what he uncritically accepted from Hegel and the wider tradition of European social theory, namely a stadial theory of society and of human 'progress'. Marx was so keen to look forward beyond capitalism that he could not see the wider aspects of the past and present that structured future possibilities. Characteristically, after the sentence that predicted the end of slavery in the United States along with the rise of free labour, Marx and Engels (1973 [1850]: 297) went on to make the vaulting claim that the same mechanism would bring an end to wage labour in Europe: 'Wage labour will

be abolished in Europe in just the same way, as soon as it becomes
not only unnecessary for production, but in fact a hindrance to it.'
Marx's later theoretical work became focused on the demonstration
of that 'truth'.

Marx's theory depended upon a tightly coupled account of the
operations of the capital–labour relation and the constraints it placed
upon state action. But what if capitalism was not as tightly coupled
as Marx supposed, and what if state action became integral to its
development and not subordinate to it?[7] In that case class formation
would be different from Marx's model in just the same way in which
the development of society was different from Hegel's. As we will
go on to show, colonialism and its legacy yielded a different process
of wage labour formation in Europe. In part this process is related
to the colonial and imperial patrimonies, which were incorporated
into welfare provision and social reforms designed to address the
contingencies of exchange relations for domestic populations, but not
for the wider imperial polities. In other words, a caste-like relation
was superimposed on the universal class relations anticipated by
Marx. This process reached its apogee in race relations in the United
States, as Du Bois would argue, and after the Second World War was
reimported into European domestic polities, where it now structures
the politics of immigration.

The Capitalist Mode of Production

In the previous section we argued that social theory can be held
to critical standards of adequacy with respect to both normative
and explanatory claims. We also suggested that the significance of
immanent critique is that it does not depend upon a fully formed
replacement theory, and therefore there are lessons to be learned
from the nature of the earlier formulations that may be lost in
subsequent developments. Marx did not need a fully developed
class theory to identify the evident fragility of the social structures
of civil society endorsed by Hegel. Nor did he need a theory of class
to express the fact that poverty was central to the problem of that
fragility. However, making poverty the problem of class enabled
Marx to see that it contained its own solution: specifically, it could
be solved through the agency of a self-conscious proletariat. Even
if we disagree with this purported solution, matters of poverty and

inequality continue to beset modern civil society, and we have to find other solutions for them.

For the remainder of this chapter we want to consider Marx's 'settled' theory of class and its problems. So far we have engaged with Marx's early writings and political comments on social and political events up to the 1850s. For most scholars of Marx, the subsequent decades represented an intensive period of study, which culminated with the publication of the first volume of his magnum opus, *Capital: A Critique of Political Economy*, in 1867. We do not want to get caught up in a debate over whether this represented an epistemological break as a result of which a true science of society was established.[8] Nonetheless, Marx's later writings do indicate the emergence of a specific object of study, that of the mode of production and, specifically, the *capitalist* mode of production.

It is easy to see why the rediscovery of the early Marx had such an impact: it helped to make sense of Marx's own description of *Capital* as a critique of political economy and not simply of capitalism. Immanent critique, then, shifted from philosophy to classical political economy. At the same time, however, it made that analysis increasingly Eurocentric. The early Marx viewed classical political economy – for example, the writings of Smith, Ricardo, and Malthus – as being part of the alienated self-understanding of the bourgeois social order. He initially rejected the labour theory of value, which was the basis of classical political economy, but subsequently accepted it in his own analysis of capitalism (Mandel 1971). A problem remained insofar as classical political economists claimed a false generality for their explanatory categories, proposing them as laws that held in all societies. For example, Smith (1970 [1776]) identified exchange relationships as having a 'natural propensity' for truck and barter, while Malthus (2018 [1803]) outlined an 'iron law' that held for all human populations and seemed to tie the living standards of workers to subsistence. This was a condition, Malthus argued, that could be ameliorated only to a marginal degree, and then only through strict moral self-discipline.

This morality of thrift enjoined upon the poor was tied to an opposite morality for the rich. To avoid the crisis of overproduction or underconsumption that concerned Hegel, the rich must consume more, since any redistribution to the poor in the form of higher wages would be squandered through an increase in procreation, which, by increasing the supply of labour, would bring wages back to subsistence level. Any generosity from the wealthy to the poor would be wasted. This analysis not only absolved the state from seeking Hegel's 'general remedy' for that which had a 'general cause' – since the deeper analysis of the general cause showed that a general remedy would worsen the problem; it also limited private charity. Those inclined to charitable relief must look to the moral hazard of the poor, if they did not want their private remedies to worsen the problem.

According to Marx, the laws of political economy were, in truth, laws that operated under historically specific social conditions, namely those of the capitalist mode of production, which was distinct from pre-capitalist forms. The labour theory of value was to be understood as a theory of value circumscribed by capitalist conditions of production and exchange and had no validity outside those conditions. Thus Marx did not argue that labour was the source of all value; he argued that labour power was the source of value *under capitalism*. The ills of modern society were not, therefore, irremediable consequences of immutable laws. They could be addressed by changing the conditions – that is, the capitalist social relations – under which the laws operated in forms specific to those conditions.

This was not to say that exchange relationships as such were peculiar to modern capitalism; obviously they were not. However, it was those features that were peculiar to it that interested Marx.[9] He argued, for example, that exchanges between petty producers – say, of agricultural products surplus to household subsistence needs – of the kind that arise in a peasant economy can be understood relatively unproblematically, in terms of the utility that the products exchanged have for each party. But, while capitalist production depended on the usefulness of the products offered for sale (otherwise no one would buy them), it was not oriented towards simple exchange relations. Capitalists *produced to exchange*, and only indirectly to meet needs; moreover, only the needs capable of taking the form of a commodity could be met. The capitalist began with money and ended with money, and the rationality of the process depended upon the sum being greater at the end than at the start. The capitalist, in offering products for sale, could not be satisfied by that 'equality' of exchange typically found in simple exchange relationships. Like the labourers they employed, the activities of capitalists were alienated in the sense that production was oriented to making money as a means to ends realised outside the activity of production itself. Or, as Marx suggested, the capitalist mode of production institutionalised money as an end, such that capitalists had to act as if they had the personality of a miser.

It was this difference between simple commodity production and capitalist commodity production that, Marx argued, was mystified in political economy. What was the source of the surplus that the logic of capitalist production required? According to Marx, classical political economy sought the answer in the 'sphere of circulation', that is, in exchanges in which the capitalist 'buys cheap', but 'sells dear'. Profits were identified with differences in the socially necessary labour times embodied in different products. It was perhaps most easily understood in the trading relations between different markets. Products that were cheap in one market could be more expensive in another owing to different local conditions of production. Those differences would be a source of profit for anyone able to take advantage of them. However, this was to identify profits in exchanges *across* different markets, not *within* a market. If the consequence of trading was to expand the market, unifying conditions of exchange through competition, this source of profit ultimately must disappear. In this way Marx could register the significance of imperialism as a means of opening up other countries to trade and expanding the market, and at the same time he could still argue that imperialism did not capture the underlying process of capitalism. Marx sought an answer to his conundrum *in* the competitive market; in other words, he tried to identify a situation analogous to that of buying cheap, selling dear within the operation of a competitive market. Imperialism, in his view, derived from and was secondary to capitalism's central social relationship, which could be expressed independently of it.

This is not to say that Marx failed to recognise that capitalist markets have all sorts of imperfections. Rather, for theoretical purposes, he accepted the characterisation of competitive market processes that classical political economists offered and formulated his answer within the scope of that characterisation, in much the same way as he did in his internal, immanent critique of Hegel. Classical political economy (and, later, neoclassical economics too, for that matter)[10] associated power in market exchanges with monopoly, or deviations from perfect competition. In this way competition could be represented as a process that dissolved 'unnecessary' power. By contrast, the force of Marx's analysis was to identify issues of power – or, more specifically, exploitation – as constitutive to market exchanges in their 'ideal' statement. For Marx, then, competitive exchange relations, rather than being the answer to the problem of power, appeared to be *an expression of power* once they were properly understood.

Marx argued that the answer to the conundrum of surplus value lay in the peculiar character of labour under the capitalist mode of production: labour was both the determinant of value in the exchange of a commodity and itself a commodity, exchanged according to the socially necessary labour time to (re)produce it. The difference between the value contributed by labour to the particular commodities whose trade was the object of capitalist production and its own value as a traded commodity was the source of the surplus; and this, in turn, was the rationale of large-scale capitalist production. Basic to capitalism, then, was an underlying structure of *two distinct kinds of market*: the market for the commodities produced by labour and the market for labour power itself, as a commodity.

The transformation of money and commodities into capital, argued Marx, required

> the confrontation of, and the contact between, two very different kinds of commodity owners; on the one hand, the owners of money, means of production, means of subsistence, who are eager to valorise the sum of values they have appropriated by buying the labour power of others; on the other hand, free workers, the sellers of their own labour power ... with the polarisation of the commodity market into these two classes, the fundamental conditions of capitalist production are present (Marx 1976 [1867]: 874)

The two kinds of markets had as their corollary two classes in receipt of two kinds of income – profits and wages – that were the expression of that social class relation. Hegel's 'integrated' commercial estate was now revealed to be internally polarised into two classes, structurally opposed to each other.

Marx analysed the issue of polarisation from both sides – that of the market for commodities and that of the market for labour power as a commodity – and from the angle of the relation between them. The competitive processes of the market for commodities imposed upon capitalists the need to gain a competitive advantage. This advantage could be only temporary, as other capitalists would follow suit. According to Marx, capitalists would seek to cheapen the price of commodities by transforming the conditions and techniques of production, thereby reducing the socially necessary labour time. This process, involving as it did the investment of capital, was perforce a form of capital accumulation and its embodiment in new productive capacities through the reinvestment of profits. Production became more centralised and organised in factories, where labour was submitted to the discipline of machine production once machino-facture replaced manufacture. At the same time, production was also a process of the concentration of capital, as some capitalists went out of business or were absorbed by their competitors.

Marx linked these processes to crisis tendencies in capitalism where the relations of capitalist production came into contradiction with the development in the forces of production (Cohen 1978). These were not contingencies in the operation of capitalist exchange relations, but necessary developments which deepened the problems intrinsic to those relations, at the same time as a temporary solution was afforded. The processes of competition were not routine and even, but gave rise to cycles of boom and bust with centralisation and concentration of capital as their outcome. Each crisis appeared to create the conditions of recovery, but Marx argued, in reality, the situation was one in which capitalism progressively created conditions where its contradictory character became increasingly evident.

There was, according to Marx in volume 3 of *Capital*, a general 'tendency for the rate of profit to fall', and any 'countervailing tendencies' that offset it could be only temporary (Marx 1981 [1894]: 317ff.). The expansion of the market through foreign trade and the incorporation of new territories that offered opportunities of profit in the 'sphere of circulation' would eventually reproduce the conditions that operated within a single market. Thus globalisation – imperialism – was for Marx an inherent tendency of capitalism, but one that always replicated the problems to which it appeared as a temporary solution. Alternatively – or, better, simultaneously – capitalists may seek to increase the rate of exploitation of workers or to reduce wages below the value of labour power. But here capitalism confronted directly its internal contradiction, namely the class struggle it generated.

Just as there were processes of concentration and centralisation of capital, so there were processes of concentration and centralisation of labour. These gave rise to the formation of a proletariat conscious of its identity and, in that identity, opposed to capital. Marx argued, as we have seen, that the condition of capitalist production was the existence of a class of 'free labourers, sellers of their own labour power'. As his analysis of Hegel showed, Marx considered this class to have been created in a long and often brutal process of expropriation from its customary rights and petty ownership of means of production. In this process, labour had many historically contingent forms, which, as the capitalist mode of production expanded, were gradually absorbed into what was in Marx's view the dominant capitalist form: wage labour. For example, factory production may coexist for a time alongside small handicraft forms of production. The latter, however, must accommodate the conditions of capitalist production as 'external' conditions, modifying their prices in line with those of their capitalist competitors. Gradually the superiority of capitalist production must drive petty producers into the ranks of those who offer themselves for hire.

This analysis underpinned Marx's treatment of primitive accumulation in the closing section of *Capital*, volume 1. There he addressed various forms of expropriation associated with the emergence of capitalism and the creation of a proletariat out of dispossessed agricultural workers and petty producers, as part of the enclosure movement of late feudalism. The section contained a chapter on the birth of the industrial capitalist able to take advantage of this surplus population, which in turn was ready for employment as a result of draconian laws against vagabondage: such laws, which existed in England since the end of the fifteenth century, prescribed branding, enslavement, and the death penalty for repeated offences. There was also a chapter on the 'modern theory of colonisation' – that is, what Marx called the theory of 'true colonies' or 'virgin soil colonised by free immigrants' (1976 [1867]: 931). There Marx dealt with policy recommendations for the pricing of land in Australia. The aim of these recommendations was to secure the economic conditions for working the land through the creation of wage labour in the colonies. The problem was that the abundance of land meant that those brought in as free labourers were potentially able to abscond and become petty producers in their own right.[11] In the absence of the conditions for wage labour, capitalists had resort to different forms of forced labour, including enslavement. But, for Marx as for Hegel, this was only a contingent aspect of the development of the capitalist mode of production. We, by contrast, argue that it was integral to the formation of different kinds of labour and to the development of a racialised division of labour.

The Real Subordination of Labour

We have already seen that social theorists treated enslavement as a feature of earlier societies, only contingently related to the emergence of modern commercial society. In many respects, Marx was no different. His scathing criticism of bourgeois morality meant that he had little patience for humanitarian arguments for the abolition of the slave trade. Abolition, in his eyes, coincided with economic arguments intrinsic to the capital–labour relation. As capitalism developed, the logic of its underlying class relation was increasingly powerful, and enslavement and colonialism were subjected to its constraints.

Lucia Pradella has recently criticised a dominant tendency, even among commentators sympathetic to Marx, to regard him as providing the notion of a self-enclosed or implicitly national economy. She argues that Marx offers instead an international analysis of a world-polarising and ever expanding system in which there is 'permanent recourse also to methods of primitive accumulation' (Pradella 2013: 117). This is correct, but does not get to the heart of the problem we are identifying here. The problem is, specifically, how primitive accumulation is itself organised through the idea of class polarisation, which Pradella embraces. This problem continues to locate colonialism and imperialism in a developmental process in which they are subsumed to a logic defined by the relation of capital and free, commodified labour power. It has the paradoxical effect of incorporating imperialism in Marx's theory and at the same time preventing it from being central to it.

This is clear in an appendix to volume 1 of *Capital* where Marx (1976 [1867]), in order to capture the subordination of labour to the capital–labour relation, made a distinction between *formal* and *real* subordination.[12] In the former, capitalists took over labour processes developed before the emergence of capitalist relations, for example handicraft, or the putting-out system, while in the latter the labour process was transformed through the logic of capitalist production itself. Primitive accumulation elsewhere is understood in relation to the same process.

Marx's point was about the transformation of small-scale production – for example, the kind where the employer worked alongside the employees while directing them – into large-scale factory production, where the numbers of workers were much higher and the separation between employer and employee much sharper. Individuals would resist absorption into capitalist conditions of work and, historically, there have been extensive class struggles and forms of resistance to the formal and real subordination of labour, for example machine-breaking and other acts of sabotage. On the other side of the equation, there were bourgeois attacks upon 'poor relief' for the 'able bodied' that would enable their subsistence outside capitalist employment (see p. 91 in this volume). But these were class conflicts that capitalism must overcome as *external* limits to its development. By contrast, in his account of the formal and real subordination of labour, Marx was concerned to identify forms of class struggle that were intrinsic to the real subordination of labour and therefore constituted *internal* limits to capitalism and its expanded future development.

Marx's arguments about the internal contradictions of capitalism can be represented as a theoretical construct of 'pure capitalism', abstracted from the 'noise' of contingent aspects of the historical development of capitalism (Harris 1939). As Marx (1973 [1852]) explained in 'The Eighteenth Brumaire', there existed a diversity of social groupings and important internal differentiations within groups, and this diversity reflected the historical circumstances in which capitalism emerged. However, in its 'pure' form, capitalism was defined by the polar class relation between capital and labour. It is important to recognise that Marx intended the construct of pure capitalism to approximate the conditions and relationships to which capitalism increasingly tended. The concept of pure capitalism was not that of an ideal type in Weber's sense (more on this later); in other words it did not have a fictional status and did not involve the eschewal of any developmental tendencies. According to Marx, 'concept' and 'reality' converged in the development of capitalism. As Erik Olin Wright (1985: 8) puts it, for Marx, 'the real movement of capitalist development would ... produce an effective correspondence between the abstract and concrete categories of class analysis'.[13]

Marx (1976 [1867]: 788) wrote that, in the process of capital accumulation, the capitalist 'progressively replaces skilled workers by less skilled, mature labour-power by immature, male by female, that of adults by that of young persons or children'. A further consequence of these competitive pressures was to produce a surplus population – surplus, that is, to the needs of capital for labour. This surplus population operated as a reserve army of labour: it was available for work during periods when the demand was high and returned to its ranks when demand slackened. Through these processes, together with the consequences of the reorganisation of production techniques in the drive to cheapen commodities, the various, historically contingent differences in the qualities and character of labour were dissolved. Thus Marx argued that, although there were conventionally established judgements that determined, say, different remunerations for men and for women, with the advance of capitalism these differences would be eroded and common circumstances would ensue. The same situation should apply to racialised differences.

At the same time, as work became increasingly dominated by the logic of capitalist production, concentrated in factories, and put through the discipline of mechanised production, where the worker was 'an appendage of the machine', there was greater uniformity in the conditions of work. The progressive development of capitalism brought about circumstances in which the differences between workers were eroded and what they had in common came increasingly to the fore. The concentration of employment in factories and the formation of new communities of industrial workers around their places of employment created conditions in which new forms of solidarity and awareness of common interests could develop.

Crucial to the development of this common consciousness was the way in which the market for the two kinds of commodity that defined capitalism operated: workers confronted a situation in which the returns on their work were tied to subsistence. The condition of the proletariat, when employed, was poverty. As Marx (1973 [1857/8]: 604) stated, 'it is already contained in the concept of the free labourer that he is a pauper'. The only response of classical political economists to this situation, according to Marx, was to urge workers to accommodate their 'numbers to the means of subsistence' (Marx 1976 [1867]: 788). Even during periods of prosperity, when wages may rise in real terms, that advantage was quite out of proportion to the surplus generated, which accrued to the capitalist. Moreover, the crisis tendencies of capitalism were such that any increase in the wages of labour above the reproduction costs of labour could be no more than temporary. This was a situation that could engender fatalism.

Marx solved the incipient problem of fatalism by arguing that, in the process of debating the price of its labour with the capitalist, the proletariat would inevitably start from false premises, but would come to recognise that its circumstances were a consequence of the capitalist mode of production itself, and not of the contingencies associated with individual employers. An amelioration of the circumstances of the proletariat within the capitalist wages system was impossible and, for that reason, its struggle must be revolutionary; its aim should be the very abolition of the wages system. 'The working class', Marx (1974 [1865]: 148) wrote, 'is revolutionary or it is nothing.' The economic laws of capitalism turned the scale against workers, with the consequence that they must organise themselves politically. The pursuit of their immediate interest – an improvement of their circumstances – would bring them to the realisation that such an interest cannot be met. Then they would have to recognise their fundamental interest: the transformation of capitalism, with its system of bourgeois private property. Since the abolition of private property was also the abolition of the exploitation and domination of one class by another, the fundamental interest of the proletariat was a truly universal interest. Its revolution presaged the establishment of a universal human community. But its avant-garde would be the European proletariat, and the community would include others insofar as they had been subsumed under the process of proletarianisation. By this token, resistance to colonialism and its forms of imposition were assigned to processes of 'formal' subordination and were considered external to the universal process of proletarianisation and its transcendence.

Class Struggle and Politics

There are many criticisms that can be mounted against Marx's treatment of class struggle, and a great deal of effort among those inspired by it has been devoted to dispelling them. At its simplest, Marx's theory was a poor account of the history of wage differences. What he regarded as 'conventional' differences – for example, those associated with gender or race – has remained remarkably resistant to the solvent of commodification. Moreover, forms of employment appeared to have grown more differentiated, as Abram Harris (1939) first indicated; and it was precisely this differentiation, not anticipated by Marx, that created the conditions for various kinds of inequalities in opportunities for access to jobs of different qualities.

This inevitably disrupted the process of learning through struggle that Marx had described.

Moreover, the constraints upon the state appear to be associated with political mobilisation rather than imposed by economic requirements. Many capitalist countries have developed welfare arrangements that represent, to a greater or lesser degree, what Gösta Esping-Andersen (1991) calls the 'decommodification' of labour. Direct support for children, support during periods of unemployment and illness, and pensions in old age are typical, especially in the welfare states of imperial and post-imperial Europe. In addition, those states have developed systems of public education designed to support investment in 'human capital', which in turn implies more differentiated forms of labour than anticipated by Marx.

Capitalism would seem to sustain a variety of such forms, with no obvious centrality and no determinate role (in Marx's sense) other than of commodified free labour (Holmwood 2016). In some contexts free labour is decommodified, in other contexts unfree labour flourishes. A variety of types of politics, national and international alike, sustain these differences. One response to the situation is to argue that the central process of Marx's theory is correct (Braverman 1974; Fröbel, Heinrichs, and Kreye 1980) and that there are various countervailing factors, which will eventually give way with the further development of capitalism. (This would be a repetition of Marx's arguments about the formal and the real subordination of labour.)

Another response is to suggest that ideology functions to deflect workers from the development of solidarity across differences (Therborn 1980). But it is important to recognise that, for Marx, ideology was not a closed, self-referential system of ideas that could normatively secure unsatisfactory social arrangements. This idea is a later sociological invention, in which the failure of an anticipated material development can be explained by a normative process. However, if the material development is different from what was anticipated, the development itself is a better explanation for the reproduction of inequality. In any case, Marx was outlining the congruity of material and normative aspects, not the possibility of using the latter to explain the failure of revolutionary agency. Although he mentioned that the ideas of a ruling class were the ruling ideas of an epoch, change across epochs and the dynamic internal to ideology in its relationship with social arrangements were central to understanding change as social learning. Bourgeois freedoms were important because they identified an 'ideal' to strive for – one that would be adopted and appropriately revised by the proletariat; but they came into conflict with the reality of bourgeois institutions, which were not the realisation of those freedoms but diminished them.

The bourgeoisie must also live 'in thought' the alienation of its false claims to universality, an alienation that the proletariat experienced practically. When the 'solution' to alienation is made available but is seen to require the transformation of bourgeois institutions, some may cleave to a perception of their interests as embodied in those institutions; but they can do so only at the cost of their own humanity, by being less than what they imagined they might be. It was precisely this dynamic that allowed members of the bourgeoisie to act against their narrow class interests by committing themselves to social changes that would overcome alienation; and their acting this way would not be a form of false consciousness. By that token, proletarian false consciousness could be only a temporary moment in the development of a more adequate understanding. Thus Marx and Engels (1956 [1844]: 53) wrote: 'The question is not what this or that proletarian or even the whole proletariat at the moment considers as its aim. The question is what the proletariat is, and what, consequent on that being it will be compelled to do.' False consciousness could never be a permanent condition that would stabilise capitalist social relations.

Marx's judgements about mere bourgeois reforms took their force from the sociological context of his analysis of capitalist development. In his later writings he did not pay much attention to the specific nature of the state under capitalism, but his diagnosis was similar to the one he had proposed in his discussion of Hegel and the condition of the Mosel wine growers. The separation of the state from civil society, which seemed to establish its independence and neutrality, masked its dependence on civil society and on the class relations that the political and juridical system and the activities of state personnel maintained. Since the maintenance of the existing form of class relations was tantamount to the preservation of exploitation, any claim to a wider legitimacy was undermined.

As Marx and Engels (1976 [1848]: 69) wrote in *The Communist Manifesto*, 'the executive of the modern State is but a committee for managing the common affairs of the whole bourgeoisie'. Political power was concentrated in a centralised national state, where it could be exercised in the interest of capitalism as a whole (although of course this was based on the understanding of the developmental tendencies of capitalism presented here). Implicit in this model was the idea that the state was the vehicle for a class-conscious bourgeoisie. For the most part this condition of the state was latent – the bourgeoisie expressed its particular interests in the form of a general interest – but, with a growing political crisis, the underlying reality of class power may actualise itself in a direct repression of the workers' movement.

It should be stressed that the identification of the proletariat as a universal class was not by definition a matter of the privileged epistemological status bestowed upon it by oppression. It was not *through self-identification as the proletariat* that it had acquired that status. That oppression was not self-evident and, indeed, was identified as a consequence of a sociological analysis that proceeded from the examination of claims for the legitimacy of inequalities in the light of the underlying social processes by which those inequalities were produced and transformed. This analysis was not immediately validated by reference to members of the proletariat, but by the process in which the proletariat was formed as a class. The proletariat was formed through the capital–labour relation; and transcending that relation would necessarily amount to transcending proletarian status.

The conscious adoption of proletarian self-identity was, then, a form of consciousness *within* capitalist social relations. Marx (1974 [1875]) was quite clear about this. For example, he rejected slogans such as the 'rights of labour' on the grounds that they merely embodied the other side of private property relations instead of transcending them. Proletarian identity could be only a transitional identity, one moment in the process of social transformation. The new, post-capitalist society would be characterised by a 'withering away' of class identities, including proletarian. Marx summed up his views in a letter to Weydemeyer in 1852. There he claims to have shown '(1) that the existence of classes is bound up with particular historical phases in the development of production, (2) that the class struggle necessarily leads to the dictatorship of the proletariat, (3) that this dictatorship itself only constitutes the transition to the abolition of all classes and to a classless society' (Marx 1983 [1852]: 62–3). Since proletarian identity was a product of exploitation, its decline should indicate reduced exploitation.

For Marx, then, reform, if it was to be real, would have to be revolutionary. But, no matter how we look at it, it would be difficult to conclude that his estimation of the limited possibilities for reforms within capitalism was correct even at the time when he advanced it. In a certain sense, estimations that Marx was the last of the classical political economists are correct (Campbell 1996). Marx managed to transcend the limitations of these economists' universal claims only by granting that their categories were appropriate for understanding capitalism, and thereby tied himself to their gloomy predictions about reform within capitalism.

In the 1840s, when Marx engaged with parliamentary debates in his articles in the *Rheinische Zeitung*, the context of public policy was quite different from the one in which he wrote *Capital*. In the article on the condition of the wine growers of Mosel, he castigated the economic doctrines that prevented the state from ameliorating their plight. As he embraced the supposed 'rational kernel' of those doctrines, he came to understand that the state's intervention was impossible, given the existing structure of civil society and the state–civil society relation under capitalism. However, by the 1860s, parliament in Britain was discussing the implementation of policies explicitly excluded by the doctrines of classical political economy – for example progressive taxation and the formation of public utilities. In the 1860s European empires were at their peak, and this created expanded state budgets and possibilities for their disbursement on domestic projects.

Although it is well known that Marx eschewed the writing of blueprints for the new society, believing that it would be forged in the heat of struggles, he did leave some clues. Much of the 'Critique of the Gotha Programme', for example, was taken up with a criticism of the principles that had been drafted in 1875 for the unification of various factions into the German Social Democratic Workers' Party. Those principles seemed to Marx to reify labour as the source of all value and labour's 'right' to the 'undiminished proceeds of labour'. In the course of demonstrating their vacuity, Marx formulated different claims for the proceeds of labour in any 'new society' after capitalism. These claims encompassed funds for investment and expansion of production, a reserve to insure against calamity, and a fund for administration, which would be diminished 'commensurately with the development of the new society'. There would also be a requirement for funds to support people unable to work.

More importantly, there would be 'an amount set aside for needs communally satisfied, such as schools, health services, etc.'. Marx went on to comment that 'this part will, from the outset, be significantly greater than in the present society. It will grow commensurately with the development of the new society' (Marx 1974 [1875]: 345). Finally, he challenged the assumptions made about the distribution of the remaining resources according to an 'equal right' of individual producers. This, Marx stated, remained a bourgeois conception. A 'right', he argued, was a standard applied equally to individuals who were unequal (and hence 'individuated') in other respects. Their rights as workers were abstracted from other aspects of their concrete particularity; as Marx commented, 'one worker is married, another is not; one has more children than another, etc, etc.' (347).

The Gotha programme was initiated four years after Bismarck had led the reunification of Germany and the creation of a new German empire. By the early 1880s, Bismarck was proposing a form of 'state socialism' (*Staatssozialismus*) with a stratified and non-universal system that provided health, accident and disability, and old age insurance, as well as the regulation of working conditions. This was a status-based system of benefits that in effect represented incorporation into a system analogous to that of 'estates'.

Conclusion

In this chapter we have argued that Marx's account of the global significance of capitalism was organised around a strongly Eurocentric account of social class. Of course, he was aware of the impact of capitalism on other communities and was always scathing of commercial interests and of the dispossession and exploitation that followed in their wake. However, our concern has been to show how this account was organised around a *telos* of class struggle that placed the dialectic of capital and commodified free labour power at the centre. Colonialism and imperialism were construed as effects of that dialectic, notwithstanding that the latter was not realised in the form Marx outlined. In the Gotha Programme, Marx confronted the emergence of new possibilities for welfare arrangements that might incorporate the estate of no estate in new hierarchical relations. The possibilities of private action (charity) and state action were expanded within the bounds of European nations. The patrimony of empires – whether private or in the form of colonial taxes – was made available in the metropoles, albeit not for the populations subject to taxation and other modes of extraction in the wider empires. The estate of no estate remained the condition of colonised others in the wider territories of empires. They were members of the imperial political community but had no claim within it. Nor were their interests represented in Marx's class analysis.

4
Weber
Religion, Nation, and Empire

In this chapter we look at the work of the German sociologist Max Weber and his legacy in contemporary sociology. Among the writers addressed in this book, Weber has had the greatest influence in the field; only a few sociologists deny his importance today. This influence is found across different schools, for example in critical theory, interpretivism, and even Marxism. Concerning Marxism, Weber's focus on the historical conditions of social processes opens up an engagement with Marx's concerns that is missing from sociologies firmly tied to contemporary issues. For interpretivists, Weber was one of the first theorists to set out the elements of a rigorous approach to a social scientific methodology outside the strictures of positivist science. Critical theorists, for their part, embrace each of these themes in Weber's work, but also find an address of the rationalisation of culture that complements Marx's treatment of the economy and of politics. Outside these different schools, Weber is regarded as the author of one of the most powerful defences of academic freedom and value-free social science and as an advocate of the dispassionate analysis of social issues in terms of their consequences rather than in terms of motivating ideals.

We argue that these claims are seriously misleading. But Weber's lasting significance in the development of modern sociology is secure. His importance was also recognised in his own time (Käsler 1988; Radkau 2011). His reputation among contemporaries was based upon the intellectual weight of his contributions to sociological histories of law, religion, and in particular the rise of modern capitalism. It was also occasioned by his impassioned interventions in the politics of the university and its role in public life, as well as in the wider politics of the time. Indeed, those who attended his public lectures or the 'salons' organised by Marianne Weber, his wife, recollect a charismatic presence, someone who could grip his audience even when the topic was dry. The dispassionate advocate of value-free social science was a passionately engaged speaker and interlocutor, at least in the eyes of those concerned to protect his reputation.[1]

The politics of his time was intense. Weber's life spanned the period that saw Germany's unification in 1871 under its first chancellor, Otto von Bismarck, right after the Franco-Prussian War, then its territorial expansion and consolidation, both in Eastern Europe and in Africa and the Pacific. The ten years before unification had brought about wars with Denmark, Austria, and France, while expansion into distant territories would cause conflict with other European empires. The outcome was the First World War in 1914–18 – a war between European powers that put an end to the short-lived German empire, dividing its overseas territories among states such as Britain and France. Weber died of pneumonia in 1920, at the age of 56, just after the formation of the new Weimar Republic in 1919 in the midst of socialist agitation and political disintegration. He had contributed to the development of the new constitution, and before his death was even touted as minister of the interior (Mommsen 1974; Radkau 2011). The new Weimar Republic proved to be unstable and collapsed in 1933, after the Nazi Party's seizure of power. The territorial ambitions of the Nazi government precipitated the Second World War, which led to defeat, the division of Germany between the Soviet Union and the West, and a full revelation of the horrors of the Holocaust.

Weber's early death was advantageous to his reputation. He had been known in the United States, where the university system was modelled on the principles of Wilhelm von Humboldt, the German educationalist who had reformed the Prussian school and university system in the early nineteenth century. In the interwar period many North American sociologists used to study in Germany for a while. Yet Weber was by no means a major influence on US sociologists; his role was enhanced through the importance acquired by scholars whom he influenced. For example, in the 1920s Talcott Parsons studied in Heidelberg, where Weber's legacy was strong, and began translating some of his work. In *The Structure of Social Action* (Parsons 1937), he treated Weber as one of the core founders of modern sociology. However, it was not until after the Second World War that Weber's reputation in sociology was established. He was presented as reconnecting German intellectual traditions with liberalism, whereas figures such as Hegel or Nietzsche were regarded as anti-liberal and therefore tainted by the nationalism that had swept Germany in the interwar period, prompting university rectors, for example, to collaborate with the Nazi regime (Hartshorne 1937; Noakes 1993).

The fact that Parsons's nemesis, C. Wright Mills, was similarly a staunch advocate and helped to translate key essays by Weber on politics, social structure, and religion (Gerth and Mills 1948 [1918]),[2] contributed to the dissemination and wide reception of Weber's thought. This happened before the postwar expansion of higher education in the United States, the United Kingdom, and other anglophone countries. Weber was placed on both sides of the divide (as it was perceived) between the 'sociologies of order' associated with Parsons and the 'sociologies of conflict' associated with Mills, whereas Durkheim was assigned to the former and Marx to the latter. In consequence, Weber was both a resource and a bridge (Antonio and Glassman 1986). Paradoxically, the liberal spirit connected with the expansion of public higher education in the postwar period and the consolidation of sociology as a discipline became attached to the figure of Weber, who represented a different age, one in which the university was part of a status order. Indeed, his essay on 'science as a vocation', published in the volume of essays edited by Gerth and Mills, explicitly argued that the democratic spirit of the United States had the unintended consequence of transforming the university into a 'state capitalist enterprise'. The traditional role of a professor, according to Weber, had 'plutocratic requirements' of independent income that sat uneasily with the condition of an academic under an employment contract: 'An extraordinarily wide gulf, externally and internally, exists between the chief of these large capitalist, university enterprises and the usual full professor of the old style. This contrast also holds for the inner attitude … Inwardly as well as externally, the old university constitution has become fictitious' (Weber 1948 [1918]: 131). Weber represented the 'old university constitution' in the face of the new.

This ambivalence in Weber's personality is now considered the key to his sociological sensibility (Scaff 1992). But the ambivalence is rarely transferred to the conceptual frameworks he bequeathed to contemporary sociology. These are straightforwardly associated with his contributions to understanding the rise of modern capitalism, the theory of the forms of legitimate domination and the modern state, core concepts of action, social relationships, and the methodology of ideal types. Yet these were all formed in the context of Weber's engagement with issues of empire and German national interest in competition with the interest of other imperial states.

Capitalism and Social Structure

Karl Emil Maximilian Weber was born in 1864 in Thuringia, into an upper middle-class family. His father was a lawyer and later pursued a parliamentary career, first in the Prussian Chamber of Deputies and later in the German Reichstag. His mother was active in social work with the church and in poor law administration in the locality. As we have already mentioned, Weber was born seven years before the unification of Germany, lived through the German empire (1871–1918), and died in 1920, just as the Weimar Republic was being established. The empire was the context of his intellectual and scholarly career, and yet it rarely figures explicitly in discussions of his work (but see Mommsen 1984 [1959] and Zimmerman 2006).

It is conventional to divide Weber's career into two halves separated by a period of debilitating ill health, which caused him to give up his formal teaching duties as a university professor (while retaining the title). However, he remained highly productive, and the first period concluded with one of his most important books: a collection of essays titled *The Protestant Ethic and the Spirit of Capitalism* (Weber 1930 [1904/5]). Earlier during this period he wrote articles on the history of economic organisations and the treatment of contemporary problems in agriculture and industry in Germany. In the same year, 1904, he published his first major essay in methodology, '"Objectivity" in Social Science and Social Policy', which expounded a theory of ideal types (Weber 1949 [1904]). The period of ill health ended with a four-month trip to the United States that he made between August and November 1904 in Marianne's company. On that trip he met W. E. B. Du Bois (Scaff 2011; McAuley 2019).

Weber had become a university lecturer (*lektor*) in 1892; in 1894 he took up a professorship in political economy in Freiburg. There he continued his empirical study of the situation of agricultural workers in the eastern part of the German empire. He first undertook this research for the Verein für Sozialpolitik, which had been founded in 1873 as the main social science association in Germany; he had become a member of it in 1888. In 1895, on the occasion of his professorship in Freiburg, he gave an inaugural address in which he put forward his concerns about the situation of German agricultural workers in the east and the threat posed to them and to the entire nation by the movement of Polish peasants into areas that had been depopulated by internal migration and by German emigration to the United States. He also laid down the principles that he thought should govern the approach to 'national economy': it should be concerned with historical developments and should promote German interests. Weber wrote: 'the economic policy of a German state, and the standard of value adopted by a German economic theorist, can therefore be nothing other than a German policy and a German standard' (Weber 1980 [1895]: 437).

Weber's orientation to Germany's national interest, his interest in the implications of various forms of economic organisation, and his views on the role of religion in the rise of capitalism were deeply interconnected. In his Freiburg address, for example, he expressed concern about the role of the Junkers, aristocratic German landowners in Prussia, where the economic backwardness of the large estates – including plantations that grew sugar beet – was displacing independent German peasants from the villages. The Junkers employed Polish seasonal labour in conditions that Weber regarded as degrading and unacceptable to the local German population. As economic conditions deteriorated, German day labourers moved out and were replaced by Polish day labourers. In the villages, too, German peasants were replaced by Polish peasants. For Weber, the issue was both economic and cultural. The Polish population was Catholic and, he argued, culturally backward, in contrast to the local German population, which was mainly Protestant; local German Catholics were incorporated into Polish churches and were 'lost to the cultural community of the nation', as Weber (432) put it. Protestant Germans in the east were touched by the 'spirit of freedom' to move on, while the Polish peasant stayed, 'not despite, but on account of the low level of his physical and intellectual habits of life' (434).

One of Weber's specific prescriptions for the situation in Prussia was to encourage modes of internal colonisation and settlement through the creation of peasant smallholdings for native Germans in these areas, thereby reinforcing the borders of the German state and the dominance of native Germans over the local Polish population (Poland itself was divided between Russia, Austria, and Prussia, and would not be united until after the First World War). The concern to Germanify the Polish population in the eastern lands coincided with similar policies towards Jewish people settled in the contested areas of Prussia, Poland, and Russia. As Abraham (1992) has argued, while Weber did not exhibit the same virulent anti-Semitism as many scholars of the time – for example the eminent historian Heinrich von Treitschke – he nonetheless regarded Jewish identity and Polish identity as equally problematic for the development of a national identity. In his view, such an identity was necessary if the country was to unite behind the project of German national greatness.

Weber's interest in rural social structure featured also in the trip he made to the United States a decade later. The ostensible purpose of that trip was for him to give a lecture at the Universal Exposition in St Louis on the topic of capitalism and rural society in Germany (Weber 1948 [1906]).[3] In the lecture he drew parallels between the United States and Germany. In part, this was a consequence of the movement of German peasants off the land and their migration not only to urban areas in Germany but also to the United States. In both countries, Weber's interest was in the impact of capitalism on agriculture; and he indicated a parallel between the decline of the manorial estates of the Junkers and the collapse of the plantation system of slavery in the United States after the Civil War. He predicted the growth of a monopoly over land ownership (as owners would draw rents) and of new farming entrepreneurs seeking to make profits out of the use of the land. This separation of ownership and entrepreneurship would provide greater resilience in the face of agricultural crises; but, according to Weber, it would also be a new source of 'plutocracy', 'once all free land has been exhausted' (Weber 1948 [1906]: 383). A new 'political aristocracy' (replacing the plantation aristocracy of the South and generalised across the United States) would emerge, and therefore, Weber argued, the United States was convergent with 'old' Europe.

The Webers' trip to the United States was highly significant as a visit to a 'settler society'. It was also relevant from the perspective of German empire and its incorporation of settler colonies of its own, in Africa and the Pacific region (primarily in New Guinea and Samoa). The trip was punctuated by Weber's interest in issues arising from the dispossession of indigenous peoples and in the 'problem of the colour line', which he discussed with Du Bois. While some scholars, for example Scaff (2011), have remarked positively on Weber's engagements with African American scholars such as Booker T. Washington and Du Bois, Christopher McAuley (2019) argues that, despite Weber's apparently positive comments about Du Bois, their views were radically different, especially concerning the role of forced labour in the development of capitalism. Andrew Zimmerman (2006) also argues that Weber's time in the United States enabled him to develop his specifically anti-Polish sentiments into a more generalised political economy of race and culture (see also Boatcă 2013).

As Zimmerman (2010) argues, the sociologists of the Verein für Sozialpolitik were interested not only in Germany's agricultural conditions but also in the development of capitalist agriculture in its African colonies – especially in Togoland, which opened an opportunity for a sociological experiment. The experiment required the development of cotton plantations, much as Marx had anticipated. The sociologists made contact with Booker T. Washington in order to understand the post-slavery labour arrangements that were being promoted at his Tuskegee Institute for the industrial training of African Americans (the Webers visited the Institute, too, on their US trip, though they did not meet Washington). The idea was that the methods used to develop wage labour among African Americans could be applied to encourage wage labour among Africans on German settler plantations in Togoland.

The dispossession of local Africans had indeed created a surplus population; but, rather than submit to forced labour or poorly paid waged work, most of them migrated from the German occupied areas. Indeed, like in other areas of cotton plantation, local handicraft production was actively destroyed, and the new system of production had to be maintained by military force (Zimmerman 2010). The idea of a 'cultural deficit' that would form the basis of a willing engagement with the colonial 'civilising mission' was therefore seriously in question. This also suggests an alternative explanation for the Poles' adjustment to poor conditions in East Prussia, namely severe restrictions on movement within different administrative districts in Prussia. Those restrictions were based on the home principle of poor relief, which continued after unification (Dross 2008). Weber attempted to explain the 'superiority' of German peasants over Polish peasants and Jewish residents of the shtetls by invoking the Germans' greater engagement with new economic opportunities. But this cultural explanation failed to pay heed to the very different restrictions placed upon the respective populations.[4]

The Spirit of Capitalism, the Spirit of Freedom

The concern with national greatness and the problem of cultural deficits associated with race or religion were the context for Weber's famous study *The Protestant Ethic and the Spirit of Capitalism*, yet these aspects are rarely addressed and form a small part of the mainstream sociological understanding of that canonical work (see McAuley 2019). It was originally published as two essays, in 1904 and 1905, in the *Archiv für Sozialwissenschaft und Sozialpolitik*, the journal of the Verein für Sozialpolitik. The English historian R. H. Tawney, who wrote the foreword to Parsons's translation in 1930, commented that 'Weber wrote as a scholar, not as a propagandist' (Tawney 1930: I(e)). This purification of Weber's intentions was further reinforced by Parsons's decision to reprint, in the 1930 edition, an 'Author's Introduction' from a three-volume posthumous collection of writings on the sociology of religion prepared shortly before Weber's death and published by his widow in 1920–1. This made Weber's approach look like a comprehensive contribution to the sociology of religion and not primarily to the cultural politics of his time.

We will return to Weber's methodological arguments about ideal types and their role in sociological explanations; these arguments were produced around the same time as the *Protestant Ethic* study. Suffice it to say at this point that, according to them, the selection of a problem for study cannot be derived from within a scientifically determined frame of reference but must follow a principle of value relevance. In other words, the motivating factor for a study should be some culturally significant problem at hand ('objectivity' being a condition for how the study was conducted and the findings reported). In his Freiburg address, Weber set out the principles associated with 'national greatness' and the 'spirit of freedom' he found in Protestantism. Taking this orientation to the problem as a given, he then presented the issue as one that can be further clarified through the scholarship that Tawney later praised.

Weber began his study by taking as self-evident the thesis that he would go on to demonstrate. He wrote that 'a glance at the occupational statistics of any country of mixed religious composition brings to light with remarkable frequency ... the fact that business leaders and owners of capital, as well as the higher grades of skilled labour, and even more the higher technically and commercially trained personnel of modern societies are overwhelmingly Protestant' (Weber 1930 [1904/5]: 35). Then he remarked that this was the case not only in countries where religious differences are due to 'nationality, and cultural development, as in Eastern Germany, between German and Poles', but also in countries where the development of capitalism has altered the distribution of population according to religious affiliation. The issue, for Weber, was how 'traditionalism' in the orientation to economic life and the meeting of needs was altered, for both the upper and the lower classes. The latter's traditional response to higher wages was to reduce working time, adjusting effort to their existing needs. This explained why compulsion and low wages were usually necessary to discipline workers and make them work. In Protestantism, by contrast, an 'inner compulsion' to work proved transformative; and this is what distinguished Germans from Poles or Africans in the colonies.

The larger issue, for Weber, was the emergence and development of the economic system of modern capitalism. Modern capitalism was a specific and historically delimited form of economic activity, whose existence could not follow simply from universal human motivations. Its development depended on the conjunction of two sets of factors: favourable material conditions; and the emergence of a specific motivational disposition – what Weber called 'the spirit of capitalism'. In order for this explanation to have force, Weber needed to identify the motivation of modern capitalism in something other than greed or the simple orientation to wealth and profit. This need followed from his argument that historical concepts 'attempt for their methodological purposes not to grasp historical reality in abstract general formulae, but in concrete genetic sets of relations which are inevitably of a specific unique and individual character' (48).

This passage has a footnote from Parsons that references Weber's methodological essays (more on them later). Yet, significantly, Parsons does not discuss Weber's curious decision to construct an ideal type of 'the spirit of capitalism' by reference to self-help manuals written by Benjamin Franklin – one of the writers of the US Declaration of Independence and someone thoroughly infused with Puritan culture as well as with the realities of settler colonialism. Weber described Franklin's texts as expressing the spirit of capitalism in its 'classical purity' and 'free from all direct relationship to religion, being thus, for our purposes, free of preconceptions' (48). The preconceptions at work in those texts, according to Weber, were just the capitalist ones of utilitarianism, and not those of religion. In other words modern capitalism needed to be distinguished from other forms of profit-seeking activities, if its 'unique and individual character' was to be captured. Like Marx, who attempted to distinguish the logic of simple exchange relationships from that of a capitalism oriented to profit, Weber argued that modern capitalism required the routine and methodical orientation to profit exemplified by the continuous and systematic activities of production and trade.

In setting up his question, namely 'How does modern capitalism originate?', Weber agreed with Marx that favourable material conditions were necessary. For example, he acknowledged that a money economy was necessary, along with independent producers relatively free from restrictions on their activities (or able to determine them themselves, through guilds), a formal rational–legal system sufficiently developed to ensure predictable contracts and their obligations, a bureaucratic administration capable of providing efficient organisation, and double-entry book-keeping (an innovation from fifteenth-century Italy), which enabled an accurate calculation of profit and loss. Many of these conditions – especially a class of small, independent producers – were also identified by Marx. However, Weber suggested that Marx and his followers took the development of a specific capitalist mentality for granted, as if it followed from the material conditions and not as having its own separate causes. Of course, each of the favourable material conditions had its own contingent development, but Weber set the limit of his explanation in terms of accepting their occurrence as necessary conditions for the development of modern capitalism, albeit by themselves they were not sufficient conditions.

What was needed, in addition, was for a specific complex of ideas with motivational power favourable to capitalism to develop. As Weber stated, 'in order that a manner of life so well adapted to the peculiarities of capitalism could be selected at all, i.e. should come to dominate others, it had to originate somewhere, and not in isolated individuals alone, but as a way of life common to whole groups of men' (55). The aim of his study was to show how a specific orientation to economic activity emerged in Protestantism. The crucial issue, for Weber, was to demonstrate that it emerged as a result of Protestant doctrine and as an unintended consequence of adjustment over time to the dilemmas posed by doctrinal injunction. These motivations were located by Weber in the Reformation – more specifically, in the associated Calvinist sects that appeared in this period. While religion tends to be understood as involving a turn away from this world and contemplation of the next, Weber made the argument that Protestantism, albeit unintentionally, facilitated the birth and development of modern capitalism and a thoroughly worldly orientation to economic life.

Once again, it was fundamental to his thesis that the transmutation of the ethical orientation of Protestantism should occur as a consequence of independent developments within the belief system itself. Weber accounted for the Reformation in sixteenth-century Europe as a movement against practices in the Catholic Church that were seen to be corrupt. There was concern about the buying and selling of indulgences – that is, of forgiveness for sins committed – and about the insistence on rites and rituals. This was associated with a sense that, as the Bible was primarily available in Latin, it was inaccessible to ordinary people and reinforced the power of the priests through a dogmatic hold over the knowledge it contained. These worries were distilled in the Ninety-Five Theses that Martin Luther composed, then nailed to the door of a church in Wittenberg in 1517. Although initially written in Latin, they were rapidly translated into German and circulated around the country in pamphlet form. In them Luther stated that salvation could not be bought or earned by good deeds, but could only be received as a free gift of God, through faith in Christ. Luther challenged the authority of the pope; he said that only by reading the Bible yourself could one truly divine the meaning of life and gain access to real knowledge. Luther also decreed that all people had to fulfil their calling by working hard and by ensuring that they were able to support themselves through labour.

A 'calling' is a moral attitude coloured by practical intent. Together with the idea of predestination, it would come to define the economic attitude that Weber believed was peculiar to the emergence of capitalism in Europe. For example, John Calvin, in his development of Protestant ideas, argued that it was arrogant to believe that anything a faithful person did in this world could affect whether he or she would be saved in the next. For Calvin, whether an individual was chosen to be saved had already been decided before his or her birth, and nothing could be done to change the decision. This was a major source of psychological anxiety. For the faithful, the most important goal was to be one of the 'elect', yet one had no power over it; an individual's actions could not determine his or her fate. At the same time, one was told to live one's life *as if* one were chosen: this would demonstrate faith in God. If someone did well in his or her chosen profession, this could be interpreted as a sign that the person in question had been favoured. While individual actions could not influence God, there were certain visible signs of grace, which came to be associated with economic success.

Calvinism transformed the idea of a calling: rather than being a simple service to God, it came to incorporate the sphere of vocation, which could take the form of actual employment. This meant that the best way one could serve God was to engage in employment that was fulfilling; and by working hard one would demonstrate fitness to enter heaven. Within Calvinism, broadly defined, money earning was seen to be an expression of virtue, and people had an obligation to do the best they could in their chosen field of activity. In this respect, Protestantism rationalised mystical contemplation: religion was now about one's activities in *this* world, not about the world to come.

According to Weber, what facilitated the emergence and development of capitalism was the distinctive character of the Calvinist belief in predestination. This was because the psychological tension of trying to ascertain whether you were one of the elect meant that the faithful were always looking for signs that they were. These signs included maintaining a careful and thrifty lifestyle and looking after your possessions – all aspects of the husbandry of God's patrimony. Economic acquisition was not simply about the satisfaction of material needs; it was now an expression of virtue and proficiency in one's calling. In consequence, labour was performed not primarily for a wage, or for subsistence, but as an end in itself. Calvinism was strongly opposed to waste and luxury, too, which fitted in with ideas about the priority of investment and the virtue of making money work as hard as its possessor.

The significance Weber's claims here is worth noting. He was breaking not only with Marx's materialist account of history but also with the idealist philosophy of history promoted by Hegel (which still enjoyed some influence in Germany). Weber's argument was both profound and ironic. The birth of modern capitalism was, indeed, an event of world historical significance. It brought about the rationalisation of life – its subjection to organised forms and calculation in all spheres – but not as an outcome of some *telos* of reason. Modern capitalism appeared in a small and seemingly insignificant sect, and developed to subvert its commitments and intentions by disenchanting the very world it believed to be infused with God's meaning.

While it was historically contingent that capitalism would emerge and be reproduced, once it was established, it would replicate on its own terms, without the sanctification brought by religious belief. 'The Puritan wanted to work in a calling; we are forced to do so', wrote Weber. For Richard Baxter, a seventeenth-century English Puritan whose writings Weber used as illustrations, 'the care for external goods should only lie on the shoulders of the "saint like a light cloak, which can be thrown aside at any moment". But fate has decreed that the cloak should become an iron cage' (181).

Weber's account has a number of important consequences. First, it served to represent modern capitalism as the consequence of a uniquely European *cultural* development, one also associated with a particular European 'personality'. Weber depicted modern capitalism as a break with traditional orientations and, in this capacity, as a civilising factor in the development of workers and citizens. To be sure, he acknowledged the negative possibilities, situations where activities become stripped of deeper meanings – at the end of his study he talked about a sense of 'convulsive self-importance'; but, as in the Freiburg address, the 'spirit of freedom' could attach itself to higher, collective purposes, such as those of the German nation. Second, Weber's argument implied that capitalism could be exported. While other places may not have initiated the 'spirit of capitalism', once it started in Europe it could be developed elsewhere as an adjunct of the export of capitalism's social structures. This has become the substance of the recent sociological theory of 'multiple modernities', which argues for an originary European modernity and a diversity of adopted forms inflected by local cultural traditions (Eisenstadt 2000).

What these arguments miss is the extent to which the modern capitalism that Weber addressed was strongly associated with colonialism. This is true of internal colonialism, where the association was manifest in the reinforcement of Germany's eastern borders through settlement and in the reinforcement of German identity against ethnic Poles and Jews; and it is also true of external colonialism, that is, German expansion into Africa and the Pacific region. The link with colonialism is further implicit in the very organisation of Weber's *Protestant Ethic* study, even though it is largely unremarked in the secondary literature. As we have seen, the spirit of capitalism is associated with settler colonialism in the United States via the figure of Benjamin Franklin, the primary source for Weber's delineation of the distinctiveness of the spirit of capitalism. It was predation, not piety, that was unleashed globally through what Lebovics (1986: 579) calls 'rapacious and rebellious men of wealth'. Indeed, the counterfactual argument subsequently developed by Weber to reinforce the claims of the *Protestant Ethic* study – namely that China experienced the favourable material conditions for the development of modern capitalism but failed to build on them because of the retardant effect of Confucianism – was flawed.[5] China, in common with other countries with a high level of economic development, such as India, experienced the deliberate destruction of its domestic manufacture at the hands of European colonists at the very time when it was forcibly 'opened' for trade (as in the Opium Wars of the 1840s and later).

In the next section we discuss colonialism as a process of the modern state and its clear presence in Weber's writings, despite its absence from the formal concepts bequeathed by him to sociology and from later treatments of his views within the discipline.

The Modern State

While reflection on the concept of the state obviously has a much longer and broader intellectual history, Weber's particular definition of it has perhaps been the most influential within contemporary scholarship. As Sheldon Wolin (1985) and others have suggested, Weber's definition of the state as a form of political association that '(successfully) claims the monopoly of the legitimate use of physical force within a given territory' (Weber 1948 [1918]: 78) is one of the most commonly accepted. Yet, in Weber and most writers after him, this definition is associated with the emergence of the state in

Europe, notwithstanding that, in all cases used for illustration, the state was a *colonial* and *imperial* state. The state did not lay claim just to a monopoly of the legitimate use of violence within a given (national) territory, but extended that violence into other territories, where it supported non-state actors such as trading companies and appropriations of settlers. In fact the techniques of violence that were used externally were also frequently applied to national populations (Cohn and Dirks 1988; Sessions 2015). What is at issue, however, is not only a matter of substance, but how political sociology has been configured to elide these aspects of the modern state.

The standard conceptualisation sees the modern state as emerging through a process of institutional differentiation whereby, as Poggi (1978: 13) outlines, 'the major functional problems of a society give rise in the course of time to various increasingly elaborated and distinctive sets of structural arrangements'. Poggi thinks that, although such an account, based as it is on a general theory of social change, cannot adequately identify and delineate the origins and nature of the state, it is nonetheless able to trace 'the diffusion of the state as an existing entity from its European heartland to outlying areas' (15). Thus, from the very outset of Poggi's analysis of the modern state, the call for a more complex historical understanding to inform such conceptualisations is itself predicated on the Weberian assumption of a qualitative difference between Europe and the rest of the world. The period seen to give rise to the modern state coincides with the period in which these states expanded and consolidated their domination over other parts of the world. Yet this external domination is not theorised as a constitutive aspect of the state – which, instead of being understood as an imperial state, is presented as a national state. This conceptual misrepresentation, which Poggi derives from Weber, does not necessarily begin with Weber but is most powerfully illustrated in his work.

Within 13 years of unification, the German state had begun the process of acquiring 'the fourth largest colonial empire at the time' (Conrad 2013: 544). The 1884/5 Berlin Conference not only inaugurated the process of European – including German – colonisation of Africa, but, according to Sebastian Conrad (2013), also formalised the idea of an 'internal colonisation' or 'Germanification' of Germany's eastern provinces. As Zimmerman (2006: 59) argues, the formerly Polish areas that had been annexed by Prussia and then settled by German colonists in the eighteenth century suffered further waves of internal colonisation well into the twentieth century. After German unification, these settlements had an increasingly explicit anti-Polish ideology and saw anxieties being expressed about the presence of 'alien Jews' (Abraham 1992). At the same time as establishing itself in Europe, the incipient German state was consolidating its hold over external territories through a variety of violent colonial expeditions, for example in South West Africa, where the Herero and Nama people were effectively exterminated in the desert regions, in Samoa, and in Qingdao in China (Steinmetz 2007).

Nevertheless, little attention is paid to this colonial activity in most discussions of the formation and development of the German state. Similarly, apart from the work of Wolfgang Mommsen (1974, 1984 [1959]) and, more recently, Andrew Zimmerman (2006, 2010), Weberian scholarship shows serious lacunae when it comes to examining the relationship between Germany's colonial activities and Weber's conceptualisation of the modern state. And even in Mommsen's work, while there is a theoretical recognition of the significance of imperialism for Weber, the colonial expansion of the German state is not discussed outside its implications for the domestic population and the need to justify Germany's overseas exploits.

Already in the Freiburg inaugural lecture of 1895, Weber outlined an economic policy that would prevent the displacement of German peasants by Polish labourers and thus would strengthen the power of the newly established German state. 'Our state is a *national state*', he asserted, 'and it is this circumstance which makes us feel we have a right to make this demand' (Weber 1980 [1895]: 436). One should bear in mind that this claim for legitimacy was directly related to the incorporation of territory beyond that associated with the German *ethnie*, even as it asserted ethnic identification over Poles and Jews. In other words, although formally Weber's definition of the state is open as to the identity of those to whom the claim for legitimacy is addressed, it operated with two exclusions: those who were subjugated through incorporation into the expanded boundaries of the state; and those internally defined as 'other'.

For Weber, the national interest trumped all other considerations, including economic ones. This was in the context of his understanding of the worldwide economic community as one in which nations struggled against one another for their very futures. In part, Weber's focus in the 1895 address was the state's capacity to act on the basis of the long-term interests of the German nation. He

recognised the important role of the Junker class in providing the
basis of Prussian dominance that had secured unification; but state-
craft required acting against the immediate economic interest of the
Junkers, because the eastern border was compromised as a result of
the demographic changes highlighted earlier.

The social basis of Junker dominance was eroded and the Junkers
needed to be reduced politically. Weber also regarded other classes
as immature. The industrial proletariat in Germany had not yet
achieved the maturity of the English working class – a maturity
demonstrated in its support for the British imperial state project.
The situation was similar for the bourgeoisie. Weber's message was
clear: 'I am a member of the bourgeois classes. I feel myself to be a
member of the bourgeoisie, and I have been brought up to share their
views and ideals' (444). However, a dispassionate analysis required
the truth. The German state was not founded on the actions of this
class, which had not stepped up to the 'great power-political tasks'
of the nation. Here Weber unconsciously echoed the Marx of 'The
Eighteenth Brumaire', with his lament that the proletariat had yet
to begin its self-education. For Weber, it was the bourgeoisie that
required educating, but 'one cannot make up in a decade for a
missing century of political education' (445). Weber did not call for a
Louis Napoleon, a great man to succeed Bismarck; in effect he asked
for the academy to assume the task of offering political education in
what was necessary for national greatness. This involved dispelling
the curse that hung over the present generation, namely 'the curse of
being posthumous to a great political epoch. Instead we shall have to
learn how to be something different: the precursors of an even greater
epoch' (447–8).

Weber went on to argue that a 'nation is favoured by destiny if
the naive identification of the interests of one's own class with the
general interest also corresponds to the interests of national power'
(442). If the nation's unification, rather than its becoming a world
power, was the end point of the political development of the state,
then, Weber suggested bitterly, it should 'have been avoided on
grounds of excessive cost' (446). The implication was that Germany
must not be left behind in the European competition for domination
but must become a colonial or imperial power in its own right. What
was important for Weber was to secure overseas territories 'before
the world was divided up into closed zones of economic control'
(Mommsen 1974: 42). These 'zones' were the spheres of activity

of other European world powers and of a nascent US empire. As Mommsen (1984 [1959]: 79) comments, Weber 'hoped to see the other great powers concede to Germany its fair share of the still free regions of the globe by means of a policy of increased armament'. The concept of a 'fair share' is, of course, moot. In this way we see that Weber's *economic nationalism* was to be executed through *imperial political ambitions* – more precisely, through expansion (Joas and Knöbl, 2013: 118–21). The 'national interest' was not the construction of a *national* state, but an imperial one. But this focus on expansion and concomitant domination was never explicitly theorised as his views of the sociology of the state developed.

Weber understood the nation as a simple natural category – he gave no recognition to historical complexity or contemporary contradiction – and presented it as the fundamental value with which a German social science should operate – despite the call for social science to be value-free. Mommsen (1984 [1959]: 48) has suggested that the 'nature of Max Weber's concept of the nation is central to his political value system'. We argue that it is better to reverse this formulation and see Weber's political value system as central to his conceptualisation of the nation. It is only this reversal that enables us to account for the fact that his concept of the nation state fails to take into consideration his commitment to Germany's being a world power, that is, an imperial state. While Weber juxtaposed the nation and imperial power, what enabled his concept to gain traction in wider sociological discourses was the omission of German imperialism – and of the imperialism of other European powers – from histories presented as national ones. As James Sheehan suggests in response to the question 'What is German history from 1866 to 1945?', it is the history of the unified nation, but it 'is also the history of experiences which do not fit within the boundaries of the nation' (Sheehan 1981: 22). Similar claims could be made about Britain, France, and other European states: all have histories that do not fit within the boundaries of a nation. The omission of those histories implicitly reinforces an exclusionary ethnic or nationalist conception of the nation, regardless of the status of other claims.

The German empire may have lasted only 30 years, from 1884 to 1915, but imperialism was a constitutive aspect of the project of nation state formation, as identified by Weber himself. Nations, he argued, were not defined merely by ethnic or cultural homogeneity, but by the act of welding a community with shared political destinies and struggles for power. For Weber, then, political struggles were not only about the assimilation of minorities at home; they were attempts to become a world power through overseas expansion. There is an obvious split between domestic populations, on behalf of which the claim for legitimacy is made, and overseas populations, who must accept their domination as 'fact'; this schism within Weber's conceptualisation of the state has remained unacknowledged. Imperial actions have to be justified at home, and part of that justification is the economic dividend that empire brings to the nation and to those whom it recognises as citizens. As Mommsen (1974: 42) states, '[o]nce the present period of international competition had come to an end, the dynamics of the economic system, the well-being of the masses of the population and, in the last resort, the degree of individual freedom as well, would all depend to a large degree on the size of the nation's colonial dependencies'. We can note that here Mommsen explicitly acknowledges the point that we are identifying as a failure of modern social theory more generally. Colonial patrimony is fundamental to understanding the social and political structures and modes of legitimation of European states.

Mommsen is making a historiographical point about the role of empire in Weber's thought. But one also needs to make an equivalent sociological point. Germany's history as an imperial power is not unique. Colonialism and imperialism have been central to the histories of European states in the modern period. Seeking a powerful political position in the world was a feature of the politics pursued by all major European powers – indeed, it is what constituted them as *major* European powers. From a sociological perspective, this meant the non-legitimate domination of others – that is, populations beyond the boundaries of the nation state. Weber's conceptualisation of the modern state has become standard in sociology and generalised beyond the context of Weber's discussion of Germany. As a result, not only did it evade the context of his discussion of Germany, but it also obscured its own wider relevance to issues of colonialism, empire, and the modern state.

A Methodology for Social Science?

Weber's political sociology was buttressed by powerful arguments for a specific methodology of the social sciences associated with his idea that theoretical constructs should be represented as being 'ideal types'. These arguments serve a conservative function with regard to criticism and, therefore, are an obstacle to any attempt to 'decolonise' his writings and the wider discipline. In fact, it is primarily through his methodological writings that Weber has become mainstream, including the incorporation of his concepts into traditions that otherwise might be understood as offering different sociological interpretations, as is the case, for example, of Marxist sociologies. Weber himself wrote that 'all specifically Marxian "laws" and developmental constructs – insofar as they are theoretically sound – are ideal types' (Weber 1949 [1904]: 103). By implication, postcolonial arguments in sociology are, from a Weberian perspective, valid insofar as they are constructed in the form of ideal types. So far, so ecumenical. What could be the reason for any concern?

Many Marxists have come to accept the 'ideal typical' nature of their theoretical constructs; but, in order to understand why, we need to consider the further arguments made by Weber about the circumstances in which a theoretical construct should be considered *unsound*. In the same piece, Weber went on to comment that

> the eminent, indeed unique, *heuristic* significance of these ideal types when they are used for the *assessment* of reality is known to everyone who has ever employed Marxian concepts and hypotheses. Similarly, their perniciousness, as soon as they are thought of as empirically valid or real (i.e., truly metaphysical) 'effective forces', 'tendencies', etc. is likewise known to those who have used them. (103)

We have already discussed Marx's views on the formal and real subordination of labour and the developmental tendencies towards a polarisation and homogenisation of labour in response to this subordination. We have also argued that Marx's understanding of those processes – his conceptualisation of the capital–labour relation, for example – was rendered problematic by the colonial context of capitalist development. The consequence was that what Marx hypothesised as a developmental tendency of mature capitalism remained unrealised. In these circumstances, Weber offers a way out. The conceptualisation can be considered valid in its status as an ideal type: the developmental tendencies are now considered to be not necessary, but contingent. In effect, empirical variations from what was anticipated on the basis of a theoretical construct call forth additional hypotheses (and their associated ideal types). They do not require the rebuilding of the theoretical constructs from which the original hypotheses derived. This is what we mean by the conservatism of the methodological arguments made by Weber. A theoretical construct is more or less useful, not more or less valid. On this argument, postcolonial criticism may give rise to new hypotheses, but it could not call into question the validity of existing theoretical constructs. It could only offer itself as a supplement. We now turn our attention to the deconstruction of Weber's argument.

Weber's argument about ideal types must also be placed in the context of his discussion of the status of social science and the consequence of its concern with the intentional meanings of actors – that is, with actors' capacities to endow the world with meaning and to take a definite attitude to the world where interests and values are at stake (Bruun 2007; Burger 1976). Social science was necessarily interpretive and, according to Weber, based upon understanding the motives of individuals. This sharply differentiated it from the natural sciences. It was understanding, not lawlike generalisation, that was the ultimate aim of sociology as an interpretive science. In other words, according to Weber, social inquiry sought to know events in their particularity, in their meanings to actors at the time, and in their unintended consequences. This was illustrated in Weber's study of the Protestant ethic and the evolution of the spirit of capitalism that it generated.

Weber was one of the first to examine and consider this difference between natural science and social science. According to him, the difference was fundamental. The objects of natural science are governed by external forces and causes. These are assumed to be regular in their interrelationships (even if we do not know those regularities, we try to discover them through experiments and other forms of investigation). If our observations are at odds with our hypotheses, we have grounds to believe that our hypotheses are *invalid*. By contrast, the objects of social inquiry are to be regarded as self-determining. They are constituted by actors, who act according to their own interpretations and understandings of the situation. For Weber, it was not that there were no causal factors involved in social behaviour but that, in some sense, those factors had to be rendered consistent with the idea that actors also attribute meaning to their actions and act in accordance with that meaning. Hence social scientific explanations had to be adequate at the level of meaning.

To say that actors attribute meaning to the world is to say that they also attribute value to it. This establishes values as entities that are significant both from the perspective of actors and from that of sociologists who study them. A natural object did not behave as it did because it thought that it was morally appropriate to do so, but actors did; and they acted for other reasons, too. But natural objects behaved the way they did on the basis of laws that were external to them; and those laws were understood from the fallible constructions of scientists. Science itself was driven forward by the attempt to accumulate more extensive knowledge of those laws. In this context, the selection of problems for research within science was related to perceptions of gaps in knowledge or anomalies in the light of imputed regularities.

Weber was explicit about this difference in his discussion of methodological issues in historical economics. He wrote that 'an hypothetical "law of nature" which is definitively refuted in a *single* case collapses as an hypothesis once and for all. In contrast, the ideal typical constructions of economics – if they are correctly under-stood – have no pretension at all to *general* validity' (Weber 1975 [1903]: 190). He emphasised that this differed from the situation in social inquiry, where ideal types 'can function as hypotheses when employed for heuristic purposes. However, in contrast to hypotheses in the natural sciences, to establish in a concrete case that an inter-pretation is *not* valid is irrelevant to the question of the theoretical value of the interpretive scheme.'[6] We return to this issue shortly, and we will see that the situation in the social sciences is even more stark. It is not only that ideal types can bypass the need for reconstruction in the light of empirical deviations; they are actively constructed in recognition of deviations.

According to Weber, the major drive in science was to explain 'particularities' as they fall under laws or generalisations. In the social sciences he reversed this process. It was not that generalisations had no role – and we will return to it; rather they were not the end that the inquiry had in view. Sociological inquiry was directed towards the understanding of particular cases. This meant that the selection of topics for research was not made by science, but by the cultural context. Weber argued that problems were chosen on the basis of their relevance to values – that is, to some culturally significant problem. We have already seen how his *Protestant Ethic* study was shaped by a desire to explain the rise of capitalism in the context of the politics behind the formation of the German state. Such structures of value relevance may be more or less stable, but they lie outside social inquiry and change independently of it.

Social inquiry may seem to follow routines similar to those of natural science, especially under the modern constitution of the university, where it is easy to imagine that the two have the same orientation. Research, once it is oriented to 'particular settings of problems and has established its methodological principles, will consider the analysis of the data an end in itself' (Weber 1949 [1904]: 112). It will lose any sense of being related to values, but this relation remains. At some point, however, 'the light of the great cultural problems moves on. Then science too prepares to change its standpoint.' New theoretical constructs would be developed in the light of new understandings of what was culturally relevant, but this would not lead to an internal reconstruction of categories. Constructs would remain valid, even if they no longer address relevant problems.

Weber's treatment presupposed that the social scientist was a member of the world under study and had the same characteristics as the objects of that world. That is, social inquirers, too, acted in the world and endowed it with values and meaning. How could one prevent those values from becoming biases? Weber argued that people, including researchers, had different values. So, since values were the standpoints of inquiry, how was objectivity to be guaranteed? Here Weber found a role for 'generalisations'. Although human action served to particularise, there was to it a common form across all situations. Paradoxically, then, generalisations were appropriate in social inquiry, so long as they were developed as concepts of action and as their 'pure types'. This was something that Weber developed fully in his later writings, which were published after his death under the title *Economy and Society* (Weber 1968).

The first part of *Economy and Society* was translated by Parsons as *The Theory of Social and Economic Action* (Weber 1947 [1922]) and began with 'types of social action' and concepts of 'legitimate order'. The intention was to lay down the building blocks that would underpin more substantive developments in the form of specific ideal types. For example, the pure types of action were instrumentally rational action, value-rational action, and traditional action (this type was based on habituation rather than on self-conscious values). These formulations have been the subject of considerable criticism, not least from Parsons (1937) and Schutz (1972 [1932]). However, the detail of these scholars' criticisms need not concern us here, since they all affirmed the appropriateness of a general scheme based on the universality of action as the necessary presupposition of an objective sociology. It is the nature of this argument that interests us rather than the possible flaws in Weber's version of it.

First, Weber claimed that the only value that enters into the construction of fundamental concepts was that associated with intersubjective, objective inquiry. The concepts were presented as analytical rather than empirical, in the sense that they applied to all cases as a basis for comparison. They represented, as Weber put it, an inquiry into the 'generic features' of a phenomenon (Weber 1949 [1904]: 77). For example, concepts of instrumental rationality and value rationality facilitated the development of the ideal typical constructions of the Protestant ethic and of the spirit of capitalism. They could serve the clarification of the relationships set out in the ideal types and the ensuing empirical study, but they were not mutually dependent. They were conditions of sociological rationality (Sahay 1972) in the sense that denying them was outside the possibility of intersubjective agreement among the community of inquirers.

But are things so straightforward? Let us take an example we have already discussed. Weber discussed issuing commands and obeying them as 'pure types of legitimate domination', where all domination involved a claim for the validity of the rule. Compliance may be due to a belief in legitimacy or to expedience (the latter may include an estimation of how much others share that belief). There are several issues here. If forms of domination are to be defined by their claim for legitimacy, the implication must be that the belief *can* secure compliance. It is difficult to construct the possibility that a form of domination is internally contradictory (as in the Hegelian and Marxian traditions, where the master–slave relation is unstable precisely because the master's claim is contradictory).

Second, whose orientation to legitimacy counts? As we have seen, Weber did not discuss modern imperial orders of domination. But how would that type be constructed? Perhaps as a mixed type, in which one claim for legitimacy applies to domestic populations and another to overseas populations? But empires rule by force and as a matter of fact, not via legitimacy. To be clear, we are not arguing that this is a problem that can be resolved within the theoretical space of pure types. For example, Parsons (1937) questioned whether 'traditional' claims were analytically distinct from 'value rational' claims, so as to constitute a type (in his view there were truly only two types: instrumental and value-rational action). At stake here is the very methodological approach inaugurated by Weber with the claim that there could be categories based on action that served the 'highly important and indispensable' 'preliminary task' of providing the general aspects of a phenomenon (Weber 1949 [1904]: 77).

The types constructed in pursuit of specific value-relevant inquiries compound the problem of categories. These are substantive ideal types, whose construction is facilitated by the 'clarity' provided by the pure types. We have already seen that Weber regarded them as theoretically sound, notwithstanding the deviation of empirical circumstances from the processes represented within the type. In part, this was because the ideal type was actively constructed in the self-conscious knowledge of such deviations. Thus

> an ideal type is formed by the one-sided *accentuation* of one or more points of view and by the synthesis of a great many diffuse, discrete, more or less present and occasionally absent *concrete individual* phenomena, which are arranged according to those one-sidedly empha-sised viewpoints into a unified *analytical* construct. In its conceptual purity, this mental construct cannot be found empirically anywhere in reality. It is a *utopia*. (90)

Since ideal types were necessarily selective, other circumstances could be represented through a different ideal type, which merely sat alongside the initial ideal type as part of the conceptual armoury of interpretations. As Kalberg (1994: 85) observes, 'ideal types accen-tuate those aspects of the empirical case of particular interest to the researcher' – which is why 'diverging viewpoints demand different ideal types'. Such a situation precludes the possibility of establishing an alternative understanding by weighing the mutually inconsistent claims of the different perspectives. Each perspective is inoculated against any criticism that taking another perspective seriously might engender.

The ideal type of European modernity, for example, was estab-lished on the basis of a selection of historical narratives that simultaneously presented a normative argument about European progress and superiority. This was the 'value-relevant' engagement from which a series of associated ideal types have been constructed.

Any criticism of that selection, for example on the grounds that significant histories may have been omitted in the construction of the type, or may contradict the evaluative scheme, can be deflected by arguing that what is now being proposed is a new set of 'value-relevant' concerns, together with their selective focus. The new representations that follow do not call into question the older ones, gathered under different value-relevant concerns. We see this in the development of new ideal types, under the idea of 'multiple modernities' (Eisenstadt 2000) that sit alongside the existing type and its evaluative scheme. There is, then, no need for any reconstruction of the original understanding of (European) modernity, although that understanding had a one-sided emphasis that neglected colonialism (Bhambra 2007).

Indeed, this is the main way in which both mainstream and Weberian sociology have deflected the criticisms of postcolonial and decolonial theorists. In a nutshell, the argument runs something like this. Mainstream theorists may point to the necessity of studying additional objects, histories, and peoples but, for them, this requires neither the reconstruction of core concepts nor revisions of previously accepted histories – just additions to them. Some of those who advocate a postcolonial approach have adopted similar arguments – which indicates how embedded these methodological assumptions have become. Saïd Arjomand (2014: 3), for example, argues that what is needed is simply 'to retrieve, modify, and extend basic concepts of Eurocentric social theory in the light of distinctive historical experiences of other world regions'. Arjomand believes that doing this could modify the place of European modernity in social theory, decentring it; but it would do so without challenging the foundational status of modernity or its supposed conceptual integrity. The effect of such a position is to proliferate descriptions of phenomena related to our understandings of 'modernity', but without regard for how the new understandings may impact on our previous views on the subject other than by multiplying them. For us, by contrast, the key question is precisely what difference taking these alternative histories seriously would make to our existing conceptualisations of modernity – that is, how it would not pluralise the standard approach but transform it (Bhambra, 2007, 2014). For example, one response to a call to 'provincialise' European understandings (Chakrabarty 2000) has been to accept that those understandings are not universal, but to retort that at least they are ours and, by being ours they are just as valid as others and we should not lose sight of the need to defend them. Our point is different: European understandings are neither universal nor 'ours', rather they were formed in colonial encounters from which they are abstracted.

In effect, a form of cultural relativism is admitted by Weber – and in sociology more widely – although he denies its direct significance for explanatory undertakings. That is, problems such as Eurocentrism, which are identified by others and may arise within universal explanations, or perhaps within particular explanations that use universal categories, can be attributed to culturally specific concerns. For Weber, addressing these problems may be of relevance to those who subscribe to specific cultural values, but need not concern others, who subscribe to other cultural values. This approach establishes a double form of protection for Eurocentric explanations, given the conflation of European cultural values with issues of universal relevance. These explanations cannot be challenged, as they constitute culturally relevant facts; and a challenge does not have to be admitted when it is held to derive from the value structures of other cultures. This separation seems to establish an in-principle possibility of agreement on what is presented as 'facts' and 'consequences', while value-relevant interests need not be resolvable, as they derive from factors specific to cultures that are beyond adjudication. Weber's statement on the matter was clear:

> It has been and remains true that a systematically correct proof in the social sciences, if it is to achieve its purpose, must be acknowledged as correct even by a Chinese – or – more precisely stated – it must constantly *strive* to attain this goal. ... At the same time, our Chinese can lack a 'sense' for our ethical imperative and he can and certainly often will deny the ideal itself and the concrete value judgements derived from it. Neither of these two latter attitudes can affect the scientific value of the analysis in any way. (Weber 1949 [1904]: 59)

At issue for us, then, in addressing neglected colonial histories, is not simply a matter of substance, that is, of 'new' – or at least newly understood – histories. It is also a matter of sociological method. Can these new histories make a difference to our previous understandings? And how might those understandings change fundamentally as a result of our taking different histories seriously? These questions bear directly upon the doctrine of value relevance, since this is what determines both the selection of research topics and the appropriate methodology for conducting any study. It is evident that empire and colonialism, for example, were not value-relevant concerns for the European social theorists we have considered here. At the same time, any claim that the theoretical constructs we use should be understood as ideal types insulates them from the unwanted intrusion of postcolonial critique. Such criticisms are rendered external to the ideal type; they are to be addressed separately if at all, within another, distinct ideal type and without affecting the validity of constructs developed independently. New conceptualisations are placed alongside existing ones, in a multiplication rather than reconstruction of theoretical constructs, and are presented as if they have no implications for previous formulations.

Conclusion

The question is raised whether theoretical constructs can be insulated from critique by reference to the (different) value-relevant concerns from which they derive. After all, the promulgation of an ideal type precedes its critique, and the idea that it can be insulated would seem to suggest a restriction on the possibility of learning. Following the themes of this book, is the question of colonialism an explanatory issue or just an issue of value relevance? Is it only because people from formerly colonised countries have entered the western academy and the western public sphere that colonialism is becoming an issue in this cultural space? Can the world of scholarship change without explanatory issues also being at stake? If there are explanatory issues, they necessarily imply a need for reconstruction and learning.

The Weberian approach makes learning an issue for others, who come to understand the logical requirements of a form of analysis from which they were previously excluded. This is the force of Weber's claim about the culturally different Chinese colleagues, who *must* accept the 'facts' in order to be admitted as colleagues. What they might bring to the conversation is not an opportunity for Weber to learn – or for the other members of the Verein, for whom his essay was intended as a methodological prospectus, to learn. Weber is indifferent to the concerns of his Chinese colleagues. Their 'ethical imperative' can be ignored (not least because it might call into question western understandings of power and domination). To the extent that their concerns are seen to be assimilable to the universal framework, they are acceptable additions to it. However, should they explicitly call into question the universality of the framework, they are deemed to fall outside sociological rationality. At best, this is a poor account of learning, one that involves no reconstruction of understandings and of selves. We will return to it in the conclusion to the book.

5

Durkheim

Modernity and Community

In this chapter we address the work of the French sociologist Émile Durkheim. Of the founding figures of classical sociology, he is the one whose star has waned the most. Part of the reason is the way in which his work was incorporated by Parsons (1937, 1951) into a synthetic general theory of action. The critical response in the 1970s to Parsons's approach took issue with the apparent conservatism of his position and the inability of his scheme adequately to address issues of conflict and change. In mounting this response, critics sought either to detach Weber from the grand synthesis or to introduce Marx as a neglected source for an alternative approach. In this way scholarship began to articulate a Durkheim–Parsons tradition (Giddens 1976) as a distinct but narrow position in sociology, to be countered by an alternative and more radical tradition.

The paradox of this interpretive shift is that it is in fact much easier to see continuities between Parsons and Weber, especially in their common concern to establish categories of action as being foundational for social theory. Indeed, it is Durkheim who stands out as denying that role for action and claiming that to begin from such a standpoint will lead sociological inquiry astray. What Parsons took from Durkheim and sought to shoehorn into Weber was the former's interest in functional explanation – something that the latter had repudiated. The 'Durkheim–Parsons tradition' would seem no more stable than a 'Weber–Parsons tradition'. Indeed, those who attempted a reinterpretation of the classics in order to reinvigorate the discipline often began from a Marx–Weber alignment and ended up with something remarkably similar to what Parsons had proposed, namely the integration of action theory and functionalism as part of a general foundational theory. This is perhaps most evident in Jürgen Habermas's (1984, 1987) two-volume synthetic approach to 'action' and 'system' derived from Weber, with its categories partially moderated by western Marxism, and from Parsons, with its culminating argument for functional principles of social integration and system integration. It is also mirrored in Anthony Giddens's (1984) theory that the constitution of society is grounded in the duality of 'action' and 'structure'. This theory is organised through four functional principles of structuration remarkably similar to the four functional imperatives of Parsons and Habermas (Holmwood and Stewart 1991, Holmwood 1996).

We do not intend to rehearse such arguments about the putative foundations of modern sociological reason. We criticised them in the previous chapter, when discussing Weber's methodology, and we will pick them up again in the conclusion. The problem, from our perspective, lies in the claim that there is a set of sociological categories such that one can separate them from the circumstances in which they are developed and at the same time use them to represent sociological modernity. This is common to all approaches to general theory and not specific to any particular attempt, whether Weber's, Parsons's, or anyone else's. In any case, we will argue in this chapter that Durkheim was very far from being aligned with such views. His 'rules of sociological method' are rules of thumb rather than foundational principles and, as Cormack (1996) puts it, they constitute an exercise in the rhetorical construction of sociology. Nor is the separation of Durkheim from Parsons a matter of repudiating the charge of conservatism in order to discover what Frank Pearce (1989) calls the 'radical' Durkheim. In effect, Pearce is interested in recuperating a nascent social democratic orientation in Durkheim. Yet it would be equally true that this orientation exists in Parsons's own sociology. Now that the radical zeal of some 1970s sociology has passed, being overtaken by the broader wave of neoliberalism and neoconservative politics, it is easier to see Parsons as also operating with a social democratic sensibility (Nielsen 1991; Holmwood forthcoming). Indeed, there are those who regard Durkheim's social democracy as conservative precisely because he was interested in reforming capitalism rather than overcoming it (Lehmann 1993).[1] For us, such issues are beside the point, since social democracy is itself bound up with the colonial and imperial conditions of the polities in which it emerged (Bhambra and Holmwood 2018).

The problem we are addressing is different: the role of colonialism in the development of modernity and its implications for social theory. We are interested in the nature of Durkheim's thought in this context. This will mean less interest in the standard categories that frame the problems of modernity (e.g. the amelioration of class conflict as a source of division in the community) and more focus on the implications of Durkheim's arguments for understanding multicultural difference after decolonisation. Specifically, we will reflect on how Durkheim's 'social-ism' can be deployed in this context. In fact Durkheim barely mentioned colonialism. His lectures on professional ethics and civic morals, were delivered regularly across the decade 1890–1900, when he was also writing *The Division of Labour in Society* (Durkheim 2013 [1893, 1902]) and *The Elementary Forms of Religious Life* (Durkheim 1995 [1912]).[2] Moreover, these lectures represent a reworking of themes first developed in 1893 in the first of these works. Yet in none of them are the topics of colonialism and empire broached, despite Durkheim's focus on the French state at the height of empire. There are no direct justifications of empire, as one finds in Weber for example. Nonetheless the absence of a discussion of empire bears directly upon other of Durkheim's claims.

This absence is matched by a correlative silence in the secondary literature. Kurasawa (2013) is an exception, but his study is mainly focused on the Durkheimian school, founded by Durkheim and developed by his nephew, Marcel Mauss. We argue that the key to Durkheim's attitude to colonialism and empire – and to grasping its relevance, too – lies in his approach to religion. Whereas Marx and Weber, in their different ways, each understood the development of modernity as a process of secularisation – Weber called it the 'disenchantment of the world' – Durkheim had a significantly different approach. His interest was in religion less as a system of ideas and beliefs and more as a quotidian set of practices and rituals expressive of *collective belonging*. In this way issues of solidarity in all societies were related to collective practices that were typically particularistic. From this relation Durkheim found clues to the nature of social solidarity and the need for it in modern societies; and it bears stressing that, far from putting religion in conflict with a secular language of rights, he found these clues to solidarity in religion itself. In fact, as we shall see, Durkheim converted utilitarian individualism into a 'moral' individualism and imbued it with a quality that it *shared* with religion. To be sure, Durkheim (1969 [1898]) suggested that the 'religion of humanity' had replaced that of specific gods. However, what interests us is its specific substance *as religion*, and thus the space he made available for what one may call, albeit anachronistically, an interfaith dialogue between rights and religion.

As a consequence of the colonisation of Algeria and other North African countries, France currently faces a 'Muslim question' – as do other European countries and the United States. We will outline continuities across the issues that face Jews and Muslims in Europe and across the different responses of Marx, Weber, and Durkheim to point out what is distinctive about Durkheim's position and makes it relevant to current issues of race and religion. This outline will also serve as an introduction to the next chapter, which discusses Du Bois and the idea of a global 'colour line' as part of his response to the 'Negro question'. Indeed, Karen E. Fields, who translated Durkheim's *Elementary Forms*, imagines a conversation between Du Bois and Durkheim on the basis of the convergence of their concerns (see Fields 2012). We will return to this topic. As Albert Memmi (1965 [1957]) suggested some time ago, hatreds motivated by religion and race are formed within a more general category of fear of difference, 'heterophobia', which originates in colonial domination. Paradoxically, Durkheim's sociological approach developed some resources towards understanding such phenomena, despite his not addressing colonialism directly.

We start by approaching these issues via a discussion of Durkheim's context and the purpose of sociology in his early work *The Rules of Sociological Method* (Durkheim 2013 [1895, 1902]). Then we go on to discuss his ideas about the division of labour and solidarity in *The Division of Labour in Society* and *Suicide* (Durkheim 1952 [1897]). Finally we move to the development of his position as set out in *The Elementary Forms of the Religious Life*. These works are his major monographs. They are supplemented by articles published in *L'Année Sociologique*, the in-house journal of the Durkheimian school, set up by Durkheim himself (Clark 1968). Unlike Weber, Durkheim was a prolific teacher and his posthumous publications contain numerous lecture courses in which he elaborated upon various themes in his books.

Milieu, Sociology, and Social Reform

We have already seen in our discussion of Tocqueville that, after the Revolution in 1789, France was beset by political instability and the recurrent overthrow of governments. Durkheim lived most of his life under the Third Republic, which replaced Louis Napoleon's Second Empire – the regime that Tocqueville experienced at the end of his life. The circumstances of the Third Republic's coming into being were not propitious. It was imposed by the German chancellor, Otto von Bismarck, after France's defeat in the short Franco-Prussian War, in 1870. This imposition caused a three-month insurrection of radical workers in Paris; the new national government was forced to decamp to Tours. The insurrection was put down by Prussian troops at the end of May 1871. As we saw in the previous chapter, the Franco-Prussian War led to the consolidation of a unified German state and empire and opened a period of expansion overseas, especially in Africa, which would be divided among competing European powers at the Berlin Conference of 1884/5. As a consequence of the Franco-Prussian War, France lost part of its territories in the north, which became the German imperial province of Alsace–Lorraine. The populations in this region spoke French and a variety of Germanic dialects. The region was repatriated after the First World War, when policies of Francisation were imposed. But, for all the psychological blow that defeat in the Franco-Prussian War represented, the Third Republic endured for a relatively long time – until the Second World War. In 1940 Nazi Germany installed the Vichy government.

David Émile Durkheim was born in 1858, at Épinal, in the Vosges department of the Alsace region.[3] He came from a Jewish family with eight generations of rabbis; his father, Moïse, was a rabbi too. Vosges was not part of the territory annexed by Germany; it was occupied by German troops between 1870 and 1873, but they withdrew after that date. Durkheim was immersed in Jewish traditions and, although he described himself as an agnostic, he continued to recognise the Jewish calendar of holy days and to travel back to Épinal to celebrate them with other family members. In spite of its German origins, the Durkheim family identified strongly as both French and Jewish. As Fournier (2013) describes Durkheim's background, he was strongly imbued with French patriotism and shared the common sense of national humiliation after the defeat to Prussia and the annexation of territories. Durkheim's patriotism was sublimated; it did not take a nationalist form, as did Weber's. But this changed at the onset of the First World War, with his involvement in writing pamphlets against German national culture (Cotesta 2017). His only son, André, died in battle in the autumn of 1915. Durkheim died in 1917.

Most commentators are agreed that Durkheim's sociology was formed by his attitude to the initial instability of the Third Republic (La Capra 1972; Wallwork 1972; Lukes 1973; Jones 1999; Fournier 2013). The workers' movement was fiercely anticlerical and the country appeared to be divided not only on class grounds but also on religious grounds, between Protestants, Catholics, and people opposed to the role of religion in civic and political life. Commentators are also agreed that Durkheim's sociology was oriented towards finding the contours of a new social and political settlement, designed to 'heal' the nation. Ivan Strenski, for example, suggests that, for all the emphasis on the idea of *society*, 'sometimes when Durkheim says "society", we should read him to mean 'nation' as well or even above all else' (Strenski 1997: 154). Certainly Durkheim did not consider empire as part of 'French society', although when he uses the term 'society' he normally has in mind some smaller group, not a whole nation. More on this later.

Durkheim was not directly involved in public politics until the Dreyfus affair. This was a scandal triggered by accusations of treason launched in 1894 against Alfred Dreyfus, a high-ranking Jewish officer in the French army. The case divided France and revealed severe anti-Semitism, as well as hostility to what was regarded as an individualism intolerant of authority and the army. Dreyfus had been imprisoned on the basis of forged documents, which purported to demonstrate his guilt. His name was not cleared until 1906, after major campaigns by Dreyfusards on his behalf. Durkheim became involved in these campaigns, albeit at a tangent – 'let us forget the Affair itself', he said at the start of his most significant intervention (Durkheim 1969 [1898]). This was a searing attempt to justify the principles of 'moral individualism' and 'religion of humanity' behind the actions of the Dreyfusards. Otherwise he leaned towards moderate socialism, a position he believed to be entailed by the moral individualism he espoused. He had met the young Jean Jaurès at his lodgings in Paris in 1876, when both were seeking entry into the elite *École normale supérieure,* and the two formed a lasting friendship.

Jaurés would go on to lead the French Social Democratic Party. Nominally a Marxist, he would steer the party in a more moderate direction than that espoused by the German Social Democratic Party, for example.

Durkheim pursued his interest in politics mostly through academic work. He was looking to find, in sociology, a science of reform that would rectify the inequalities and injustices that moved Jaurés into action, making him shift from liberal republicanism to socialist republicanism. To some degree, this shift reflected the same sort of bifurcation of the workers' movement that we identified earlier around Marx. But, if Marx had anticipated that the workers' movement would coalesce around a strong revolutionary attitude fostered by increased social polarisation and the difficulty of winning reforms, the situation appeared to be very different in the last quarter of the nineteenth century. The middle classes remained strong and politically influential, and the working class was more differentiated. Marx had anticipated that the material conditions of capitalism and the logic of capitalist production operated as a constraint on the possibility of reform, but Durkheim and others discerned that the opposition to reform was ideological more than material.

In some ways, Durkheim's argument for a science of reform laid claim to a major trope of Marx's dialectics.[4] Sociology, too, would have the task of revealing the underlying nature of social development in order to facilitate policies that would help its realisation. This meant explaining how misunderstandings could arise and be maintained, and at the same time developing a sociological alternative to ideological positions that informed opposition to positive public policies – positions that Durkheim labelled 'pathological'. According to him, the problem turned around a misconceived form of individualism, which undermined the much needed sense of solidarity. The dominant influence on public policy was a kind of utilitarian individualism that encouraged egoism; it was transplanted from economics and reflected its powerful status among social science disciplines. Marxist-influenced socialism recognised the need for solidarity but addressed it in a particularistic manner, which risked turning it into a kind of collective egoism. What was needed was a social or moral individualism, which sociology had the task to explicate. This placed the new discipline of sociology in direct conflict with the two major intellectual currents of the time: liberal individualism inside the academy, Marxian socialism outside it.

We have some way to go before we can properly understand Durkheim's claims. They were set out in his first major published study, *The Division of Labour in Society*, and he returned to elaborate on them throughout his life, including in an extended reformulation of his thesis in a preface to the second French edition of the book in 1902 (Durkheim 2013 [1893, 1902]), written when he was reformulating his lectures on 'professional ethics' and 'civic morals'.[5] Once reform was understood to be possible, Marxism itself was cast as utopian and sociology took on the task of explicating the possibility of a different socialism, now properly scientific.[6] Moreover, when the working class was seen as *what it was* rather than as *what it must become* (i.e. through the lens of its *telos*), it was possible to notice that other kinds of mobilisations were possible, for example those of nationalism or racial difference.[7] At the same time, nationalism and racial difference were represented as contingencies vis-à-vis a process whose 'lonely hour of the last instance', as Althusser (1977a: 113) famously put it, 'never comes'; and thus political interventions on the basis of Marxist claims become opportunistic (in the pejorative rather than Meadian sense) and undetermined by science.

Method

The medical analogy suggested by the idea that sociology might heal social ills was explicit throughout Durkheim's work. In his *Rules of Sociological Method* (Durkheim 1933 [1895]), he drew on recent developments in medical science to distinguish phenomena that were 'pathological' from others that were 'normal' (Hirst 1975). Thus he wrote about two types of fact that are dissimilar: 'those that are just as they ought to be, and those that ought to be different from what they are – normal and pathological phenomena' (Durkheim 2013 [1895, 1902]: 50). In this context, the task of sociology was propaedeutic: to develop an understanding of the normal functioning of the social body so as to propose remedies that could cure its pathologies. Durkheim wrote: 'for societies, as for individuals, health is good and desirable; sickness, on the other hand, is bad and must be avoided' (51). It is in this sense that his sociology was necessarily oriented towards reform even as it betrayed an underlying commitment to order.

Indeed, in the circumstance of a *normal* functioning of society, Durkheim argued that the 'preference for rule and order is naturally preponderant' (Durkheim 1961 [1902–3]: 101). The interests of individuals and society come together in a properly functioning order, such that 'to deny a morality other than that implied by the nature of society is to deny the latter and, consequently, oneself' (Durkheim 1974 [1906]: 38). This may raise an existential question, but one that Durkheim dismissed: '[S]hould a man deny himself? This is a legitimate question, but we shall not examine it. We shall postulate that we are right in wishing to live' (38). His 1897 study of suicide showed that different rates of suicide could be explained by different states of social functioning. Individual unhappiness, which was linked to some forms of suicide, had social causes; hence addressing those causes would contribute to individual happiness – and achieving an aggregate of individual happiness was the focal point of utilitarian individualism (although of course utilitarian individualism misunderstood the *social* conditions of happiness).

This abbreviated introduction to Durkheim's approach already contains specific clues to what was distinctive about it. First, he sought to establish a role for sociology as a science of society, and also its contribution to public policy. Unlike Weber, however, he argued that the principles informing public policy could be provided by that science and were to be derived from an understanding of the functioning of society. This frequently attracts (wrongly) the view that Durkheim was putting forward a positivist justification of sociology, although the need for that science was prescribed by the specific nature of the pathologies evident in modern society. The positivist interpretation was seemingly reinforced by the fact that Durkheim was necessarily setting out the nature of the sociological orientation in contrast to the orientations of actors. After all, the distinction between the 'normal' and the 'pathological' derived its force from the idea that people were currently and contingently living the pathologies that sociology sought to uncover. Consequently their meanings and motives were bound up with those pathologies; they were expressions that served to reproduce the pathologies rather than resolve them.

Durkheim also rejected the argument that sociology was primarily an interpretive undertaking, as it was for Weber. However, unfashionable though these arguments may seem, they do have the immediate consequence that social functions must be established through comparative analysis – which, for Durkheim, did not mean presenting different societies in an order of stages of development (see chapter 1). Indeed, it is a puzzle for many commentators that Durkheim failed to discuss societies intermediate between the most elementary and the most complex (Poggi 1972; Allen and O'Boyle 2017). But, if this is a puzzle, it was nonetheless a feature of Durkheim's approach that derived from his specific use of comparison to distinguish the normal from the pathological in his treatment of the problems that confronted the French Third Republic (and similar societies). In other words, far from presenting modern society as the culmination and final stage of social development, his comparisons were focused on what was specific to it and what was missing from it or what it was deficient in, as it appeared to its members; and they were based on an analysis of the commonalities of all societies.

Durkheim's 'rules' are best understood as provisional commentaries on the nature of problems that sociology must necessarily confront, rather than as foundational claims about the discipline (Gane 1999). If they are taken in the latter way, they risk being understood as a now superseded set of principles of a positivist science. Understood this way, his purposes are misrepresented and insights relevant to a sociology with a different philosophical reconstruction are lost. His interest in reform meant that he must address society *as it is* and *as it should be*, the latter being the focus of sociology in its propaedeutic role. In terms of current philosophy of science (Outhwaite 1987), Durkheim would have to be understood as a realist rather than as an empiricist (see also Jones 1999). The normal is real (that is, established as necessary by science), but not necessarily realised. The pathological exists, but is not real (that is, it is not necessary). It is this characteristic of Durkheim's thought that leads to his being described as a 'master of dialectics' (Peyre 1960). His dialectics was sociological rather than philosophical or historical, but it did have an analogue in Marx, who has also been characterised as a scientific realist (Bhaskar 1979; Outhwaite 1987). That said, we should also here reinforce a point that will occupy us later. For Durkheim, unlike for Marx, religion was not to be regarded as illusory but, as Fields (1995: xvii) comments, it was 'real'. Religion was not one of the 'pathologies' of modern life; it would be a guide to the nature of modern solidarity.

The distinction between the normal and the pathological also operated in a way that paralleled the distinction between 'science' and 'ideology' in Marx. In the first instance, this distinction was associated by Durkheim with the 'objective' and 'subjective' characteristics of a phenomenon. He began *Rules* by designating sociology's object of interest: social facts. These he described as 'ways of acting, thinking and feeling which possess the remarkable property of existing outside the consciousness of the individual' (Durkheim 2013 [1895, 1902]: 20). He gave examples such as forming contracts, using currency, the practices of a profession, and the use of language and argued that, although these are part of the willed behaviours of individuals, they exist independently of them: 'even when they conform to my own sentiments and I feel their reality within me, that reality does not cease to be objective, for it is not I who have prescribed these duties; I have received them through education'.[8] He went on to comment that such facts are not biological because they are about meanings and actions, and are not psychological because they are collective rather than individual.

As Durkheim stated, social facts

> constitute a new species and to them must be assigned exclusively the term *social*. It is appropriate since it is clear that, not having the individual as their substratum, they can have none other than society, either political society in its entirety or one of the partial groups that it includes – religious denominations, political, and literary schools and occupational corporations, etc. (21)

The property that social facts are collective did not mean for Durkheim that they are general in the sense of necessarily exercising their constraint on *all* members of society. Anything that was general was necessarily collective; but, *for something to be collective, it need not be general*. Society was divided into different groups. Nor was Durkheim denying individual consciousness. As he put it, 'no collective entity can be produced if there are no individual consciousnesses; this is a necessary but not a sufficient condition. In addition, these consciousnesses must be associated and combined in a certain way. It is from this combination that social life arises and consequently it is this combination which explains it' (86).

Durkheim's first and most famous rule derived from his claim that sociology's domain was a distinct substratum of social facts: 'consider social facts as things' (29). It was in this context that Durkheim distinguished between 'science' and 'ideology'. People necessarily form impressions and ideas about their circumstances. Accordingly, 'because these notions are closer to us and more within our mental grasp than the realities to which they correspond, we naturally tend to substitute them for the realities, concentrating our speculations upon them … Instead of a science which deals with realities, we carry out no more than an ideological analysis.' This was because such ideas were products of everyday experience, hence 'their main purpose is to attune our actions to the surrounding world'. In this situation, ideology can be more or less systematic. However systematic the elaboration of our reflections, they will remain ideological, unless they are oriented in the proper manner to social facts. Given that modern society is strongly characterised by the development of ideas of individualism, Durkheim was here indicating the need to shift liberalism away from ideology and put it on a scientific footing. This was a kind of liberalism he would later characterise as 'moral individualism', in recognition that social facts were also *moral* facts.

This is an area in which Durkheim is most strongly criticised, especially from the perspective of those who argue that sociology needs to be interpretive and grounded in the meanings of actors. The objections were evident to Durkheim and he answered some of them. A society in which the individual is valued will have difficulty understanding the social as something prior to the individual. Yet it was precisely in terms of this priority that Durkheim argued that the 'sacred' status attributed to the individual could properly be understood. Paradoxically, too, there will be hostility to the very discipline and to the method necessary to demonstrate this view.[9] Indeed, according to Durkheim, economics was a discipline that constructed 'abstractions' based upon actors and their putative rationality. Notwithstanding that concrete circumstances deviated from what might be expected given those abstractions, as 'pure types' they purportedly expressed what would be rational in the circumstances. Thus deviation from market models could not be understood as an indication of the 'irrationality' of the models; on the contrary, it provided the basis for circumstantially rational policies.

Durkheim was not making an empiricist point. Equally, he agreed that circumstances could manifest pathologies, but his alternative to abstractions based upon the actor was sociological realism. Economists and sociologists were themselves members of society who depended on its ways of functioning; and they may prove unable to bring their understanding of their discipline's methodological demands to the required level. Current social problems indicated a need for sociology, but it was possible that that need would not be met. Thus Durkheim commented that the understandings he deemed ideological

> are as a veil interposed between the thing and ourselves, concealing them from us even more effectively because we believe it to be more transparent. Such a science can only be a stunted one, for it lacks the subject matter on which to feed. It has hardly come into existence, one might say, before it vanishes, transmuted into an art. (30)

We can illustrate what Durkheim intended by reference to his study of suicide, published a few years later (Durkheim 1952 [1897]). Our purpose is not to provide a detailed evaluation of the book (see Pope 1976). Durkheim's claim to science allows fallibilism: a methodologically sound argument may fail to hold empirically, and therefore may be in need of correction.[10] For the moment, we are concerned with the methodological argument, not with the substance of its empirical claims. Durkheim's choice of suicide as a topic of study was to the point. After all, suicide is seemingly the most individual of acts and, therefore, on the face of it, inauspicious for sociological explanation. Durkheim began with a definition separated from everyday understandings: 'the term suicide is applied to all cases of deaths resulting directly or indirectly from a positive or negative act of the victim himself, which he knows will produce this result' (Durkheim 1952 [1897]: 44). The definition was specifically designed to refer to actions such as those associated with military valour, where the self-understanding of individuals did not involve the formulation of a motive of suicide.

In line with his discussion of social facts in *Rules*, Durkheim was interested in the number of such acts within a society or a group – that is, in the collective total or *rate* of suicide as a new, *sui generis* fact. Moreover, different rates of suicide were to be explained by properties of the society or group, or what was described in *Rules* as the 'pressure' of social facts. This pressure, 'which is the distinctive sign of social facts, is that which all exert upon each individual' (Durkheim 2013 [1895, 1902]: 85). This was because, for Durkheim, society was not to be understood as a sum of the actions of individuals, 'but the system formed by their association represents a specific reality which has its own characteristics' (86). For the purposes of his study of suicide rates, Durkheim identified two dimensions of a *system* formed by association: integration and regulation. These dimensions were then characterised by the strength or weakness of the respective relations. This yielded four types of suicide, according to whether it reflected egoism (low integration), altruism (high integration), anomie (low regulation), or fatalism (high regulation). Integration referred to the degree of interaction among group members, while regulation referred to the strength of moral sentiments and injunctions.

Pope (1976) argues that key aspects of the argument are somewhat confused, although, as we shall see, the nature of what Durkheim argued is clearer in the context of what he had proposed in *The Division of Labour in Society*. For example, according to Pope, it is difficult in practice to distinguish integration and regulation. After all, the strength of moral injunctions is likely to vary with the degree of interaction among the group. In consequence, it is hard to separate anomic from egoistic suicides independently of the prior identification of the cause applied to explain them.[11] Moreover, there are some doubts as to whether the different rates that Durkheim finds among Protestants, Catholics, and Jews are evident in the data he cites.[12] In addition, his discussion of 'domestic anomie', which related to how the absence of children or the death of a partner reduces domestic interactions, disclosed gendered differences – for example higher rates among married women than among married men but lower rates among widowed women than among widowed men – and might have benefited from an investigation into men's and women's different experiences of marriage vis-à-vis the dimension of regulation.[13]

Pope (1976: 191) also comments that, 'though everywhere using the term and addressing himself to its basic nature, Durkheim (somewhat curiously) never defined society'. These points will be addressed in the next section, where we shall see, *contra* Pope, that Durkheim was clear. 'Society' was a system formed by associations. This system was to be understood as a simple or as a complex organisation – what Durkheim called the division of labour – and therefore also as a *system of systems of association*. Although Durkheim was accused of reifying the idea of society, he most frequently used the term to indicate the substratum of social facts. While he was interested in different systems of association and the relations among them, he was far from arguing that they formed coherent 'totalities' – societies – even for theoretical purposes. 'Society', then, was a shorthand – and not straightforwardly a shorthand for the 'national society', as Strenski (1997: 154) argues. However, to the extent that colonialism bears upon Durkheim's concerns, his framing of the question never extends beyond the national.

Types of Solidarity

In this section we discuss Durkheim's *Division of Labour in Society* (henceforth *Division*) in the light of the rules of sociological method he developed while reflecting on it (and in anticipation of *Suicide*). He began with a discussion of 'the problem', which was the coming to social 'self-consciousness' of the principle of the division of labour, especially as it operated in the organisation of modern industry. Modern industry 'involves increasingly powerful mechanisms, large-scale groupings of power and capital, and consequently an extreme division of labour' (Durkheim 2013 [1893, 1902]: 33). Durkheim credited Adam Smith with the recognition of this principle; but, in his own time, the principle had become obvious to all. Moreover, 'those economists who study its causes and evaluate its results, far from condemning such diversification or attacking it, proclaim its necessity. They see in it the higher law of human societies and the condition for progress.'

From the outset, Durkheim set the approach of sociology in contrast to that prevalent among economists of his day (Steiner 2011). Moreover, he defined the division of labour more widely, so as to encompass not just the organisation of the economy but also the differentiation of institutions such as the family, political admin-istration, the law, education, and science. Each represented a separate (and linked) system of association. Like Weber (1948 [1918]) in his discussion of 'science as a vocation', Durkheim pointed to the division of science into multiple disciplines and to specialisation as a feature of the activities of the scientist. While Durkheim sought to identify the positive social functions served by the division of labour, he was aware, as we have seen, that it could also manifest pathological forms and this could apply to the constitution of the academic division of labour itself. Put simply, economics as a disci-pline had not clarified its relation to social facts, and therefore had failed to elaborate a distinction between pathological and normal forms of the division of labour. In consequence, in many cases it promoted pathological forms, exacerbating social problems rather than resolving them.[14]

In his preface to the second edition of the book, Durkheim (2013 [1893, 1902]) characterised the problem of modern society, succinctly, as one of 'legal and moral anomy' (8), which was especially evident in the area of economic activities. There was, he argued, an absence of collectively binding ethics and direct regulation of activities. The consequence was anarchy and disorder; the law of the strongest prevailed – a situation counter to what he proposed as the normal functioning of society. Yet dominant ideologies – including those within academic disciplines such as economics – compounded the problem. In part, the problem involved the nature of specialisation itself, and an associated problem of 'alienation' was brought about by too much specialisation (Durkheim 2013 [1893, 1902]: 36). Durkheim argued that this was a consequence of unequal power in the enforcement of contracts. The solution he proposed, of developing collective ethics and regulation, or social solidarity, was something he sought to show as being integral to modern society when properly understood; but misunderstandings served to disrupt its development.

A standard sociological representation of *Division* is that Durkheim sought to differentiate two types of society, *mechanical* and *organic*, which he associated with early and modern societies respectively. For this reason, he is usually said to rely upon a stadial theory of society. But, if his theory were truly stadial, it would be one of a most curious kind, indifferent to the variety of intermediate phases or stages and to the differences between them, and interested only in the two ends of the stadial development. One example will suffice; and it draws on postcolonial theory. Allen and O'Boyle (2017: 35) make the following claim: 'Durkheim's central categories neatly separate the world into the "primitive societies" of the colonial periphery and the "advanced societies" of the capitalist core.'[15] Of course, some of the secondary sources used by Durkheim, for instance the American anthropologist Lewis Morgan's book *Ancient Society*, were available as a consequence of colonialism, and they contained a stadial theory. But this is an aspect that Durkheim studiously ignored. Besides, there are plenty of non-stadial main sources in *Division*, such as the Old Testament and histories of German and Frankish tribes.

Indeed, Durkheim does not construct a 'societal type' of mechanical solidarity, although some secondary accounts created one on his behalf (Poggi 1972).[16] To some extent, the idea that Durkheim was contrasting two types of society is reinforced by misreadings of his study *The Elementary Forms of Religious Life*, where he undertook to explain religion through the prism of totemism – 'the simplest and most primitive religion that is known at present' (Durkheim 1995 [1912]: 1) – as practised by indigenous peoples in Australia. By extension, it would appear that this had been his intention in *Division* too. Yet in *Elementary Forms* he stated explicitly that his purpose was 'to explain a present reality that is near to us and capable of affecting our ideas and actions. That reality is Man. More especially, it is present-day man, for there is none other that we have a greater interest in knowing well.' If Locke articulated stadial theory by declaring that in the beginning all the world was America, Durkheim's response was that *in the end we are all Australian*.

In short, in *Division* Durkheim wanted to identify something held in common across all societies, and he sought to do it with the help of comparisons that explained apparent differences. The common element was solidarity, and the differences were set out in relation to mechanical and organic forms. But Durkheim was clear: his focus was modern society, in which the division of labour had progressed most, yet the features associated with mechanical solidarity also remained significant within it. We have already seen that Durkheim understood society as a 'system formed by associations' and that there can be a multiplicity of such systems within any society. Multiplicity – evidenced by the division of labour – was characteristic of modern society, he argued; but, if we take mechanical solidarity to be associated with a society with a low degree of the division of labour (that is, with little differentiation between systems), two things will follow. First, differentiation will produce its own characteristics, which are not found where the division of labour is undifferentiated. Second, some of the component systems in which there is differentiation will reproduce the characteristics attributed to mechanical solidarity. As a result of this argument, Durkheim has been attributed two distinct types of society, when what he described is *two different types of situation* found across different societies. Incidentally, this diffusion also explains what may look otherwise like a rather promiscuous use of secondary sources, derived from a variety of societies.

Durkheim's dialectical strategy operated by unfolding these arguments through a distinction between 'repressive' and 'restitutive' sanctions. In effect, he provided a sociological definition of criminality and of the function of punishment, in order to establish the social character of these two phenomena and their common elements. Punishment derived from the sentiments elicited in a group; and it is the nature of these sentiments – *la conscience collective* ('the collective consciousness') – that interested Durkheim. Repressive sanctions were those that 'consist essentially in some injury, or at least some disadvantage, imposed on the perpetrator of a crime. Their purpose is to do harm to him through his fortune, his honour, his life, his liberty, or to deprive him of some object whose possession he enjoys' (Durkheim 2013 [1893, 1902]: 55). He distinguished this type from another: sanctions that 'do not necessarily imply any suffering on the part of the perpetrator, but merely consist *in restoring the previous state of* affairs, re-establishing relationships that have been disturbed from their normal form'.

In the modern period, these types correspond to penal law on the one hand, civil, commercial and other similar forms of law on the other (penal sanctions are removed from a domain of activities as a result of the further division of labour). Durkheim indicated that in repressive law the sentiments elicited were immediate, revealing the strength and general nature of the collective bond, whereas in civil law the nature of the obligation – say, in a contract – needed to be spelled out in the process of determining redress, thereby indicating that the sentiments were not general. By the same token, not all norms are granted status in law. Truthfulness, for example, may be desirable in everyday associations, but only in specific circumstances will it be brought into the domain of restitutive and repressive sanction – for example in cases of disclosure of relevant information that bears upon a contract or in cases of swearing an oath before God in a court of law.

Criminality is associated with different acts in different societies, but the fact that all societies stipulate punishment for certain acts indicated to Durkheim a common underlying cause. At the same time, the focus of punishment was different in different areas of law and not related to a judgement of the severity of the consequences of the crime, as indicated by the distinction between penal and civil law. Thus the punishment for homicide elicits the most severe sanction in modern societies, while an economic crisis can cause more serious disruption but generates no penal sanction. As Durkheim stated, 'in the penal law of the most civilized people murder is universally regarded as the greatest of crimes. Yet an economic crisis, a crash on the stock market, even a bankruptcy, can disorganize the body social more seriously than the isolated case of homicide ... an act can be disastrous for society without suffering the slightest repression' (58–9). The utility of the sanction, therefore, cannot be its explanation. Finally, Durkheim concluded, 'punishment constitutes essentially a reaction of passionate feeling, graduated in intensity, which society exerts through the mediation of an organized body over those of its members who have violated certain rules of conduct' (74).

The increased division of labour, then, does not remove the significance of repressive sanctions, but displaces them as the number of associations in which membership is not general throughout society increases. This is the source of the differences between mechanical and organic solidarity. In the former, which is exemplified by a tribal society, differentiation is limited. The group is defined by its lineage and has ritual practices and symbols associated with membership. The *conscience collective* is shared by the entire clan and all members bear a strong resemblance with one another that derives from continuous association. Repressive law dominates. Responses to violations are immediate and, according to Durkheim, vengeful. In contrast, where the division of labour has increased, members participate separately in different groups and have different spheres of activity. Even in the family there can be discontinuity, as households separate in order to create new units and some members may live for a time outside a domestic unit. Not only is the *conscience collective* differentiated and less general, but the members of society have separate experiences and therefore differentiated individual consciences. However, the differentiation of activities entailed that the members of society were mutually dependent through the interdependence of the very functions that underlay differentiation.

In this context Durkheim describes two types of positive solidarity: 'the first kind links the individual directly to society without any intermediary. With the second kind, he depends upon society because he depends upon the parts that go to constitute it' (101). One is an organised set of beliefs and sentiments common to all members, the other is a system of different and special functions. However, Durkheim observed, 'these two societies are really one. They are two facets of one and the same reality, but which none the less need be distinguished from each other.' In consequence, each of us, according to Durkheim, has two consciousnesses, 'one which is common to our group which we share in its entirety, which is consequently not ourselves, but society living and acting within us; the other that, on the contrary, represents us alone in what is personal and distinctive about us, what makes us an individual.'

In effect, with this Durkheim was elaborating here the two dimensions that came to be associated with his study in *Suicide*: integration and regulation. Integration – the amount of interaction among members of a group – bears the imprint of mechanical solidarity, while regulation – the specification of rules of conduct – bears the imprint of organic solidarity. The bulk of *Division* was concerned with how these dimensions were articulated in modern society and with possible pathologies associated with them. This engaged Durkheim constantly across his writings – from *Division* through *Suicide* to *Professional Ethics and Civic Morals*; and the last book, which consisted of a series of lectures, was used to reinterpret the earlier one through a lengthy preface to its second edition. This filled out the solution to pathological forms set out in *Division*, and we now turn to his discussion of pathological forms.

Modern Community and Its Discontents

In the previous section we have argued that Durkheim did not intend to produce a *typology of societies*, but to distinguish two *types of solidarity* that he found in a variety of combinations in different societies. The purpose of his analysis was to lay bare the problems confronting modern society and the misunderstandings bound up with them. The main target of his critique was individualistic approaches, be they classic liberal or utilitarian, which emphasised individual liberty. Given that the development of the division of labour and the multiplication of differential systems of association pointed to the need to strengthen the rules that secured regulation, these understandings of individualism presupposed opposition to regulation; therefore they were part of the problem, not its solution. 'In vain one may claim to justify this absence of rules by asserting that it is conducive to the individual exercising his liberty freely', wrote Durkheim in the preface to the second edition of *Division*.

'Nothing is more false than the antinomy that people have too often wished to establish between the authority of rules and the freedom of the individual. On the contrary, liberty (by which we mean a just liberty, one for which society is duty bound to enforce respect) is itself the product of a set of rules' (Durkheim 2013 [1893, 1902]: 9). Justice, then, has a specifically sociological determination.

Durkheim shared the utilitarian concern for individual happiness. Indeed, he devoted one chapter of *Division* to the topic. But he denied that it could be understood as a psychological drive with social consequences. Rather, individual happiness had social causes. Moreover, it depended on the moral constitution of societies and not on the degree of development of their division of labour.[17] All societies had the possibility of securing happiness for their members, since happiness derived from what Durkheim called the 'charm' of a common life together. Thus, he wrote,

> a life lived in common is attractive, yet at the same time coercive. Undoubtedly constraint is necessary to induce man to rise above himself and superimpose on his physical nature one of a different kind. But, as he learns to savour the charm of this new existence, he develops the need for it; there is no field of activity in which he does not passionately seek after it. This is why, when individuals discover they have interests in common and come together, it is not only to defend those interests, but also so as to associate with one another, and not feel isolated in the midst of their adversaries, so as to enjoy the pleasure of communicating with one another, to feel at one with several others, which in the end means to lead the same moral life together. (18)

The passage is significant in several respects. In the first place, Durkheim attributed individual happiness to social causes, namely to the character of solidarity, thereby indicating the relevance of mechanical solidarity in modern life: people lead the 'same moral life together'. At the same time he placed all this in the context of 'interests' and 'adversaries', which was the domain of egoism, albeit of the collective kind. Durkheim was concerned that class conflict indicated an absence of regulation that would moderate differences of power in the contractual relation. Here happiness required a regulation of the interests that would inspire the collective action, which transcended egoism. As he argued, 'society has no justification if it does not bring a little peace to men – peace in their hearts and peace in their mutual intercourse. If, then, industry can be productive only by disturbing their peace and unleashing warfare, it is not worth the cost' (Durkheim 1957 [1890–1900]: 16). How did Durkheim resolve these tensions?

It follows from what we have argued so far that Durkheim's socio-logical analysis involved the articulation of organic and mechanical solidarity within modern institutions. Mechanical solidarity remained a significant aspect of modern community, but it could no longer easily function as an aspect of the *conscience collective* of all members. For example, the family was characterised by mechanical solidarity and a unity of feeling. Thus, in his lecture course on *Moral Education* (Durkheim 1961 [1902–3]), Durkheim discussed the role of the punishment of the child within the family and the school. Repressive sanctions were appropriate for the very young child, where the impact could be modified by tenderness between the parent and child, but inappropriate in the school, albeit that the function of all punishment was to reinforce the moral significance of the rule that had been transgressed. In any case, the child was meant to be prepared for a life in the wider society.

In modern societies the family could not be the solution to the problem of anomie. The fact that the family was increasingly separated from the sphere of paid work meant that there were sections of the day that its members spent outside the domestic sphere; the details of life were now beyond the family's purview. Moreover, the family unit was created anew in each generation, hence there was a time when individuals were outside its influence. Durkheim (2013 [1893, 1902]: 19) wrote: 'nowadays the family is dispersed with each generation, man spends a not inconsiderable part of his existence far removed from any domestic influence'. As he put it in his lectures on professional ethics and civic morals, 'the lives of a host of individuals are passed in the individual and commercial sphere. Hence it follows that as those in this milieu have only a faint impress of morality the greater part of their existence is passed divorced from any moral influence. How could such a state of affairs fail to be a source of demoralisation?' (Durkheim 1957 [1890–1900]: 18).

Durkheim referred to 'man' (*homme*) in the generic sense, but there can be no doubt that what he was describing was gendered. The participation of men and women in the different activities associated with the division of labour was unequal and, of course, also different in different social classes (Lehmann 1994). French women were not granted suffrage until 1944. If Durkheim was oblivious to these inequalities, they were at least revealed by his categories and his data. We have already remarked that, in *Suicide*, men and women exhibit different rates of suicide despite their apparently similar domestic circumstances. In a situation where a possible general problem of anomie was ascribed to men by virtue of their participation in (unregulated) public life, women's restricted participation in the public sphere and confinement to an increasingly privatised domestic life made them more vulnerable to the pressures that Durkheim otherwise attributed to the forced division of labour. At the very least, the experience of men and women and their involvement in different systems of association were dissimilar, and therefore, on Durkheim's arguments, likely to have different consequences.

Durkheim's view was that the family might be thought of as having the characteristics of a mini-society to some degree, but the general problem he was describing could not be resolved simply by an aggregation of such mini-societies. For Durkheim, there was something outside individuals and their families (which, much later, Mrs Thatcher, the utilitarian British prime minister, would deny). However, the solution could not be found directly in the collective consciousness, since this consciousness expressed itself in the form of mechanical solidarity. With the development of the division of labour, its role had become specific – no longer general. At the same time, distinct spheres of activity, especially in the economic realm, had developed without an adequate framework of regulatory rules. The general role of collective consciousness was now 'enfeebled', replaced as it was by the functional interdependence of the division of labour itself. The problems, according to Durkheim, resided primarily in the dimension of regulation.[18] It is in this context that, having established the *normal* forms of solidarity and their relation to the division of labour, he offered an account of the *abnormal* or *pathological* forms of this division: 'if normally the division of labour produces social solidarity, it can happen, however, that it has entirely different or even opposite results' (Durkheim 2013 [1893, 1902]: 277). One such form, the anomic division of labour, occurred when the appropriate regulation was absent. Another form, the forced division of labour, occurred when the problem was in the nature of the rules themselves: 'it is not enough for rules to exist, for occasionally it is these very rules that are the cause of evil' (293). A third, unnamed form ('another abnormal form') occurred when there was division without corresponding function.

Once again, the three forms were not designed by Durkheim to be mutually exclusive, and all three may be at issue in modern society. However, it was fundamental to Durkheim's analysis that the primary problems of modern society be associated with anomie. For example, he returned to the problem he addressed initially in relation to restitutive law and the comparative disruptions caused by economic crisis and by homicide. Economic crisis, he suggested, was a problem of absence of regulation, and therefore of an anomic division of labour. So, too, was the class conflict between capital and labour, which he attributed to the unregulated power of the employer, especially in large-scale industry. But Durkheim acknowledged that the situation may look different from the perspective of labour: 'this tension in social relations is due in part to the fact that the working classes do not really desire the status assigned to them and too often accept it only under constraint and force, not having any means of gaining any other status' (279). Finally, working class alienation was sometimes a matter of integration rather than one of regulation. This was the domain of the third abnormal form, in which the division of labour had been pushed too far. As Durkheim put it, 'the individual, bent low over his task, will isolate himself in his own special activity. He will no longer be aware of the collaborators who work at his side on the same task, he even no longer has any idea at all of what that common task consists. The division of labour cannot therefore be pushed too far without becoming a source of disintegration' (280).

At this point we need to note the absence of any discussion of colonialism and its bearing upon Durkheim's claims in general. For example, we saw in our discussion of Tocqueville that the French administration of Algeria (and also of the Caribbean and Indian Ocean colonies) involved colonial plantations and forced labour. Given that Durkheim was concerned with the expression of power within contractual relations as potentially indicative of a forced division of labour, it is striking that he failed to address the forced division of labour within territories under French jurisdiction, where no dialectical argument was necessary in order to demonstrate that the situation was *forced*. This problem is compounded, as we shall see, by the fact that Durkheim's solution to the pathological forms thrown up by modernity involved participation in the regulatory frameworks that connect the state and civil society. Strenski's (1997) argument that, in Durkheim's eyes, society is essentially a national society has force especially at this point, even if colonialism and empire are not central to Strenski's own analysis. Moreover, the state's regulatory frameworks, which Durkheim recommended in a desire to solve the domestic pathologies in France, were precisely the instruments that disrupted the solidarities that had secured social relations in the overseas territories before colonial domination.

Durkheim's solution to the problems that faced modern societies was to consider their different institutional modes – for example the family, civil society with its economic organisations, and the state (Wallwork 1972). His manner of proceeding included judging whether a particular set of institutional arrangements was necessary and sufficient to produce the desired results. Given the multiplicity of systems of association that characterises the division of labour in modern societies, it followed that the problems could not be addressed in a single sphere, but would require a comprehensive set of reforms. One of Durkheim's primary concerns was for the organisation of civil society and of the institutions intermediate between the individual and the state. Here he needed to address 'anomie' in the economic sphere through the development of occupational groupings.

But, since his analysis made room for the possibility that the rules themselves are part of the problem, Durkheim was far from arguing that the solution was simply one of regulation. That solution would have rendered his socialism anaemic. The position of workers vis-à-vis employers needed to be addressed both with regard to inequalities of power and with regard to social status. In effect, the treatment of economic anomie had to resolve issues about the forced division of labour, or else one pathology would just be replaced with another. In addition, since any regulatory mechanism needed an intermediary agent to enforce it, the solution that Durkheim sought ultimately required the engagement of political authority, which itself had to be justified in a manner consistent with the regulatory mechanisms of the parts. In other words, the professional ethics of the regulation of occupational activities was interconnected with the civic morality of the organisation of public life. The state was the ultimate 'guardian' of the regulatory frameworks and drew its legitimacy from the sanctity of individual rights, which were expressed as a form of moral individualism.

Durkheim argued that trade unions represented a first step towards the regulation of occupational activities; and they should not be understood as a separate organisation of workers without the employer, but as federated organisations of unions and employers

– as an expression of the creation of systems of association between workers and employers. This necessarily mitigated the power that determined the employment relation, but also stopped trade union activity from representing the collective bargaining power of a single group of workers and encouraged the unions to rise above individual or collective egoism (Durkheim 1957 [1890–1900]: 12). Durkheim saw an analogy with the guilds and corporations of medieval Europe that had become an obstacle to the development of the division of labour and a constraint upon an individual's choice of occupation. Professional ethics in the organisation of the different branches of industry was, for Durkheim, a reinvention of modes of association that secure the same functions of regulation: the need is moral rather than economic. The problem could not be overcome by transforming all private property into collective property since the issue of the regulation of employment would remain (30). Durkheim proposed administrative councils, boards, and tribunals organised regionally and across different branches of industry.

Part of Durkheim's difficulty was that he was dealing with institutional forms that, in other circumstances, had been seen as problematic and in need of change, only for him to argue that they needed to be reinvented for new circumstances. A similar situation arose in the discussion of civic morality, which was concerned with the relationship between the individual and the state. We do not need to dwell on Durkheim's account of the emergence of the state as a distinct institution with authority over secondary groups. The crucial issue for him was the process by which the development of the state and that of individualism, having different trajectories, were brought together. This, he argued, was a matter of 'determining the relation of individuals to this sovereign authority, to whose control they are subject' (47). In this context, Durkheim argued, 'the principal duties under civic morals are obviously those that the citizen has towards the State and, conversely, those the State owes to the individual' (48).

While the state and the individual can be opposed to each other, opposition does not define them as classic liberalism argued. In Durkheim's judgement tyranny was, however, a real possibility. What is more, that possibility was being actualised in the French empire, where the relation of the colonised to the sovereign authority was one of domination. But Durkheim also argued that the development of the division of labour produced a sense of individuality and that political authority was necessary to uphold the framework of obligations and duties. Yet the relation between coloniser and colonised was antagonistic in principle, and the non-antagonistic form of the relation between state and individual was reserved for the metropole. Durkheim was seemingly unaware of the contradiction; for example, he argued that 'our moral individuality, far from being antagonistic to the State, has on the contrary been a product of it. It is the State that sets it free' (69). In his view this was not only a sociological deduction but a thesis practically demonstrated: 'it is the state that has rescued the child from patriarchal domination and from family tyranny; the state that has freed the citizen from feudal groups and later from communal groups; it is the state that has liberated the craftsman and his master from guild tyranny' (64). However, Durkheim was aware that, just as there could be pathologies associated with the organisation of economic activities, social malaise could have political malaise as its consequence. The cause was the same in both cases: an absence of secondary associations in civil society.

Durkheim considered human rights to have taken on a sacred character and to have become a religious phenomenon in that respect, notwithstanding their seemingly secular nature. He was opposed to the idea that the state should embody the religious values of a specific faith, since common religious belief was no longer general. But, as his study of suicide showed, he expected religion to provide protection from anomie for some members of society. Religious communities were among the secondary associations that were seen to be positive, but they could not operate as a solution to commercial anomie because they were not fully involved in commercial activities. Moreover, if the state derived legitimacy from its embodiment of individual rights and their support, a complementary question would arise about the nature of the collective sentiments through which individuals provided the state with solidarity. Here Durkheim postulated a role for 'patriotism'. This potentially displaced the problem of adversarial relations, moving it from the commercial sphere into that of relations between states, where it would be expressed in warfare and self-sacrifice – the ultimate demand upon members of society and their moral values.

Durkheim looked beyond the French nation to see how the 'religion of humanity' was developing in the relations between states. Mindful perhaps of the territorial annexation of Alsace–Lorraine, Durkheim proposed that states – or nations – need not find their destiny in geographical expansion, even if that was the current situation of France, with its imperial territories. The conflicts between European powers contributed urgency to his claim:

> everything justifies our belief that national aims do not lie at the summit of this hierarchy – it is human aims that are destined to be supreme ... If each state had as its chief aim not to expand, or to lengthen its borders, but to set its own house in order and to make the widest appeal to its members for a moral life on an ever higher level, then all discrepancy between national and human morals would be excluded ... Societies can take their pride, not in being the greatest or the wealthiest, but in being the most just, the best organised and in possessing the best moral constitution' (74)

In this way, Durkheim argued, patriotism could become a 'fragment of world patriotism' (75). Patriotism would be expressed not outwardly, but towards internal affairs and the reforms that Durkheim advocated.

Durkheim concluded his discussion of patriotism with a prescient remark: 'to be sure, we have not yet reached the point where this kind of patriotism could prevail without dissent, if indeed such a time could ever come' (75).

Moral Individualism, Nationalism, and the Question of Religion

Durkheim's discussion about the state and about interstate competition for the promulgation of the 'best moral constitution' was poignant. It was markedly different from Weber's nationalist invocation of greatness in global power politics.[19] As we saw in the previous chapter, Weber was acutely aware of the imperial ambitions of the German state and regarded them as legitimate in the competition with France, Russia, and Britain for dominance in Europe and elsewhere. Weber promoted the interest of the 'German people', and did so in explicitly nationalist terms. As Abraham (1992) has argued, this action included support for ethnic policies on the eastern border, against both Poles and Jews. If Weber's views were not as virulently anti-Semitic as those of other academics with whom he was associated, for example Sombart and Treitschke, he viewed the formal exclusion of Jews from the professions and the civil service (which meant also from academia) with some equanimity.

For the most part, secondary commentaries on Weber have neglected the significance of these aspects of his thought. With Durkheim we face a different situation. It was as if he was oblivious of the fact that the state he represented as being ordered under the 'values of humanity' was an imperial state. France had invaded Algeria in the 1830s, as we saw in our discussion of Tocqueville. Algeria was made formally a part of France in 1848 and, from 1881, came under the direct authority of the Ministry of the Interior (Evans and Phillips 2007). France also had long-standing colonies in the Caribbean and in the Indian Ocean and, after the Berlin Conference of 1884/5, took its share of African territories – the 'spoils' negotiated at that conference. From the 1850s on, it engaged in colonisation in Indochina (in Cambodia, Vietnam, and Siam), an action that brought on military defeat in the late 1880s, in the Sino-Chinese or Tonkin War. There were further military conflicts in the 1890s, when Durkheim was working on his lecture courses on civic morals and professional ethics. The death of General Rivière in battle in 1883, while engaging with Vietnamese fighters in Hanoi, provoked anger in France at the temerity of those who resisted colonial rule, but also a reaction against colonialism within the French National Assembly (Munholland 1978).

Durkheim remained silent in the face of this turmoil, as did the secondary literature on his work. Yet surely this turmoil bore on his proposed solutions to the problems of anomie and integration. All his solutions depended on the effective and ethical role of the state. In his own time, however, the state was associated with divided justi-fications and with groups that embodied the different claims. There were nationalist justifications from the military, and these functioned like the ones endorsed by Weber in his call for national greatness in Germany. On the other hand, there was the professional ethics of science, legal functionaries, educationalists, and other members of the intelligentsia who advocated a secular republic with constitu-tional human rights. Durkheim's solutions in the sphere of economic activities were also entangled. He had noted the growth of large-scale economic organisations; this was not just a matter of size, but also one of geographical reach. Colonialism, albeit not necessarily military adventurism, was bound up with commercial interests; and it also structured the French state. Durkheim failed to address colonialism, but colonialism was bound up with the problems he sought to resolve.

Some of this problematic came to a head in the Dreyfus affair, where Durkheim (1969 [1898] intervened significantly against the anti-Semitic and Catholic reaction to an individualism presented as predominantly 'un-Godly' – or, more properly, un-Christian. Individualism here was associated with 'unpatriotic' commercial interests and functioned as a code for Jewishness, and therefore as a trope of anti-Semitism. Dreyfus had been accused of passing secrets to Germany and found guilty by a military court that had covered up the guilt of another officer and made Dreyfus the scapegoat, as was revealed later. The anti-Dreyfusards believed that both military honour and the interests of the state were being challenged, so they closed ranks (as might have been anticipated from Durkheim's own account of solidarity). Durkheim joined the side of the Dreyfusards – the 'intellectuals' of his title ('Individualism and the Intellectuals') and an embodiment of professional ethics and civic morals. Dreyfus's rights as an individual and the injustice to which he was subjected were set against the authority of the state and its military corps. Those rights had to be defended because they were the foundation of the state's claim to legitimacy. As Durkheim (1969 [1898]: 22) wrote, 'there is no reason of State which can excuse an outrage against the person when the rights of the person are placed above the State'.

However, Durkheim's understanding of liberal rights was not a standard one and transcended the terms in which the Dreyfus affair was debated. Although he regarded the Enlightenment's ideas of individualism – those associated with Kant and, in France in particular, with Rousseau and with the 1789 Declaration of the Rights of Man – as superior to those derived from utilitarian philosophy, they all shared the same foundation: they looked at the human being in the abstract. Durkheim believed that the tradition that had led from Kant to Hegel and then to Marx developed in the direction of socialism. But it also triggered problems around the relationship between the individual and society and around the reification of the state, as was evident from authoritarian tendencies in Rousseau and in the wider French revolutionary tradition; Tocqueville had pointed to these problems too. In part, this situation was due to a failure to develop the sociological nature of individualism; for in sociology, unlike in utilitarian philosophy, the rights of individuals could both define and require the legitimacy of the state.

One development of the Enlightenment's ideas was to oppose individual autonomy and judgement to authority, and especially religious authority. Like Weber, Durkheim accepted that the 'spirit of freedom' had a direct relationship with Christian thought. For this reason he criticised the seemingly religiously motivated anti-Dreyfusards for their failure to understand that individualism was part of their own tradition and not antithetical to it. However, his argument was stronger. Once properly understood, in sociological fashion, secular individualism was in fact a *religious* phenomenon too. This was a striking idea, and it may seem odd to many readers today. It was reminiscent of Comte's desire to establish a religion of humanity, with all its anachronistic trappings of calendar and liturgy (Pickering 1990). But it was precisely this aspect of Durkheim's thought that both captured a need of his day and opens space for an engagement with postcolonial sociology. Durkheim's endorsement of a secular position was not part of a stadial philosophy of history; in fact, notwithstanding his own agnosticism, it made room for the recognition of religious belonging as a component of modern solidarity.

In order to understand just what was distinctive about Durkheim's argument, we need to look at his last major work, *The Elementary Forms of Religious Life*. Ostensibly this was a study of totemism among indigenous peoples of Australia, as described in ethnographies from the time.[20] Durkheim selected this topic of study in order to show religion in its simplest, most elementary form. Of course, this assumption is easily criticised as a presumption inspired by belief in the superiority of western thought. However, Durkheim sought to construct a sociology of knowledge where the categories of thought – space, time, number, cause – were seen to derive from religion (Bloor 1982).[21] The sociological condition for the availability of the ethnographic studies was, of course, the existence of a European colonial settlement in Australia. While Durkheim had no explicit comment on this, his intention shortens the distance between 'us' and 'them' and reveals 'us' in 'them'.[22] He tells us clearly instead that he sought to 'comprehend the religious nature of man, that is, to reveal a fundamental and permanent aspect of humanity' (Durkheim 1995 [1912]: 1).

This idea of 'the religious nature of man' replicated a central feature of his sociological method: he regarded religion as real, not as something false and superseded in the development of modernity. In this way his choice to study beliefs and practices, bizarre and exotic as they may seem to readers, had polemical force. 'There are no religions', he commented, 'that are false' (2). All religions involved improbable claims and descriptions, and nothing would be easier than to demonstrate their 'errors'. Yet the beliefs associated with them persisted and, in order to understand why that was so, we have to understand the function they served and the need they met. How, for example, do we explain the belief in a 'soul' that survives the body and can live on (270)? Religious beliefs and practices were various, and they were equally improbable. It might be possible to rank religions according to some criterion or another, but what would be the point, if 'all are equally religious'? And he went on:

> if I address myself to primitive religions, then, it is not with any ulterior motive of disparaging religion in general. These religions are to be respected no less than the others. They fulfil the same needs, play the same role, and proceed from the same causes: therefore, they can serve just as well to elucidate the nature of religious life and, it follows, to solve the problem I wish to treat. (2–3)

In 1895, in *Rules*, Durkheim had pointed to the nature of social facts, that is, their independent existence. They precede any given individual and continue after any individual's death. Almost two decades later, in *Elementary Forms*, he asserted that religion provided a way of thinking about this condition of all social life; and the fact that it did was evident in the idea of a soul. Australian tribes did not believe in an all-powerful God; but they did believe in a soul that lived on and was reincarnated in the newly born. As a corollary, 'belief in the immortality of souls is the only way man is able to comprehend a fact that cannot fail to attract his attention: the perpetuity of the group's life. The individual dies, but the clan survives, so the forces that constitute his life must have the same perpetuity' (Durkheim 1995 [1912]: 271).

Durkheim was a self-described agnostic and an assimilated Jew (Lukes 1973; Strenski 1997; Fournier 2013). He wrote from the perspective of science, but did not regard science as displacing religion. The process of secularisation involved endowing human rights with a religious character. Seen in this light, human rights are collective and general. But this did not mean that they replaced religion. The old religions could no longer claim to be collective and general, but they remained as important sources of solidarity. Thus, in the conclusion to *Elementary Forms*, Durkheim argued that the common representation of religion and science as irreconcilable was itself based on a scientific misunderstanding, which could be dispelled by attuning science and the scientists to what a religious life entailed. 'Believers', he argued, 'sense that the true function of religion is not to make us think, enrich our knowledge, or add representations of a different sort and source we owe to science. Its true function is to make us act and to help us to live' (Durkheim 1995 [1912]: 419).

In effect, Durkheim postulated a pluralism of religious solidarities – between Catholics and Protestants, Christians and Jews – within a secular republic ruled by the norms of a religion of humanity, which encompassed all that plurality. In this way Durkheim answered the 'Jewish question' more profoundly than did Weber or Marx. Weber, as we have seen, adopted a position that was, at best, one of assimilation into a dominant cultural model: the nation, both Christian in its traditions and German in its ethnic identity. Marx (1975 [1842a]), for his part, addressed the Jewish question as it was discussed by the Hegelian philosopher Bruno Bauer, and did so from the perspective of human emancipation (Durkheim would have appreciated this from his own position on Hegelianism and its orientation towards socialism). But the issue for Marx was the need to emancipate the state from religion – that is, to establish a secular state. He cited Tocqueville to the effect that the political emancipation of Jews had taken place in France and in the United States but was incomplete insofar as the social divisions of civil society remained. Bauer had argued that, for Jews, religious freedom would mean providing them with special rights, different from the rights of Germans who were not Jewish. Marx noted, like Weber, the break-up of the old shtetls in the east: this triggered a partial assimilation of Jewish people as they moved into other regions of Germany, where the restrictions placed on their ability to participate in a wide range of occupations pushed them into commerce. In this context, Marx adopted the anti-Semitic trope of 'the Jew' as a metaphor for the private commercial and antisocial interests that emergent capitalism represented. Human emancipation required social emancipation, which involved emancipation from 'Jewishness', both as indicator of an outmoded religion and as symbol of a class relation that must be transcended.

Durkheim offered something radically different – and yet … There is something timid about Durkheim's response, alongside his failure to treat issues of Islam and the inclusion of Muslims, especially in the context of France's colonies in North Africa.

Algeria was, after all, French by colonial incorporation, yet Muslim Algerians were not offered political emancipation. It was unlikely that Durkheim was unaware of their situation, which included both political suppression and material deprivation (300,000 had died of starvation in Algeria after a famine in 1867: see Evans and Phillips 2007: 31). He was a member of the Union for Truth, which had up to 1,000 members. It met between 1905 and 1913 and held 'open conversations' that were subsequently published (Pedersen 2014). This was a gathering of the intelligentsia similar in social character to the Dreyfusards. Fournier (2013: 487, 519, 540–2) mentions Durkheim's contributions to debates on church and state, Marxist socialism, internationalism, and public service. Lukes (1973: 534–5) tells us that Durkheim was a regular attendee. Neither mentions Algeria or colonialism.

However, Jean Pedersen describes the Union as holding regular discussions on German nationalism in the light of the unwar-ranted annexation of Alsace–Lorraine, as well as on French and wider European colonialism. Most members deplored nationalism as it was expressed in Germany, but they justified colonialism as a civilising mission and even outlined a 'right to colonialism', as did the political economist Charles Gide, for example. Pedersen does not talk directly about Durkheim's role, but she refers to his objec-tions to one of Gide's more forceful points. Gide had stated that, without colonialism, 'all of North Africa would still be barbaric, all of Central Africa would still be delivered to frightful little Negro potentates and slave merchants, [and] all of North America [would still be delivered to] Apaches!' and had noted Durkheim's objection in the proceedings; Durkheim had declared that 'he [Durkheim] had never known what constituted a savage people'. Gide overrode this comment by observing that there was a distinction between 'civilised' and 'uncivilised' people and 'the former had a duty and a right to colonize the latter' (cited in Pedersen 2014: 17).[23]

Durkheim raised the 'rights of the person' above the rights of the state, but it seems that the colonised had no such rights. It would be incorrect to say, with Cotesta (2017), that Durkheim neglected their rights to national self-determination, since that would imply that 'human rights' require a national embodiment. Durkheim's wartime denunciation of the 'German mentality' was not a form of racism (Cotesta 2017). After all, 'German' was a self-description of this mentality: it was used by nationalists such as Treitschke, who talked about the individual's subordination to the state. Nor was Durkheim's argument 'jingoistic' (Allen and O'Boyle 2017: 31), since it was consistent with his discussion of patriotism in *Professional Ethics*. However, given that Algeria was part of France, it was striking that Algerians were treated as subjects rather than citizens. At least in part, this was because they were Muslim. They could be naturalised individually as French citizens, as if they were foreigners, but they had to give up the authority of Muslim religious law (Bousquet 1953: 599). The colonised subject was a French national but not a citizen (Saada 2011). After full incorporation into France in 1881, Algeria was divided into three departments that sent deputies to the National Assembly in Paris. However, only adult male *settlers* could vote at the 'national' (that is, imperial) level; Algerians were excluded (Evans and Phillips 2007: 33).

In short, Durkheim's neglect of colonialism caused him both to misrepresent republican human rights and to fail to grasp the nature of nationalist sentiments, which would beset Europe. He was a child during the Franco-Prussian War and died during the First World War – that is, during a crisis for humanity – while propounding the religion of humanity. His scientific method cut through much that was obscure to contemporary writers, but ultimately could not rise above the limitations of Durkheim's own field of vision. One of these was the failure to register the centrality of colonialism and empire to any diagnosis of his times.

Conclusion

Karen E. Fields (2012), who recently translated Durkheim's *Elementary Forms* into English, imagines a dialogue between Durkheim and W. E. B. Du Bois. She identifies as Afro-American, in recognition of her heritage as an American of African descent, not as an African who is also American; and she sees in Durkheim someone who got close to the unveiling of the racial order of modern society and its sociology. Durkheim and Du Bois were direct contemporaries. They did not meet, yet they might have done. Both attended the Universal Exposition in Paris in 1900. As Fields comments, Du Bois had precious few interlocutors in US sociology in 1903, when he wrote about the colour line in *Souls of Black Folk*. To many of his fellow Americans he was less than fully human. But in Durkheim he would have found a sociologist who sought to demonstrate, through a study of indigenous people in Australia, what it was to be fully human.

Both sociologists, Fields suggests, came to their craft as 'outsiders', with characteristics ascribed to them by 'majority' others on the basis of a presumed and racialised collectivity. Du Bois would have understood Durkheim's need to be patriotic in the face of looming war. As Fields (2012: 251) puts it, for Du Bois, 'along with a double-consciousness went what can be called "double death" – dying once for America and once for Afro-America'. Durkheim was part of a committee that recorded the deaths, injuries, and service of Jewish soldiers in the First World War. Fields draws further parallels between their positioning as a function of racialised difference. Ultimately her claim is that Durkheim's treatment of France's Jewish question and Du Bois's treatment of the Negro question are analogous. She concludes that 'Durkheimian ideas find themselves on Du Boisian terrain: In studies of race, the notion of double-consciousness jostles that of collective identifications produced in social life' (260).

We have argued nevertheless that Durkheim answered the Jewish question only to fail before the Muslim question. In each case, it was a question asked of Jews and Muslims by other Europeans, just as the Negro question was asked of African Americans by white Americans of European descent. Jews and Muslims were present in Europe by historical processes that preceded modernity. Africans were brought to the United States by a process that belongs to modernity – colonialism – just as some Muslims have become part of Europe through colonial incorporation and domination within multicultural empires. Durkheim did not acknowledge those processes. As we shall see in the next chapter, Du Bois began from the position of African Americans within the nation and its colour line, but transcended Durkheim's limitation and recognised the global colour line traced by colonial modernity.

6

Du Bois

Addressing the Colour Line

In the preceding chapters we have been considering writers whose status in the development of modern social theory is secure and largely unquestioned. Our purpose has been to show how their engagement with the development of modernity was shaped by the colonial histories of the societies they used as the basis of their sociological concepts. The writers in question remarked upon those histories and at the same time effaced them, as they identified what each one took to be the central feature of modernity: the society of equals, the capital–labour relation, rationalisation, or modernity as moral community. As we have also argued, their references to colonialism and empire are left out of the mainstream secondary literature that sought to delineate the foundations they have created. In these respects, the fact that W. E. B. Du Bois has been neglected until very recently is a manifestation of this same situation.

Du Bois was a contemporary of Weber and Durkheim, though the long span of his life meant that he was active well beyond the period 1890–1920, which is considered foundational for sociological theory. His magnum opus, *Black Reconstruction* (Du Bois 1935), was written just at the time when Talcott Parsons (1937) was promoting the idea of a founding generation of classical social theorists. However, our concern is not simply to right a wrongful omission. During the past decade Du Bois has been well served by new accounts of his relationships with sociology and political science – accounts by writers such as Aldon Morris (2015), Robert Vitalis (2015), Christopher McAuley (2019) and José Itzigsohn and Karida L. Brown (2020). Our interest here is to see how his work bears directly upon the themes we have been discussing in the other writers. Put very simply, we can see the theories we have discussed so far as involving universal claims that have been confounded by the particularities of racialised difference. In Du Bois we trace the opposite movement, which goes from a deep and embodied engagement with a specific society organised around racialised differences to a universal claim about the construction of a global 'color line' in colonialism. Du Bois was, indeed, an 'African American pioneer of sociology' (Saint-Arnaud 2009).

Du Bois's first major work was a survey and an ethnographic study: *The Philadelphia Negro* (Du Bois 1967 [1899]). As we shall see, this work can be read in the context of Tocqueville's arguments about the generalisation of racial prejudice in the United States. The migration of African Americans from the South, after the Civil War and the failure of Reconstruction, exposed them to *de facto* prejudice in northern cities that was equivalent to the legalised discrimination practised in the South. This was a kind of prejudice already experienced by long-standing communities of free African Americans present in those cities. It also put them in competition with European migrants in the same cities, just as Tocqueville said it would. Wherever they found themselves, African Americans were a minority, both in the cities they inhabited and in the general population. Tocqueville depicted enslavement and the dispossession of indigenous people as forms of tyranny. He also suggested that there was a form of tyranny that was possible in democracies: that of the majority over the minority, a form that electoral politics can produce. It is significant, however, that he did not address this as a problem that would be confronted by African Americans after the abolition of slavery. Indeed, he was so convinced of the reality of racial prejudice that he could imagine only their continued oppression or the possibility that African Americans somehow consolidated their numbers and formed a majority in a separate state – in other words, complete segregation. He wrote: 'If we assume that Whites and emancipated Negroes are to occupy the same land and face each other as foreign peoples, it is easy to see that the future holds only two prospects: either Negroes and Whites must blend altogether or they must separate' (Tocqueville 2004 [1835]: 410).[1]

As we have already argued, Tocqueville described the situation of 'mingled races' as impossible. Du Bois, however, had to live it and, in living it, he made it central to the development of his sociological inquiries and political commitments.[2] Alongside his scholarly work, Du Bois was active in politics in a variety of roles, including as a founder of the National Association for the Advancement of Colored People (NAACP) and as editor of its monthly magazine, *The Crisis*. He was a delegate to the newly established United Nations, got involved in pan-African congresses, and worked as an antiwar activist for much of his later life. Persecuted by the McCarthyite campaign in the 1950s and disillusioned about the possibility of racial equality in the United States, Du Bois spent the last years of his life in Ghana at the request of its president, Kwame Nkrumah. Du Bois joined the Communist Party of America on the day he left the United States for Ghana, as a symbolic gesture towards previous accusations that he had been a member of the party.

Du Bois's personal integrity is clear. He had had an ambivalent attitude to the First World War and US involvement in it. Unlike Weber, who was a staunch advocate for the national cause, Du Bois regarded participation in the war as necessary to the furtherance of African American claims for equal citizenship. African Americans should participate as *Americans* and, as participants, should be granted the same rights and respect as other citizens. His experience of the failure of this strategy took him in more radical directions, including towards pacifism. In his later autobiographical reflections on the period of the First World War he wrote:

> I am less sure now than then of the soundness of this war attitude. I did not realise the full horror of war and its wide impotence as a method of social reform. Perhaps, despite words, I was thinking narrowly of the interests of my group and was willing to let the world go to hell if the black man went free ... Possibly passive resistance of my twelve millions to any war activity might have saved the world for black and white. (Du Bois 1995 [1940]: 407–8)

Du Bois, as we shall see, would connect black interests to saving black and white. This puts him in contrast with white sociologists and their positive orientation to colonialism and empire.

Colour Prejudice

William Edward Burghardt Du Bois was freeborn, in 1868, in Great Barrington in the northern state of Massachusetts. This was five years after the Emancipation Proclamation had begun the process of abolishing slavery across the former Confederate states and three years after the end of the Civil War. At the age of seventeen, at a time when Jim Crow laws were undoing the gains of Reconstruction, Du Bois travelled south of the Mason–Dixie line, to study at Fisk University in Tennessee. Fisk had been set up in the aftermath of the Civil War and was an educational institution 'open to all regardless of race' (though that, in fact, made it a primarily black institution). There Du Bois obtained an education in classics and in the liberal arts, graduating in 1888. His public comments at his commencement – part of graduation at the time – were on Otto von Bismarck and the way in which he 'had made a nation "out of bickering people"' and should be seen as 'a model for African Americans' (Lewis 1993: 77). Bismarck had just presided over the 1884/5 Berlin Conference, in which the African continent was divided among European powers. On this Du Bois had no comment at the time. He continued his studies at Harvard, where he was taught by the pragmatist philosopher William James, and in 1895 he became the first African American to gain a PhD from that institution. During this period of study he also spent two years at the University of Berlin. His PhD thesis was submitted under the title 'Suppression of the African Slave Trade to the United States of America, 1638–1870'.

After graduating, Du Bois worked initially in historically black universities and undertook research for white institutions such as the University of Pennsylvania. His first job was a chair in classics at Wilberforce University – the oldest college for African Americans in the United States – where he was employed from 1894 to 1896. This was followed by a position at the University of Pennsylvania, a historically white institution where he held 'the unheard of title "assistant in sociology" without office or teaching responsibilities' (Lewis 1993: 179). That is, he was an untenured affiliate researcher forbidden to teach white students on the grounds of being an African American. It was in this context that Du Bois undertook the research to be published in 1899 as *The Philadelphia Negro*.

The Philadelphia Negro was a sociological study of African Americans in Philadelphia in the context of their long-standing presence in the city. The problem, as set out by Du Bois, was that in Philadelphia there was a group of some 45,000 African Americans 'who do not form an integral part of the larger social group' and whose 'segregation is more conspicuous ... and so intertwined with a long historic evolution' (Du Bois 1967 [1899]: 5). The questions that organised the study were formulated so as to determine both the real condition of the group, including its internal stratifications, and how the group was shaped by its physical and social environment. Du Bois was eager to establish from the outset that 'a slum is not a simple fact, it is a symptom' (6) and that 'every group has its upper class' (7). However, this hierarchy among African Americans occurred in the wider framework of their general separation from the white residents of the city, such that a position of advantage within the group was at a relative disadvantage by comparison with an equivalent position among whites in similar occupations. Du Bois (2007 [1940]) would come to refer to this phenomenon as the caste organisation of class stratification. In this way he sought to dispel the prevalent view that simple poverty was the natural condition of African Americans and to point to the social conditions of poverty as well as to the diversity of classes within African Americans as a group. He asked the reader to ignore extreme statements and instead to 'seek to extract from a complicated mass of facts the tangible evidence' on the basis of which 'to describe, analyse, and, so far as possible, interpret' the issues of concern (Du Bois 1967 [1899]: 8).

The first two chapters of the study focused on the historical context of the African American population in Philadelphia from the early sixteenth century onwards. Du Bois presented the establishment of slavery, the early arguments for abolition and emancipation, and the rise of freedmen in the late eighteenth century. News of the Haitian revolution in 1794, he suggested, resulted in 'forbidding the export slave trade' and in an increased number of petitions to the Legislature and to Congress requesting the immediate abolition of slavery, the rescinding of the fugitive slave laws, and full emancipation (22). While those involved with the petitions were censured, the conditions of African Americans in the city, 'although without doubt bad, slowly improved' through the establishment of schools, churches, insurance, and benevolent societies (23).

Over the nineteenth century there was increased movement into the city as a consequence of immigration from Europe and of the fact that African Americans were escaping the conditions of slavery and servitude in the South. This created a volatile situation, especially after the Emancipation Proclamation conferred political rights to African Americans without bringing any change to their social conditions and stymied the progress that had been made in earlier years.

As Du Bois noted, those 'who want votes for specific reforms will not themselves work besides Negroes, or admit them to positions in their stores or offices, or lend them friendly aid in trouble' (383). His central purpose, as Elijah Anderson (1996: xvi) sets it out, 'was to enlighten the powerful in the city about the plight of black people in an objective, social scientific way'. He hoped that this would then enable them to work together to improve the conditions of African Americans in the city.

The bulk of the chapters addressed the general condition of the population – both as individuals and as groups – and the facts were collected through the use of maps, census data, statistics, and in-depth interviews carried out by Du Bois as he walked the streets of the Seventh Ward (Anderson 1996). He presented detailed information on the size and growth of the African American population in Philadelphia over the preceding century and comparative data for other cities in the United States. This information indicated that, 'of all the large cities in the United States, only three have a larger absolute Negro population than Philadelphia: Washington, New Orleans and Baltimore' (Du Bois 1967 [1899]: 53). Further demographic investigation revealed a marked excess of women to men. According to Du Bois, this situation reflected the fact that women's opportunities for employment in domestic service were greater than men's opportunities for employment in the industrialising city, especially in the context of increased migration from Europe.

Examination of the age structure and 'conjugal condition' of the community (as Du Bois called it) revealed disproportionate numbers of both young people and single people (the latter included widowed and separated women). This, Du Bois suggested, largely accounted for the social problems attributed to the African American community. Those were discussed in greater detail in a chapter titled 'The Negro Criminal'. Subsequent chapters addressed the educational opportunities available to African Americans, their occupations and economic conditions, and health statistics, including birth and death rates. Moving from individuals to groups, Du Bois looked at the family – its size, income, property, and conditions of life – the church, societies and cooperative businesses, and other institutions in the city.

The substantive chapters concluded with a discussion of the kinds of impact that the social and physical environment had on issues of crime and pauperism and on the relations between the races. In a chapter on colour prejudice, Du Bois showed how this kind of factor 'is a far more powerful social force than most [white] Philadelphians realise' (322) and 'costs the city something' (351). In this way Du Bois pointed out the effects of prejudice on the life chances of African Americans and emphasised that the thwarting of aspirations constituted an important part of the explanation for the broader social and political instability in the city.

> The connection of crime and prejudice is ... neither simple nor direct. The boy who is refused promotion ... does not go out and snatch somebody's pocketbook. ... The connections are much more subtle and dangerous; it is the atmosphere of rebellion and discontent that unrewarded merit and reasonable but unsatisfied ambition make. ... How long can a city teach its black children that the road to success is to have a white face? How long can a city do this and escape the inevitable penalty? (351)

Significantly, here Du Bois was inaugurating an approach to criminal behaviour that would subsequently be elaborated upon by Robert Merton (1968 [1949]) in his Durkheimian theory of anomie. Merton constructed a typology of deviance associated with the presence or absence of commitment to the American value of success (as described by Tocqueville) and with the presence or absence of the means to achieve it. Criminality, in this framework, was a form of 'innovation' that followed from a commitment to the outward signs of success (e.g. money) in situations where the legitimate means of achieving it were blocked (in Du Bois's argument, they were blocked by colour prejudice).[3]

The Philadelphia Negro was the first empirical sociological study of a specific group within the United States; other surveys had been more limited, being devoted to specific social problems and their solutions (Lengermann and Niebrugge 2007). Its focus on social relations marked it as a distinct contribution to the emerging discipline of sociology. In the final chapter, Du Bois located the 'Negro problem' in the facts of slavery and segregation, which constituted American civilisation. He stated that this problem could be resolved only by redressing the broader issues that were its context. Contrary to prevailing eugenic theories that saw the problems encountered by African Americans as a consequence of their genetic heredity, Du Bois placed the causes in the wider environment, namely in the historical circumstances of slavery and segregation and in the ongoing prejudice attached to colour. Indeed, just as the Jewish question was formulated by Europeans as they attempted to assimilate Jews, rather than by Jews themselves, who sought equal citizenship *as Jews*, so the Negro problem – as seen by Du Bois – was a problem of white Americans in the face of legitimate claims for equality. We will return to and develop this idea in the next section.

Upon completing his research for *The Philadelphia Negro*, Du Bois was appointed professor of economics and history at Atlanta University – a historically black university committed to an inclusive education – where he was responsible for establishing the sociology department and for running the Atlanta Sociological Laboratory. Earl Wright II (2002a, 2002b) has argued that the Atlanta Sociological Laboratory was the first American school of sociology and that it ought to be understood as such, in preference to the more usual presentation of the Chicago School as the first such institution. The Chicago School is usually said to begin with William I. Thomas and Florian Znaniecki's study *The Polish Peasant in Europe and America*, published between 1918 and 1921, which tends to be regarded as the first ethnographic empirical sociological study (see Thomas and Znaniecki 1996 [1918–21]). Such an accolade – awarded to a study that was published 20 years after *The Philadelphia Negro* and that was significantly weaker in terms of methodology, organisation, and rigour – is symptomatic of a wider problem in accounts of the birth of US sociology.[4] As Anderson and Massey (2001: 3) argue, US sociology did not begin in the University of Chicago in the 1920s, but at the University of Pennsylvania in the 1890s. Du Bois's *Philadelphia Negro* 'anticipated in every way the program of theory and research that later became known as the Chicago School' (4).[5] Even earlier, Bracey, Meier, and Rudwick (1973: 9) had observed how ironic it was that, although Du Bois 'was part of the mainstream of American sociology as the discipline was emerging at the turn of the century', he should find himself 'relegated to the periphery of the profession'. But we shall see that this relegation also derived from the fact that Du Bois did not *anticipate* Chicago School theory, as Anderson and Massey suggest: he developed instead something distinctive in its own right, which challenged that theory.

Under Du Bois's leadership, the Atlanta Sociological Laboratory 'engaged in urban sociological research investigations directed at ascertaining the physical, economic, and social condition of urban African Americans' (Wright 2002a: 173). With this, it complemented the research institutes at Tuskegee and Hampton, which focused on the conditions of African Americans in rural locations. The Laboratory produced scholars and scholarship engaged in the social scientific investigation of the living conditions of African Americans in the United States (Morris 2015). During this period, Du Bois also published *Souls of Black Folk*, in which he developed the idea of 'double-consciousness' and discussed his significant disagreements with Booker T. Washington's Atlanta Compromise Speech.

Double Consciousness, Domination, and Equality

The Souls of Black Folk, published in 1903, redefined the terms of interaction between African Americans and Americans of European descent. It started by pointing to the significance of the colour line as being the most fundamental issue of the twentieth century. The stultifyingly slow march of progress since emancipation, as Du Bois presented it, required analysis of 'that dead weight of social degradation' that was borne by all African Americans and was 'partially masked behind a half-named Negro problem' (Du Bois 1997 [1903]: 41). As in his earlier work, Du Bois framed what was presented as the Negro problem as a shared problem in the history of the nation.

In the first essay Du Bois asked the reader to reflect on what it meant for African Americans to be constantly regarded as a problem in the world, both from the perspective of white Americans and from that of their own self-understanding as African Americans who lived under that reality: 'How does it feel to be a problem?' (37). Going on to ask what it means to see oneself only in the terms in which others see you, Du Bois diagnosed the condition as one of alienation. In African Americans, this condition produced both a divided self and a double consciousness. 'It is a peculiar situation,' he stated, 'this double-consciousness [*sic*] ... One ever feels his two-ness, – an American, a Negro; two souls, two thoughts, two unreconciled strivings' (38).

According to Du Bois, this sense of 'two-ness' was a product of the history of the nation and its institutions of slavery and segregation. While emancipation was initially presented as opening a possibility to resolve the division, this had not come to pass. 'The Nation', he stated, 'has not yet found peace from its sins; the freedman has not yet found in freedom his promised land' (40). Some have seen an echo of Hegel and the master–slave relation in Du Bois's framing of the problem (Gilroy 1993; Lemert 1994; Meer 2019). Du Bois would certainly have been familiar with Hegel's dialectic of freedom – both from his exposure to American pragmatist thought through William James and from his period of study in Berlin. However, the dialectic of freedom in the United States is unresolved. The 'master' does not recognise his potentiality in the person of the 'slave'. Du Bois's discussion of double consciousness is mindful of the fact that white Americans do not understand themselves to be self-limited in their relation to those they had enslaved.

A better comparison would be with the emerging idea of the social self. This idea, associated with pragmatism, would be developed later by George Herbert Mead (1934). In Mead's language, the social self develops in relation to two phases of the self: the consciousness of the 'I', which arises in an immediate, reactive, response to the attitudes of others, and the 'me', which involves a reflective adoption of the attitudes of others; and there is also the 'generalised other' – the regulatory authority or voice of social sanctioning of the organised community. From the perspective that Du Bois develops (and he does so independently of these ideas), the issue of double consciousness is that the 'generalised other' represented a racialised order that African Americans could internalise only in the form of a divided (social) self, whose 'me', projected onto them by white Americans, was radically different from the 'me' of their own community. White Americans live neither as divided selves nor in recognition of their own limitation. Nor do they recognise how they limit others. Indeed, they do not see those others.

In these respects, Du Bois can be said to develop a form of standpoint epistemology in which the specific experience of domination yields a vantage point for understanding the nature of the system that maintains that domination.[6] It is a position that has been attributed to Marx in his account of proletarian class consciousness within the capital–labour relation (Lukács 1968). However, while for the standpoint of the proletariat in Marx's account a necessary dialectic resolves the contradiction that exists on both sides of the relation, for Du Bois's racialised division there is no such solution. Nor does the oppressed group constitute an emerging majority. Du Bois was raising issues of inequality, injustice, and recognition – profound issues, similar to those that exercised Marx in his early writings. The idea that the oppressed not only were central to social reproduction but would grow to become a majority in the societies that oppressed them offered Marx the possibility to conceive of a solution to that oppression. However, Du Bois confronted a situation in which a deep injustice was committed by a majority against a minority, in the absence of any self-development by which the majority in question might understand the need to redress that injustice. This was compounded by the fact that the universal language of rights through which the majority understood itself was implicated in the production and reproduction of the injustice visited on the minority. As we will see, Du Bois himself turned briefly to class as part of a possible solution before he started looking for an international majority by reconstituting the colour line as a global phenomenon.

For white Americans, Du Bois argued, it was as if African Americans live behind a veil, unseen but visited by the consequences of a vicious neglect. From behind that veil, they saw both themselves and the veil, which separated them from others. They had to live in 'white' society, and so they understood it as well as their own. They knew how they had to behave in the former, they knew how they lived in the latter, and they had to move between them. The divided self and its double consciousness, then, were a consequence of the particular form of alienation produced by a society organised along hierarchies of racialised inequality. That division, in turn, produced a radical doubling of the self that could become the fount of moral and creative energies, and these could reinvigorate what it meant to be American. 'We the darker ones', Du Bois (1997 [1903]: 43) wrote, 'come even now not altogether empty-handed: there are today no truer exponents of the pure human spirit of the Declaration of Independence than the American Negroes.' African American self-consciousness and self-organisation were necessary to overcome oppression.

The poetic allusions of many of the essays in Souls of Black Folk were accompanied by prose that displayed the actual and palpable gains of Reconstruction and the activities that African Americans engaged in to remake the nation during this period. In particular, Du Bois focused on the work of the Freedmen's Bureau, set up in 1865 by an act of Congress to support newly emancipated African Americans and poor whites in the South in the aftermath of the Civil War, which he regarded as 'one of the great landmarks of political and social progress' (51). Under its auspices, the labour of the enslaved was transformed into contract labour, free schools were raised for African American children, equality before courts of law was promoted, and some land was distributed to freedmen, although this action was soon blocked. The college institutes of Fisk, Atlanta, Howard, and Hampton were also established during the same period. Despite its promise, the Bureau was not able to fulfil its ambitions because, according to Du Bois, it saw 'its work as merely temporary, and Negro suffrage as a final answer to all present perplexities' (60). As will be discussed in the next section, for Du Bois emancipation meant more than freedom from enslavement. It meant also being able to enjoy the opportunities that freedom brought about. This required social and economic equality alongside suffrage. This particular argument was to become a key point of contention with Booker T. Washington.

Washington was born under slavery in 1856, heard the Emancipation Proclamation read out in 1865, lived through Reconstruction and the violent backlash against it embodied in the Jim Crow laws of 1876, and died in 1915 (Washington 1945 [1901]). On gaining his freedom, he worked his way through school and, in 1881, became the first head of the Tuskegee Institute – a normal school for training 'colored teachers' in Alabama that had been established under Reconstruction. He rose to prominence as a leader of the African American community, raising funds for the Tuskegee Institute and for the project of building schools in rural African American communities. He was recognised by African Americans for his ability to garner funds from wealthy white philanthropists (such as Andrew Carnegie) and celebrated by the latter for his views in favour of accommodating the social realities of segregation (Harlan 1988).

Washington (2007 [1909]) believed that, as African Americans were greatly outnumbered by whites, the best they could hope for was to build up support among sympathetic whites and to prove themselves worthy of a deferred equality. In a speech delivered in 1895 that came to be known as 'the Atlanta compromise', Washington urged African Americans to improve their current economic conditions through hard work and industry and by acquiring the education necessary for this task. He felt that they should sacrifice their desire for immediate social and political equality and, instead of pursuing 'a seat in Congress or the state legislature' or wishing 'to spend a dollar in the opera house', they should prepare themselves for the *eventual* exercise of such privileges. 'The wisest among my race', he stated, 'understand that the agitation of questions of social equality is the

extremest folly, and that progress in the enjoyment of all the privileges that will come to us must be the result of severe and constant
struggle rather than of artificial forcing' (Washington 1895).

Booker T. Washington was perhaps the most renowned African
American leader of the post-emancipation period and probably the
last great African American born under slavery. Du Bois lauded
him 'as the one recognised spokesman of his ten million fellows,
and one of the most notable figures in a nation of seventy millions'
(Du Bois 1997 [1903]: 63). He asserted that, while previous African
American leaders had probably not been known outside their
community, save Frederick Douglass,[7] Washington 'arose as essentially the leader not of one race but of two – a compromiser between
the South, the North, and the Negro' (67). It was the nature of the
compromise, however, that led to criticism of Washington and gave
renewed impetus to debates on the meaning of emancipation in
African American thought. As we saw in the chapter on Weber, it
is significant that German sociologists who looked for a model for
labour on German colonial plantations looked to Washington rather
than Du Bois, notwithstanding Weber's polite exchanges with Du
Bois on his American visit (see Morris 2015; McAuley 2019).

Much of Du Bois's research focused on the barriers to economic
advancement for African Americans and, initially at least, his
aims appeared to converge with Washington's. But, in *The Souls
of Black Folk*, Du Bois broke with the latter's more accommoda-
tionist approach. In the essay titled 'Of Mr Booker T. Washington
and Others', he argued that, for all the good that Washington had
undoubtedly done for African Americans, he had not dealt adequately
with the most crucial issues that faced them: the continuing injustices emanating from slavery, the lack of voting and other political
privileges, and the psychosocial effects of segregation and of the
maintenance of racial hierarchies.

Du Bois argued that Washington's pronouncements had three main
implications: 'first, that the South is justified in its present attitude
toward the Negro because of the Negro's degradation; secondly,
that the prime cause of the Negro's failure to rise more quickly is
his wrong education in the past; and, thirdly, that his future rise
depends primarily on his own efforts' (Du Bois 1997 [1903]: 71).
Du Bois suggested that each of these 'is a dangerous half-truth' and
that the supplementary truths ought not to be lost sight of: first,
slavery and race prejudice were significant factors in the current

position of African Americans; second, educational institutions for African Americans had to be literally built up from scratch, as very few had existed before emancipation; and, third, that, while African Americans had to strive for their positions, the 'environing group' needed to encourage and support their efforts, not be an obstacle to it.

Du Bois further argued that Washington's doctrine allowed whites to 'shift the burden of the Negro problem to the Negro's shoulders' and enabled them to 'stand aside as critical and rather pessimistic spectators; when in fact the burden belongs to the nation' (72). 'The Negro problem', he argued strongly, is neither the problem of African Americans nor that of white Americans; rather the problem of race was correctly identified as a problem of the nation, that is, of the social relations between citizens and of the construction of a hierarchy of citizenship.

Du Bois urged African Americans to stand with Washington when he preached 'Thrift, Patience, and Industrial Training for the masses', but to oppose him unceasingly when he 'apologises for injustice ... does not rightly value the privilege and duty of voting, belittles the emasculating effects of caste distinctions, and opposes the higher training and ambition of our brighter minds'. He concluded the essay by arguing that 'we must strive for the rights which the world accords to men' and quoted the founding fathers' statement '[t]hat all men are created equal; that they are endowed by their Creator with certain unalienable rights' (72).

With this, Du Bois inextricably linked the struggle for African American emancipation with the impetus behind the founding of the nation itself and with a wider conception of emancipation, which should have substantive equality at its core and provide for its realisation. Significantly, this conception also envisaged a commitment to intellectual desegregation and to an education in classics and liberal arts for African Americans. While Washington asked only for a vocational education and skills training, Du Bois argued for the importance of involving African Americans in philosophical and social scientific culture as part of the project of social regeneration. The piece as a whole saw Du Bois assert his right, following Douglass, to participate in the nation through self-assertion, to be a citizen *as an African American*, and to expand the meaning of citizenship and democracy on that basis. As Douglass had argued, the abolition of slavery required both that the nation be redefined and that social and political freedom be accompanied by economic measures capable of redressing the conditions of poverty in which African Americans lived – conditions created through two centuries of slavery (Foner 2005).

Du Bois was employed by Atlanta University until 1910, when he tendered his resignation in order to accept the position of director of publicity and research at the newly formed National Association for the Advancement of Colored People. This appointment opened a more politically active phase of his career (Lewis 1993), in which he increasingly recognised the need to associate the struggle for emancipation in the United States with global struggles for emancipation from colonial rule. In fact the very naming of the NAACP reflected this general orientation. As Du Bois (1995 [1957]: 91) stated, 'the "Colored People" referred to in our name was not originally confined to America'. For example, he and other co-workers at the NAACP were admirers of Gandhi and of his resistance to British colonial rule in India. Du Bois retained a strong engagement with the struggles in the United States, albeit he likened them now with wider movements, such as the pan-African congresses and broader anti-colonial struggles. He also retained his commitment to scholarship that would culminate in a major study, which was to become Du Bois's magnum opus: *Black Reconstruction: An Essay toward a History of the Part Which Black Folk Played in the Attempt to Reconstruct Democracy in America, 1860–1880* (Du Bois 1935).

Black Reconstruction

The work for *Black Reconstruction* had begun a quarter of a century earlier, with a paper presented at the American Historical Association in 1909 and titled 'Reconstruction and Its Benefits' (Du Bois 1910). Up until then, the two dominant views in mainstream historiography about the post-Civil War period were that Reconstruction had failed because the suffrage had been extended too quickly to African Americans and that southern institutions had been unjustly dismantled. This historiography, which came to be associated with the Dunning School, though it had a wider provenance, was critical of post-Civil War federal actions, considering them a tyrannical overreach, especially in the sphere of ameliorations for African Americans. Such views were instrumental to the subsequent implementation of new forms of segregation and subordination of African Americans – the Jim Crow laws – that would last until the 1960s and the later civil rights movement.[8] It was the Jim Crow laws that Du Bois experienced in the 1880s, when he first moved to the South to study at Fisk University, and then a decade later, on his return to the South to take up a new position at Atlanta University.

Du Bois was clear that Reconstruction had not been a failure but had been subverted, and the ideologies associated with that subversion had become the historiographic norm. The American Civil War did not have emancipation among its aims when it began in 1861. Yet the emancipation of enslaved African Americans was one of its outcomes and, in Du Bois's view, this was a consequence of their agency and not primarily of the action taken by abolitionists. Self-emancipation en masse forced the hand of legislators, making them legalise the actions of African Americans. Legal emancipation was followed by Reconstruction – a decade of attempts to rebuild the nation along egalitarian lines; but these attempts foundered as the white Democrats regained power in southern states and reinstituted forms of disenfranchisement and segregation along racial lines. The broader social context was one of widespread and systematic violence against African Americans that saw lynchings and the establishment of the Ku Klux Klan (Johnson 2008).

Yet Reconstruction had initially been a success for African Americans, and had also carried forward positive consequences for white Americans. Du Bois's paper emphasised three key benefits of Reconstruction: it brought about democratic government; it established free public schools; and it provided for new social legislation that addressed poverty across communities. Du Bois argued that the involvement of African Americans in drafting Reconstruction constitutions was of such significance that, even after the retrogressive movements overthrew the rights of African Americans in the southern states, much of what else had been gained remained. Indeed, the gains won by African Americans had been applied generally across society, though now they benefited white citizens disproportionately. In many cases, the only aspect of newly forged state constitutions that changed was the African Americans' right to suffrage.

Du Bois ended the paper on the benefits of reconstruction with the conclusion that 'the whole new growth of the South has been accomplished under laws which black men helped to frame thirty years ago. I know of no greater compliment to negro suffrage' (Du Bois 1910:

799). The paper was published in the *American Historical Review* the following year but, according to David Levering Lewis, Du Bois's biographer, 'virtually nothing more was ever said among white professional historians about its heterodox interpretation' (Lewis 1993: 384; see also Franklin 1980). The Jim Crow laws, which were subsequently imposed, took away from African Americans the benefits they had won but continued to bestow these benefits on white southerners. This was the very outcome that Tocqueville had anticipated as a logical corollary of the refusal to admit African Americans into 'the society of equals'. Tocqueville had also predicted that the impacts of racial prejudice would extend across the country, and he was right there too. Although it emanated from the South, Jim Crow legislation had wider consequences (King 1995).

The argument of the article was expanded and developed more fully in Du Bois's later book *Black Reconstruction*. Published in 1935, *Black Reconstruction* 'represented one of those genuine paradigm shifts periodically experienced in a field of knowledge', just as Lewis (2000: 367) notes. There Du Bois challenged every problematic claim about Reconstruction made in the dominant scholarship of the time and advanced a strong argument for the African American contribution to the rebuilding of democracy. *Black Reconstruction* gave voice to a history that had been silenced; it wrote the chief witness of Reconstruction – 'the emancipated slave' – back into that history, But Du Bois did not wish just to add another narrative to the general history of Reconstruction. His ambition was to point to the studied absence of African Americans and, while reconstructing history, also to reconstruct the nation and democracy (Singh 2004).

The significance of slavery for the social development of America, Du Bois argued, rested upon 'the ultimate relation of slaves to democracy' (Du Bois 1935: 13). In his view, this relationship demonstrated the limits of democracy in the matter of determining who was to be free, who was to be schooled, and who had the right to vote – in other words, who was considered a full citizen. Citizenship was defined in terms of whether the worker – here the black worker – had control over his or her own labour. Du Bois connected the black worker in the United States under slavery with that 'dark vast sea of human labor in China and India, the South Seas and all Africa; in the West Indies and Central America ... that great majority of mankind, on whose bent and broken backs rest today the founding stones of modern industry' (15). This, for him, was 'the real modern labor problem'. Emancipation should involve the emancipation of labour, and this, in turn, would require the freeing of that 'basic majority of workers' (16).

In *Black Reconstruction,* Du Bois began by examining the global colonial context, which united people under similar conditions of coerced and unfree labour. But he also made a fundamental point about emancipation. Marx saw emancipation as a process of bringing African Americans into the labour force on such terms that they, too, would participate in the self-emancipation of the proletariat; moreover, he believed that this latter process of self-emancipation had already begun in the class struggles of the metropole. By contrast, according to Du Bois the social and political emancipation of the colonial working class would be a precondition for the general emancipation of labour, including in the United States. This was a global argument similar to the one about African American suffrage in the South, according to which it was the actions of emancipated African Americans that produced a general improvement for all, albeit one from which they were subsequently excluded.

Going on to discuss the condition of white workers, Du Bois outlined the many ways in which their refusal to countenance equality of treatment with black workers led to the abject failure of any attempt to emancipate labour and to generalise the condition of democracy. It was the doctrine of race that 'long stood against that democracy in industry which might have emancipated labor in the United States, because it did not admit to that democracy the American citizen of Negro descent' (28). That refusal, he argued, was 'central to the plight of the white working class throughout the world' no less than it was responsible for the subordinated position of 'colored labor' globally (30). The focus on the emancipation of labour as central to general emancipation was fundamental to Du Bois's broader understanding of the Civil War – which saw black workers reclaim their own labour and, in the process, fully reclaim their own selves, too.

Du Bois described the mass withdrawal of labour mounted by those who had been enslaved as a 'general strike' against slavery: 'to stop the economy of the plantation system ... they left the planta-tions' (67). They took control of their own labour in this way, and decided how and where they would use it. In Du Bois's view, 'this withdrawal and bestowal of ... labor' was the factor that 'decided the war' (57). In part, this was a consequence of the fact that the issue was no longer whether 'Negroes ought to be free; it was that thousands of them were already free' (82). This is where Du Bois saw a new democratic movement arise in the United States – one that should do away with the 'paradox of a democracy founded on slavery' and constitute a revolution among the people (121).[9] The transformative nature of the self-emancipation embodied in the general strike can be seen in Du Bois's description of emancipation as equivalent to 'the coming of the Lord'; it was 'the fulfilment of prophecy and legend' (122) and had been brought about by the African Americans' own actions. Further, emancipation also freed white Americans of the sin they had inherited and opened the space for a full articulation of democracy.

This was the hope of Reconstruction. That it failed had little to do with any deficiency attributable to African Americans (as standard accounts of Reconstruction claimed); it was rather a result of white Americans' incapacity to work together for a common project. Du Bois observed that 'most Americans used the Negro to defend their own economic interests and, refusing him adequate land and real education and even common justice, deserted him shamelessly as soon as their selfish interests were safe' (378). These events are detailed at length by Du Bois in chapters on the participation of African Americans in the political life of the southern states and on how their involvement was obstructed and ultimately denied. No one can read the documents of the time, he argued, and suggest that African Americans were not central to 'the widening and strengthening of human democracy' (577).

Black Reconstruction stands both as a contribution to an accurate history of the period – an attempt 'to establish Truth, on which Right in the future may be built' (725) – and as a challenge to the racialised character of earlier accounts. It presented a forceful argument for the thesis that scholars should 'regard the truth as more important than the defence of the white race'. Scholarship on the period of Reconstruction may now be transformed, not least as a result of the appreciation shown for Du Bois's contribution. But there was a further and broader aim to *Black Reconstruction*. This work focuses on social theory and its narratives as much as on historiography. Du Bois wished Reconstruction, together with the mass transportation and enslavement of human beings that preceded it, to be understood as 'an upheaval of humanity like the Reformation and the French Revolution' (727), in other words as a world historical event.

As we have seen, 'emancipation' – together with its correlative, 'liberty' or 'freedom' – emerged as a key theme in European Enlightenment thought at a time when slavery was being instituted in the new world. While the idea of freedom was contrasted with the condition of slavery, the Europeans' practice of enslavement did not render suspect their political and intellectual pronouncements on the topic (Kohn 2005). Both France and the United States inscribed a commitment to freedom and liberty in their declarations of independence and documents of rights. Freedom, espoused abstractly, as *universal* freedom, was in practice circumscribed. Europeans were 'ready' for freedom, but others had not attained the requisite level. They had to prove themselves, while in subordination, for a future equality that was permanently postponed. In fact some claimed that their subordination made them unfit for equality. The dominant attitude was colour prejudice pure and simple, much as Tocqueville had described it from the other side of the colour line. Du Bois commented:

> Of all that most Americans wanted, this freeing of slaves was the last. Everything black was hideous. Everything Negroes did was wrong. If they fought for freedom, they were beasts; if they did not fight, they were born slaves. If they cowered on the plantations, they loved slavery; if they ran away, they were lazy loafers. If they sang, they were silly; if they scowled, they were impudent. (Du Bois 1935: 125)

One of the distinguishing characteristics of Du Bois's conception of emancipation is its expansive definition: he takes 'emancipation' from a narrow sense – the condition of not being enslaved – to a much wider one – the condition necessary for the fulfilment of an individual's capacities as a human being. If emancipation was previously understood in terms of formal equality, so that the Jim Crow laws, which enacted a state of 'separate and equal', could be regarded as not incompatible with emancipation, Du Bois's conception emphasised the social and economic correlates of equality that were necessary for securing full emancipation. Du Bois articulated an understanding of emancipation that distinguished, and then connected, the different dimensions of civil, political, and social rights. Whereas Washington had argued for a social uplift based on civil rights but deprived of political rights, Du Bois argued that a social uplift needed political rights in order to protect any gains that were won. In addition, he argued that political rights would be without substance unless the social and economic disadvantages caused by centuries of enslavement were rectified.

In this way Du Bois prefigured post-Second World War arguments for welfare arrangements designed to resolve class inequalities related to citizenship (see Marshall 1950).[10] In the aftermath of the Civil War and its economic costs, there was no strong movement to compensate slave owners for the loss of their property, as happened in the British and French empires after abolition, although many Americans had their confiscated property quickly returned. Du Bois is unique among the social theorists of his time in arguing both that African Americans had a just claim when they demanded that the consequences of enslavement upon their present condition be rectified, and that the realisation of this just claim produced a benefit for all.

The Colour Line and Colonialism

Du Bois's expansive notion of emancipation had been clearly formulated in his earlier contribution to the Universal Races Congress held at the University of London in July 1911.[11] Alongside participating in this congress, Du Bois delivered a paper to the Sociological Society in London that was then published in the *Sociological Review* under the title 'The Economics of Negro Emancipation in the United States'. There he argued not only for legal but also for economic emancipation. That is, emancipation was not about a particular type of labour being made illegal, but about 'the deeper question as to the slow development of that organisation of labour from a primitive to a more advanced form' (Du Bois 1911: 303). Alongside developing this line of thought, Du Bois asked his audience to consider what freedom meant, since emancipation left formerly enslaved people with nothing except their freedom – no land, no capital, no possessions. Initially a Freedmen's Bureau was created and there were discussions about a system of public education that should address past injustices methodically, but the white North and the white South, together, felt that this was too much of a burden for the 'general' (read: 'white') public to take on; the responsibility ought to fall on those who were freed.

In such conditions, freedom was quickly curtailed through sharecropping and other, newly devised forms of bonded labour. One form continues to the present; here is how Du Bois described it: 'Negroes were systematically arrested on the slightest pretext and then their labour leased to private individuals, or single individuals convicted of crime were paroled to any owner who paid his fine' (310; see also Alexander 2010). Du Bois ended his piece with a call for solidarity not just across the colour line, but across lines of economic inequality:

> In all these problems we cannot doubt lies the economic core, the old slavery which is determined to reduce human labour to the lowest depth in order to derive the greatest personal profit. Against this world-old tendency the black men of America are fighting a battle on the frontiers of the world – and for their success they ask the active sympathy of all right-thinking men. (Du Bois 1911: 313)

The Universal Races Congress was supposed to be a quadrennial event. But the Great War started, so no more congresses could take place. It was not until the 1950s that an international group of scientists, social scientists, and politicians again met to discuss race; and they did it under the auspices of UNESCO. On that occasion Du Bois's article 'Prospect of a World without Race Conflict', published in a 1944 issue of the *American Journal of Sociology*, was one of the key readings. This happened at a time when sociology departments in the United States were unlikely to recommend Du Bois as required reading – apart from those in historically black universities and colleges, of course (Morris 2015).

Du Bois resigned from the NAACP in 1934, partly because of profound disagreements with other members over the issue of segregation. From January to June 1934, as Lewis (2000) notes, he published in *Crisis* a number of articles that distinguished racial segregation from racial discrimination. He also argued that segregation was not necessarily problematic so long as it was not discriminatory. In effect, Du Bois was recognising both the obduracy of the Jim Crow laws and the efficacy of African American agency. If African Americans created better conditions for white Americans from which they were then excluded, they could create better conditions for themselves too, when segregation was imposed upon them. This was also a holding position so far as the situation in the United States was concerned, as Du Bois believed that solving the colour line internationally would be the means to address the colour line in the United States, rather than the other way around. Hence Du Bois sought to address broader questions than those oriented towards relations between the races in the United States and to consider the significance of colonialism across Africa and Asia to the situation of African Americans.

Du Bois's internationalism was not a priority for the NAACP, which remained focused on national issues. Moreover, the official position of the NAACP was 'unyielding opposition to segregation', and Du Bois's public proposal to work within segregation as well as against it created great consternation within the organisation. When he returned to the NAACP a decade later, in 1944, there was initially greater understanding and sympathy for his internationalist position, although he remained in post for just four years. His role there from 1944 to 1948 was to coordinate global efforts, particularly in the area of anticolonialism. After presenting the colour line as the defining issue for humanity in *The Souls of Black Folk* in 1903, by 1945 he came to argue, in *Color and Democracy*, that the abolition of colonialism was the most serious problem in need of resolution.

The 1944 Dumbarton Oaks Conference proposed the creation of the United Nations as an international organisation committed to resolving the problems of peace and prepared to take over from the League of Nations. In his discussion of this proposal, Du Bois highlighted the racial inequalities that structured the new organisation. The Security Council, which initially consisted of Great Britain, Russia, and the United States, invited China, the fourth member, only in the latter stages of the discussions. Du Bois (2007 [1945]: 247) commented that the 'three powers consulted for six weeks, while China was called in only for the last six days'. This slight consolidated the League of Nations' earlier refusal to acknowledge Japan as a full member on the grounds that Japan demanded racial equality (Mayblin 2017). Japan's subsequent withdrawal from the League of Nations, its pursuit of imperial hegemony in Asia, and alliance with the European Axis powers minimised its involvement in the new organisation as well.

Du Bois further pointed out inconsistencies about the countries accepted as members of the United Nations. Many of the 'free states' represented in the Assembly were not really free. For example Canada, Australia, and the Union of South Africa were 'closely integrated parts of the British Empire' (Du Bois 2007 [1945]: 248).

Their problematic inclusion was compounded by the exclusion of a significant proportion of the global population, namely those '750,000,000 colored and black folk inhabiting colonies owned by white nations' (248). Questions around the future of the colonies and the treatment of colonial peoples came under the purview of a committee that had no power of action, limited as it was by the Security Council on one side and by nation-states on the other. Du Bois's strongest criticism of the Dumbarton Oaks Conference was that it made no serious attempt to address the long-standing issues of the colonial system and modern imperialism.

At least since 1911, when he participated in the Universal Races Congress in London, Du Bois argued for the need to consider 'the disenfranchisement of American Negroes, the subjection of India, and the partition of Africa' (Du Bois 1995 [1911]: 45) within a common framework of analysis predicated on the solidarity of peoples of colour. While the United Nations was set up to establish 'government for men', as Du Bois argued, 'under this proposal something between one-fourth and one-half the inhabitants of the world will have no part in it – no power of democratic control and scarcely an organised right of petition' (Du Bois 2007 [1945]: 251).

In *Color and Democracy*, Du Bois demonstrated a keen understanding of the broader histories of colonialism and of the extractive relationships through which colonising countries had not only existed but thrived. He further drew the link between the depletion of raw materials in colonial areas and the seemingly paradoxical desire of empires for colonies. He offered an explanation for this desire and its continuation into the present: 'colonies are today areas for the investment of capital in which the investor can make a rate of profit far beyond that which comes to him from domestic ventures' (270). This was as a consequence of the limitation of profit at home once organised labour started demanding higher wages, shorter hours, and better working conditions. Du Bois was trenchant in his claim that 'the colonial system is a part of the battle between capital and labor in the modern economy' (275) and demonstrated this by referring to economic analyses of the conditions of labour in colonies.

Du Bois was prescient in his analysis of how the colonial organisation of the world was implicated in the situation of the working classes in the colonising countries and vice versa. He wrote that, when working people in European countries began to demand 'costly social improvements from their governments', the financial burdens were likely to be balanced through increased investment in (and extraction from) the colonies (276). In this way 'democracy in Europe and America will continue to impede and nullify democracy in Asia and Africa'. The social and economic improvements that he argued were necessary to realise a proper emancipation of African Americans and of other colonised people came to be part of the postwar settlement for white majority populations in Europe and the United States. These improvements were paid for from a patrimony of enslavement and colonialism. Du Bois's analysis also accounted for the particular plight of minorities in nations – specifically for the plight of Jews in Germany and of African Americans and indigenous people in the Americas. The problem of democracy, he stated, was the poverty in which most people live: the poverty of the colonised, the poverty of the smaller nations, and also the poverty within the colonising countries. Until these issues were cleared across the board, 'there can be no satisfactory development of the democratic ideal' (289).

One of Du Bois's last major initiatives under the auspices of the NAACP was to coordinate and present to the United Nations a petition on the situation faced by African Americans in the United States, in the past and in the present. This petition is known as *An Appeal to the World*, and its considerably longer subtitle is *A Statement on the Denial of Human Rights to Minorities in the Case of Citizens of Negro Descent in the United States of America and an Appeal to the United Nations for Redress*. Ninety-four pages of encyclopaedic data on the prevalence and systematic nature of lynching, on the realities of segregation, and on significant racial inequalities in education, housing, health care, and voting rights were presented to the director of the Division of Human Rights at the United Nations in October 1947. The United Nations was drafting a declaration of human rights at the time, and Du Bois asked for the petition to be translated into several languages and distributed to the various delegations. But, as Lewis notes, the petition was to be 'an early casualty of the new Cold War civil rights politics': Eleanor Roosevelt, the United States' representative, refused to support its placement on the agenda on the grounds that, in her words, 'no good could come from such a discussion' (Lewis 2000: 529–30, 534). What Du Bois regarded as the US government's co-optation of the NAACP led to his final break from the organisation in 1948.

Race, Caste, and Class

The tradition of sociology inaugurated by Du Bois in the first half of the twentieth century provided a significant challenge to dominant understandings of race and race relations in the United States, and this challenge had broader implications globally (Ladner 1973, Wilson 2006; Rabaka 2010). In particular, Du Bois contested mainstream sociological arguments that sought to explain the unequal conditions African Americans found themselves in by reference to ideas of cultural deficit or biological difference between races. He argued that 'race' should be understood as a product of racism – a prejudice that carried the associated material injustices of poverty, degradation, systematic oppression, and segregation. If this position failed to make headway in the development of sociology, a major part of the cause was that universities were themselves part of a racialised system. The much vaunted 1890–1920 generation of social theorists who created modern sociology did so in a Europe organised into a wider system of colonial domination, in which the colonial subjects of empire were at a distance from the metropoles. In the United States, by contrast, universities were themselves segregated institutions – both *de iure* (in southern states) and *de facto* (in the northern states) – and reflected the caste relations of the country in which they operated.[12]

Du Bois's presentation of the separate racialised social structures of Philadelphia – as set out in *The Philadelphia Negro* – could easily have been extended to the associated educational systems that denied him full participation in the development of US sociology. As Christi M. Smith (2016) shows, some of the institutions identified as 'historically black' – including Fisk, where Du Bois studied for his undergraduate degree, and Atlanta, where he was professor and directed the Atlanta Sociological Laboratory – had been established as 'anti-caste', integrated institutions during Reconstruction.[13] They were open to all, regardless of race and gender. They became 'historically black' through the loss of white students to institutions that operated with colour bars. Early developments of sociology in the white institutions of the United States have been associated with the 'settlement movement' and problems of the urban poor, as exemplified by Chicago's Hull House (Deegan 1988). In the same manner, sociology developed in the black colleges as a particularly relevant subject in a curriculum directed at understanding the living conditions of Americans, including African Americans (Lengermann and Niebrugge 2007; Reed 1997). As Du Bois described the situation for an article published in the *Washington Post* in 1896, the integrated colleges functioned as social settlements, interaction among black and white students being a central part of their educational mission (just as Hull House sought to bring the white middle and working classes together).

The development of a tradition of black sociology separate from what came to be considered mainstream sociology is significant in the light of a study commissioned from Gunnar Myrdal in 1944 and titled *An American Dilemma* (Myrdal 1962 [1944]). Myrdal, a Swede, was asked to look at the unequal position of African Americans in the United States. Evidently, it was too problematic to ask local scholars, let alone local African American sociologists, to conduct such a study. Nevertheless the study was in all crucial respects a joint product of Myrdal and a team of largely African American investigators, Ralph Bunche and Kenneth B. Clark among them. The subtitle of the study, given either by Myrdal himself or by his sponsors, was *The Negro Problem and Modern Democracy* – a construal that Du Bois had effectively dismantled decades earlier, as we have seen.

In *An American Dilemma*, Myrdal treated inequality in the United States as a problem of values and argued that 'the American creed' would ultimately require and sanction the assimilation of African Americans. In this way Myrdal postulated the gradual dissolution of 'the Negro problem' through the institutionalisation of the democratic values of liberty, justice, and fair treatment. However, as Ralph Ellison argued at the time, 'aside from implying that Negro culture is not also American', Myrdal assumed that African Americans 'should desire nothing better than what whites consider highest' (Ellison 1973 [1944]: 94). In addition, there was little discussion in Myrdal's study of the fact that this creed had been defined independently of the African American experience and in direct negation of it. What was needed, Ellison argued, was 'not an exchange of pathologies, but a change of the basis of society' (95). Moreover, African Americans had their own distinctive contribution to make to a common American culture.

While in public Du Bois reviewed the project positively, calling Myrdal's book 'monumental', Lewis (2000: 452, 453) suggests that he was unlikely to have been 'entirely comfortable with a race relations paradigm in which psychology trumped economics'. For some time now, Du Bois had sought to understand the race problem in terms of the institutionalised structures that maintained economic inequality. In his autobiography *Dusk of Dawn*, for example, Du Bois presented racial inequalities in the present as consequences of 'the modern African slave trade', which had in turn established 'a tremendous economic structure and eventually an industrial revolution [that] had been based upon racial differences between men' (Du Bois 2007 [1940]: 2). He traced the evolution of his own thinking about race, stating that he came gradually to the 'realization that the income-bearing value of race prejudice was the cause and not the result of theories of race inferiority' (65).

This insight led Du Bois – to the consternation of many, as we have seen above – to advocate a programme of racial segregation that would focus on eliminating economic discrimination. This was not, he was keen to clarify, 'a program of complete racial segregation', nor was it one of 'nationalism among Negroes' (99). Rather Du Bois argued for the necessity of developing the already existing segregated economy in order to enable African Americans 'to raise the social status and increase the efficiency of the group' and ultimately 'to obtain admission of the colored group to cooperation and incorporation into the white group on the best possible terms' (101). Given that so much segregation was compulsory, for example in education, it would be a better use of time and energy to 'organize and plan these segregated schools so that they become efficient, well-housed, well-equipped, with the best of teachers and with the best results on the children'. Further, Du Bois pointed out that African Americans wielded some power as consumers and he recommended that they use that power through what they buy, in order to develop a 'Negro co-operative movement' (107) to the benefit of the group. Du Bois returned time and again to the point that segregation currently exists without reason and exhorted African Americans to 'put reason and power beneath this segregation', with the aim of breaking down all segregation in the end (108). His vision of the 'co-operative commonwealth' was an inclusive one. 'It need draw no line of exclusion,' he argued, 'so long as the outsiders join in the consensus.'

With this argument, Du Bois proposed in effect a project of 'caste mobility'. He was bitterly opposed by Oliver Cromwell Cox (1959 [1948]), who described his leadership as doomed after his proposals on segregation. Cox wrote that 'segregation is a white man's principal

anti-color weapon of oppression; therefore, Negroes can have one
but quite obvious attitude towards it (501). In his view, class-based
action across the colour line could dissolve caste. Understandable
though this response may be, Cox rather missed Du Bois's point: Du
Bois had already come to a bleak view of the willingness of white
workers to make common cause with black workers and, where this
was so, to expect African American workers to display solidarity with
white workers was asking too much of them.[14] African American
workers were routinely barred from union membership; and many
jobs were available only to those who held union membership. Even
unions that sought to reach out across the colour line appeared to do
so rhetorically more than in practice. As Du Bois (1995 [1929]) had
earlier commented, the American Federation of Labor, while calling
for the unity of workers, nonetheless permitted segregated unions to
affiliate to it.

David Levering Lewis, in the conclusion of his two-volume
biography of W. E. B. Du Bois, notes that, over his long career, Du
Bois had 'attempted virtually every possible solution to the problem
of twentieth century racism – scholarship, propaganda, integration,
cultural and economic separatism, politics, international communism,
expatriation, third-world solidarity' (Lewis 2000: 571). At each turn,
Du Bois confronted the enduring nature of the colour line, but did
not give way to pessimism. The fact that he entertained caste mobility
as a possible solution is indicative of his commitment to social justice
and to the amelioration of racialised inequalities; it is not evidence of
capitulation. Just as Marx argued that the proletariat had to struggle
for reforms within capitalism before it could understand the need to
overcome capitalism, so Du Bois (2007 [1940]) argued that African
Americans had to struggle for changes within caste before caste itself
could be overcome. But this overcoming was Du Bois's ultimate goal.

Conclusion

The failure to acknowledge Du Bois as a canonical thinker within the
discipline of sociology and within modern social theory more generally
is of great significance from the point of view of the history of our
discipline. However, this is not simply about his presence within the
canon, but about the fact that sociological concepts have coalesced
into the structures they have today in the absence of his sociology

and away from its different interpretations of common problems. Ira Katznelson argues that the US academy's failure to incorporate Du Bois as more than an emblem of diversity 'has cost it – that is, us – quite a lot' (1999: 469–70). This cost is not limited to US sociology; it is global. This is not because of the hegemonic position of US sociology, but because Du Bois understood that the local constitution of the colour line in the United States was the consequence of a global colour line, which derived from colonialism. In *Dusk of Dawn* Du Bois tells us how he was called by the histories of African Americans to confront the totality of the history of his day: 'That history may be epitomised in one word – Empire; the domination of white Europe over black Africa and yellow Asia, through political power built on the economic control of labor, income and ideas. The echo of this industrial imperialism in America was the expulsion of black men from American democracy, their subjection to caste control and wage slavery' (Du Bois 2007 [1940]: 48).

Conclusion
The Fictions of Modern Social Theory

Unreasonable divisions of humankind seem to be born from reason itself, not from its opposite.

Karen E. Fields

This book has discussed the classical canon of modern social theory. We have considered how modernity has been represented, how its key social problems have been identified and described, and what methodologies have been proposed to address them. Our focus has been on European colonialism, which is the context in which modernity developed and the social theories of the modern canon were formed. But, as we have seen, colonialism has received little attention in modern social theory so far. At best, it is represented as a transitional phenomenon, which mediates between feudalism and capitalist modernity. This is a double displacement, in which the rise of European imperialism out of colonialism is neglected as well – or, as in the case of Marx, represented as following from capitalism's global expansion. The consolidation of modern social theory at the end of the nineteenth century, in the writings of Marx, Weber, and Durkheim, coincided with the highpoint of European empires and a global war between them. Yet empire lay outside the purview of mainstream social theory, except as a phenomenon associated with earlier historical periods and civilisations. Even in the work of Du Bois, a theorist who entered the canon only recently, the issue of colonialism was not immediately evident; he worked gradually towards it from the angle of race relations in the United States, which was his starting point.

The end of the Second World War encouraged the spread of secondary and higher education across Europe, the United States, and other parts of the world. It was a period in which sociology expanded and was fully incorporated into university curricula. In Europe, this began with the dismantling of empires and new agendas in domestic politics. These focused on the nation and its new social settlements, themselves associated with the growth of education. Sociology came to centre on divisions that were framed as internal to postwar developments in nation states – for example the class stratification of outcomes and opportunities, the gendered nature of public life, and the inequalities of power in the private sphere. Issues around the relation between the private and the public were extended to encompass sexual orientation and discrimination. These are of course important, even fundamental matters. But they are shaped by the historical processes that generated them, just as sociology itself was shaped by the concepts and approaches bequeathed by its traditions and history – both those that were acknowledged and those that were not. And the historical processes in question included colonialism and its legacy – in fact that legacy could not have been more evident, although it went largely unremarked in sociology.

During the period of the consolidation of sociology, most European countries faced anticolonial movements that challenged their global dominance. In Algeria, for example, there was, from 1954 until 1962, a war of independence from the French empire (and, by implication, from the European Economic Community, of which Algeria was at the time a subordinated part).[1] India had declared independence from Britain in 1947. In the subsequent decades, much of the British empire was dismantled as a result of wars of liberation in the colonies of the Indian Ocean world and across the African continent. This process continued into the 1960s, with serious repercussions for domestic politics in Britain. The same happened across southern and western Europe. Also during this period, the United States was embroiled in colonial wars in East Asia that continued into the 1960s, after France's withdrawal from Indochina. Germany, for its part, had to address the Holocaust. However, these challenges to the political structures of European modernity seemed not to impinge on what sociology perceived as its 'jurisdiction'. They were treated as political entanglements of individual nation states, not as defining features of their societies. These events were not understood as the culmination and consequence of a systematic process integral to modernity; on the contrary, modernity was represented as being independent of them.

In this book we have not attempted to deny the importance of class, gender, or other divisions that have preoccupied European sociology over the decades since the Second World War. We have sought to show how bringing the colonial context and the imperial realities of modernity into focus will produce a fundamental shift in our ways of understanding what falls under the jurisdiction of sociology. Our book has been influenced by calls to 'decolonise' the university, but what does that mean when colonialism has been so thoroughly effaced from the self-understanding of academia? For those who practise sociology in places that were under European colonial domination, what this means is relatively clear. It means addressing how their institutions were produced or reproduced as part of a colonial system and how structures and curricula were shaped by their particular location in that system. For sociologists who work in institutions of the former metropoles, the answer is less clear because the shaping of these institutions by colonialism is less obvious to them. Universities no longer provide education for colonial administrators and professionals, and the global university system is a marketplace where students are sources of revenue. Decolonising the university can easily become a marketing slogan, and the associated concerns devolved into issues of 'diversity'. Calls to address racialised inequalities are multiplied by calls to address other differences such as 'gender', 'sexuality', and 'class' and become embroiled in a politics of identity claims. Yet issues of identity are issues of social structure; and, while the structures of patriarchy or class have been examined in detail, the structures of colonialism associated with racialised difference have not received the same attention.

We seek to contribute to current debates, but we want to do it by transforming their terms. The issue is not simply to add colonialism to sociology's repertoire of topics, but to show how that repertoire must change and how the concepts and methodologies with which it is associated must be transformed. What does it mean to 'decolonise' a curriculum in which colonialism is not recognised? Paradoxically, if our book is to be understood as an attempt at 'decolonisation', it is one that has had to proceed by putting colonialism into the picture. In doing so we aim to create a different way of seeing sociology. As we argued in the Introduction, there are two possible ways of approaching the history of social theory. One is to place writers in the context of their own times and debates. This method frequently takes the form of disrupting received understandings of a particular author or set of texts; it renders them less familiar to us, and therefore potentially more challenging. The other is to bring authors into conversation with the present, to understand them as precursors of our own concerns and modes of thought.

We have been engaging with the past from the point of the view of the present. We do not take issue with the fact that the authors we have selected for treatment here are central to the construction of contemporary sociology. But we take issue with what contemporary sociology regards as central. As we have seen, colonialism and empire are absent from sociology's current jurisdiction. They were not central to the concerns of the writers we have discussed; but we have also shown that they were not absent either. Secondary interpretations of these authors have expurgated them, rendering colonialism and empire absent. To remedy this absence, we have adopted the first kind of approach in order to fulfil the objectives of the second, placing the writers of our choice into a different conversation with the present from the one normally entertained.

As we have seen, modern social theory begins by being saturated with the presence of colonialism and the interpretive issues it posed. How do we engage with others when their presence is an obstacle to our interests? How do we use others to further our own interests? These were unavoidable questions in the early modern period. As colonialism became institutionalised, those questions receded from the centre to the periphery. But even there they persisted as matters of recurrent reflection. European nations – and, as should be clear by now, these of course included the United States – were engaged in colonial and imperial projects continuously throughout self-proclaimed modernity, and so their impacts could not be denied. It has not been until the formal end of empire in the latter half of the twentieth century that these questions could be fully elided. However, the legacies of colonialism and empire remain, and they are increasingly urgent.

We argue for a renewal of social theory and sociology, not for their rejection. However, central to this renewal is to recognise and address five fictions that currently organise understandings. We present these fictions as a distillation of the lessons to be learnt from our examination of the classical tradition.

FICTION 1   The idea of stages of society

The first fiction is associated with the idea of a 'state of nature'. We saw how this idea was developed by Hobbes and Locke as part of their discussions on the possession and use of resources available in common. It seems to carry the notion of a basic humanity shared by all, but does so in order to justify inequality and differential treatment. It is a construct that depends upon the distinction between a 'state of nature' and a 'state of society', the latter being typified by the 'modernising' society of Europe. This initial construct fosters a concern to delineate the characteristics of modern society against which other societies can be described and classified. We regard the idea of a modern society as equally fictional, because it carries the imprint of the original fiction. Once stages of society are delineated, it becomes possible to arrange them hierarchically in conformity with ideas of development and progress and to associate particular kinds of social relationships with each type of society. As we saw, colonialism and its practices of appropriation – of territories, of resources, and of people – have an explicit but ambiguous place within these constructions. It is evident that colonialism is directly connected to the emergence of modern society, but it comes to be associated with a late stage of feudal society – a stage that witnessed encounters with people in earlier phases of development. The act of taking other people into possession is then understood not simply as beneficial to those who derive profit from it but also as a 'civilising' process for those who are subject to it. These people are categorised as being at a lower stage of development and an entire vocabulary of 'savagery' and 'barbarity' is applied to them, notwithstanding the brutality of those who describe themselves as 'civilised'. We need to move away from the idea of types of society that can be investigated separately from the relationships between them. We must instead understand how those connections structure ideas of difference and domination.[2]

FICTION 2   Liberty, autonomy, and modern subjectivity

The idea of progress and the normative weight attached to it take us to our second fiction, which is about the special nature of modern subjectivity. As we have seen, modern society is assumed to inaugurate a distinctive kind of subjectivity, associated with the modern individual and his or her self-determining capacity to act on the basis of reason and self-interest. This is the individual 'capable of property', in contrast to individuals who are either incapable of or indifferent to property. But the latter are a product of European colonialism; their state – incapacity or indifference to property – is not a condition that colonialism originally confronted. As we have seen, this kind of individualism is represented as having developed within a religious tradition – that of Christianity and Protestantism in particular – but it is also a development that leaves religion behind. In the tradition of modern social theory, especially that associated with Kant and Hegel, modern reason is about developing autonomy and freedom and subjecting institutions such as those of religion to a criticism led by reason. This construction is powerful because it also inaugurates the possibility of self-criticism, as is outlined, for example, in the dialectical approach of the Frankfurt School's critical theory. When critical theory regards private property as a limit on self-emancipation, it does so after having postulated that the development of private property was itself a necessary stage in the process that leads to its transcendence. The very idea of an 'unfinished' project of modernity presupposes that modernity is a civilising project and that we should look at all premodern societies as inferior precursors, beset by traditional authority and inadequate selves, and not as bases of knowledge and sources of experience from which we can also learn.

FICTION 3   *The idea of the nation state*

Two kinds of sovereignty have taken shape alongside the development of the idea of the modern individual. One is the individual as a sovereign entity; the other is political authority as a guarantor of the liberty of sovereign individuals. As we have seen, in early modern thought political authority was associated with a commonwealth that had no obligatory territorial limits. But the exercise of political authority comes to be tied to nation states, in particular European nation states. Weber's formulation is the classic expression of the position in sociology: the nation has a legitimate claim to the monopoly of violence within its given territory, legitimacy being associated with the state's responsibility for and towards its citizens (i.e. the citizens who live within that territory). But not all members of the population are regarded as full citizens or members of what Tocqueville called the 'society of equals'. Equally, all European nation states (including the United States) either were empires or participated in the construction of empires through the movement of their populations. The latter, apart from consolidating these empires, contributed to turning their societies into 'societies of unequals'. The fiction of modern subjectivity and self-criticism allows that, in the realisation of rights, contingencies of exclusion can be overcome through a process of recognition of their false limitation (i.e. false from the perspective of a proper understanding of their underlying nature). This is a standard interpretation of the extension of political rights from propertied males to all males, then from men to women, and so on. However, in the case of issues of race and ethnicity, inequalities are constructed both inside and outside the newly established boundaries of the nation. From the outside, subjects of empire are denied inclusion among beneficiaries when the patrimony of empire is distributed; from the inside, they are denied full citizenship in the newly understood nation. As a result, people who in reality share the common political heritage of empire are now represented as 'immigrants' within its metropoles and are seen as threats to the nation's solidarity and social contract.

FICTION 4   Class and formally free labour

Marx recognised that modern society was developing as a society of unequals, that is, as a class-divided society, and he associated this class division with the system of private property. On the basis of the dialectical development of the class relation, proletarian agency would develop to transform private property and to create the new society. As we have suggested, the class division that Marx described depends on the centrality of formally free labour and on the commodification of labour power in capitalist modernity. We have argued that these two features are called into question once we understand the colonial (and imperial) nature of modernity. Commodified labour power does not develop as the central form of capitalism; moreover, capitalist nation states are able to divide their populations between national citizens and colonial subjects. As Du Bois noted, this opens possibilities for a 'decommodification' of labour power within the metropole by using colonial patrimonies in the provision of stratified welfare and other collective goods. At the same time, colonial subjects are denied the status of free labour and are subordinated to various forms of indenture. In this context, enslavement represents the commodification of the labourer, while the abolition of slavery does not give rise to free labour but to new forms of indenture. Both are enduring features of modernity. For example, in the metropole indenture returns in the form of treating migrant labour as not worthy of the rights and rewards associated with the citizenship status afforded to nationals.

FICTION 5   The fiction of sociological reasoning

The present chapter opens with an epigraph from Karen E. Fields. It is perhaps easy to grasp that Enlightenment thought had its dark side, and even to consider sociology as falling both within and outside that tradition. However, the task of sociology cannot be only to reveal that dark side; it must also be to consider how that dark side influenced the practice of sociology itself. Here we argue that such influence shows up in the nature of the methodological claims that are made in this discipline. They all tend to present sociological reasoning as ahistorical and as a necessary condition for an objective inquiry. In this way sociological reasoning is assimilated to the general claim of the Enlightenment, and sociology aligns itself with a critical project that continues that claim. However, this project is not a self-critical project. We have argued that understanding sociology as historically formed would open it to learning through dialogue with those represented as 'other'. We do not argue for some form of relativism or for *multiple perspectives* – that is essentially the corollary of the dominant methodology of ideal types; we argue for a *transformation* of our own perspective as a result of learning from others. The first step in any process of learning is the recognition of a limitation in one's understanding. We have shown that colonialism has structured European modernity as well as European thought, hence recognising its significance opens an opportunity to practise sociology differently.

We hope that the critiques we have presented are both nuanced and pertinent. While our book has looked back in order to provide a different contextualisation of the work of the thinkers we address, it has also sought to give a better understanding of the categories they have bequeathed to us. Our purpose, then, is forward-looking: it is to show how we can reconstruct the concepts and categories of modern social theory so as to make them able to intervene more effectively in contemporary social problems. Modern social theory and sociology are part of the problem, but they are necessary to any solutions.

Notes

Notes to Introduction

1 Quinn (1966) and Canny (2001) suggest that the model was first applied, albeit unsuccessfully, in Elizabethan England during its colonisation of Ireland before being applied with greater success in Virginia.

2 Settler colonialism is itself vulnerable to movements of independence against the authority of the metropole, to which the settlers see themselves as 'equals' (Veracini 2010). Thus Latin American independence movements that secured freedom from Spain and Portugal occurred in the early nineteenth century. Just as in the United States, they did not dispense with the institutions that typified colonialism, such as forced labour and the continued dispossession of indigenous peoples.

3 The 'Hobbesian problem of order' that Parsons (1937) discussed was not that of Hobbes's texts; it was an analytical device meant to express the sociological problem of explaining the coordination of actions outside their framing in terms of utilitarian calculations of self-interest.

4 The book gave equal space to the Italian sociologist Vilfredo Pareto and to the English economist Alfred Marshall, but secondary engagements with Parsons's argument are, for the most part, focused on his discussions of Weber and Durkheim and on his omission of Marx. As Marx comes into the canon, Pareto and Marshall recede.

5 The colleges that came to be known as 'historically black colleges' were, initially, integrated colleges – integrated by race and gender, albeit attracting few white students. By contrast, other universities serving white students operated segregation but have not been labelled 'historically white' (Smith 2016).

6 Giddens's treatment of capitalism makes no room for a discussion of colonialism, enslavement, and dispossession, in contrast to the treatment of the writers he looks at. His only discussion of India, for example, is

about its 'traditionalism' and how its system of religious belief, including the designations of caste, condemned it to economic backwardness after developments in the centuries before Christ that had produced an urban organisation similar to that of mediaeval Europe (Giddens 1971: 173). This type of formulation is a characteristic trope of Eurocentrism. Indian civilisation is recognised and identified as advanced and India is compared to Europe, but it is compared to mediaeval Europe, that is, to a Europe that has already transcended itself. Europe has the capacity for development, while India is represented as being in suspended animation.

Notes to Chapter 1

1 Macpherson's (1962) account of the class basis of contract theory is complemented by feminist criticisms of its gendered character, notwithstanding its origins in a critique of patriarchal theory. See, for example, Carole Pateman's (1988) account of the 'sexual contract'. Her argument is extended by Charles Mills (1997) so as to outline the idea of a 'racial contract'.

2 Constructions of stadial difference, as we will see, become important adjuncts to arguments in favour of progress and the improvement of others through colonialism. They also arise in the context of the English conquest of Ireland in the late sixteenth century, when local practices were described as 'backward' and 'derelict'. The project was described by Canny (1976) as planting English virtues where they could yield Irish profits.

3 For a discussion of the way in which early settlers encountered indigenous people engaged in animal husbandry and domestic agriculture, see Jennings (1971) and Greer (2012).

4 In this way Hobbes can justify obedience to the English king before his defeat in the Civil War at the hands of the parliamentary forces, and then to the new sovereign, Lord Protector Cromwell. For Hobbes, religion is a matter private to individuals and there can be no religious justification of rule that is not circular in its logic, depending on (all too) human interpretations rather than on the revelation of God's word.

5 Self-interested motives ultimately derive from the motivation of self-preservation and can include prideful concern with one's own reputation, which indicates some degree of social recognition, as Oakeshott (1975) argued.

6 The Jamestown massacre of indigenous people of 1622 was a significant event in English understandings of the need for the violent suppression of resistance (Evans 2012).

7 In contrast to Filmer, Locke proposed that every male, and not just a monarch, is an 'Adam'.

8 In common with other writers after him, Locke did not believe that indigenous people had anything equivalent to money. He regarded Wampompeke (wampum) as ceremonial (Lebovics 1986, Cattelino 2018).

9 For example, Sir Josiah Child, a governor of the East India Company, commented: 'Plantations being at first furnished and afterwards successively supplied with people from their mother kingdoms, and people being riches, that loss of people to the mother kingdom be it more or less, is certainly a damage, except that the employment of those people abroad, do cause the employment of so many more at home in their mother kingdoms, and that can never be except their trade be restricted to their mother kingdom' (cited in Furniss 1965 [1923]: 54).

10 Locke favoured religious tolerance towards the enslaved, but denied that becoming a Christian could alter their status. See Welchman 1995.

11 Lewis and Maslin (2015: 175), by contrast, suggest that the continent had had a population of around 61 million before European contact and that this 'rapidly declined to a minimum of about 6 million people by 1650 via exposure to diseases carried by Europeans, plus war, enslavement and famine'.

12 Jonathan Swift's *Gulliver's Travels*, written in 1726, uses a similar conceit for satirical purposes.

13 For a comparative study of slavery in the United States and Russian serfdom, see Kolchin (1987).

14 Buck-Morss (2000) claims that more than 20 per cent of the French bourgeoisie was dependent upon slave-connected commercial activity, although other scholars, such as Sala-Molins (2006), have suggested that the figure is closer to one third. On the North American fur trade, Eric Wolf (1997 [1982]) writes that it began when European fishermen and sailors first bartered for fur with the local Algonquins. While they were initially active participants in the growth of the trade, 'as European traders consolidated their economic and political position, the balanced relation between native trappers and Europeans gave way to imbalance' (194). They gradually repatterned their social relations and cultural habits around European demands and expectations, and this led ultimately to their dispossession.

15 As Mehta (1999) argues, the conservative philosopher Edmund Burke is alone in late eighteenth-century England in castigating the radical abstractions that are embraced by liberal philosophers of the market (which he distinguishes from the orderly relations of established property) or by proponents of radical democracy in the French Revolution. According to Mehta, Burke regards empire, or what he calls 'Indiaism', as equally rapacious and disruptive of the coherent and established relations of Indian society. For example, Burke describes the commercial mercenaries of India as 'birds of prey' that engage in feeding frenzies and

bring their vices back to infect English institutions. Still, even for Burke, it is not an infection nurtured within the commercial society that sets its birds of prey in flight over other lands.
16 For a discussion in the context of colonialism, see Stone (2017).
17 This is a representation of 'elementary' religion that Durkheim, as we shall see, strongly contested.

Notes to Chapter 2

1 See Rogers M. Smith (1993) for a critique of the continuity of this argument in American political discourse.
2 As Frymer (2017) argues, historians do not often use the term 'empire' to describe the territorial expansion of the United States to the south and west of the north American land mass, but it was the term used by founding fathers such as Washington, Hamilton, and Jefferson.
3 This was a process that concluded during Tocqueville's lifetime with the annexation of the Republic of Texas in 1845, the purchase of Oregon Territory from Britain in 1848, the Mexican Cession in 1848, and the Gadsden purchase of 1853 from Mexico.
4 The *coup d'état* of Louis Napoleon was the subject of one of Marx's most celebrated essays, *The 18th Brumaire of Louis Napoleon*, which will be discussed in the following chapter.
5 Raymond Aron (1965) makes a similar point about the role of ideal types in Tocqueville's thought.
6 These are expressed in George Fitzhugh's (1854) *Sociology for the South*, one of the first works with the word 'sociology' in its title; it was devoted to the defence of feudal and racial privileges in the United States and its southern states.
7 Wagner (2001) argues that the American Revolution is more pronounced than the French Revolution, as it not only shifts sovereignty to 'the people' but has to create, through itself, so to speak, the very people in whom sovereignty is to be lodged. The American Declaration of Independence and new constitution are seen to bring into being an American people and an American republic. In fact, as should be evident, Tocqueville's argument is very different. American society is already a society of equals and must bring into being a commensurate politics. France has a political revolution and confronts a society of unequals; it bequeaths to modernity the trope of social revolution brought about by a political vanguard.
8 This idea of 'legality' is further elaborated on by Beaumont (1999 [1835]: 82ff.) in his discussion of the 'violence of decrees'. Native Americans were granted land under 'usufruct' – or landlord–tenant agreements – which could be rescinded by the sovereign power for any alleged infringement of the tenancy agreement.

9 Indeed, among the complaints against the king expressed in the US Declaration of Independence are those associated with settlement: 'He has endeavoured to prevent the population of these States; for that purpose obstructing the Laws for Naturalisation of Foreigners; refusing to pass others to encourage their migrations hither, and raising the conditions of new Appropriations of Lands ... He has excited domestic insurrections amongst us, and has endeavoured to bring on the inhabitants of our frontiers, the merciless Indian Savages whose known rule of warfare, is an undistinguished destruction of all ages, sexes and conditions' (quoted in Allen 2014: 28, 30).

10 In part, Tocqueville constructed indigenous peoples as 'aristocratic' by temperament, eschewing the labour and occupations that would be those of (white) America. In this respect he followed the assumptions of a stadial history, treating the evidence of husbandry and political organisation beyond hunter gathering (for example, among the Cherokees) as an adaptation to settlers rather than as an expression of features that belonged to indigenous societies. By temperament they are would-be conquerors who might adapt to the ways of those they had conquered, but cannot submit to being conquered. For a detailed discussion of complex social and political organisation among indigenous peoples in the south-west in the eighteenth and nineteenth centuries, see Hämäläinen's (2008) discussion of the Comanches.

11 This was so despite the fact that, according to the stadial theory with which Tocqueville operated, Africans would be represented as hunter-gatherers, as were the indigenous peoples in the United States.

12 Religious conversion provided no protection against slavery, which early modern Protestants justified on racial grounds – as in the case of Africans (Gerbner 2019).

13 Anna Julia Cooper, a contemporary of W. E. B. Du Bois, graduated from Sorbonne University in 1925, at the age of 67, becoming the fourth African American woman to gain a doctorate. Her dissertation was titled *L'attitude de la France à l'égard l'esclavage pendant la révolution* and was subsequently translated into English under the title *Slavery and the French and Haitian Revolutionists* (Cooper 2006 [1925]). The book presents a powerful argument that, had the white French revolutionaries taken the issue of slavery more seriously than indicated by James (1989 [1938]) and had they both abolished slavery and renounced empire, they could have shaped the revolution more favourably, in line with their declared concern for equality and liberty.

14 Interestingly, as in the presentation of indigenous peoples and Africans in the United States, Tocqueville described a 'noble' people (the Kabylie) that lived in the Atlas Mountains and a 'corrupted' people that occupied the fertile plains on which French settlers had designs. One of the paradoxes of stadial theory is that the argument for the need for progress runs alongside a romanticisation of people remote from 'moderns', who

are deemed to be 'more pure', and a denigration of people closer to 'moderns' and otherwise possible companions in modernity.

15 As Brower (2009) argues, this led Bugeaud and others to propose the introduction of enslaved people from sub-Saharan Africa as a 'docile' agricultural labour force that could replace the dispossessed local population unwilling to labour for the French settlers.

Notes to Chapter 3

1 In fact, Marx (1975 [1842a]) cites Tocqueville in his essay 'On the Jewish Question' in the context of political emancipation of Jews in Germany, but not in any of his writings on the emancipation of enslaved people in the American Civil War (see Marx and Engels 2016). We will return to the discussion of the Jewish question in Marx, Weber, and Durkheim in chapter 5.

2 In his 'Critique of the Gotha Programme', Marx (1974 [1875]: 347) wrote that the principle of the 'new society' would involve 'from each according to their abilities and to each according to their needs', thereby indicating the existence of real inequalities separate from those produced by market exchange relations. However, these inequalities would be at the service of a society that functioned for the collective good.

3 In some ways, Marx's account of republicanism in the United States and France is not dissimilar to that of Tocqueville, where 'the republic is generally only the political form for the revolutionising of bourgeois society, and not its conservative form of existence, as for example in the United States of America' (Marx 1973 [1852]: 155).

4 The Mobile Guard was a militia raised by the government from the ranks of the urban poor. See Traugott (1985).

5 Need we mention that those who are enslaved, or otherwise subject to forced labour, are outside contract, being made the property of others?

6 Such arguments influenced Marx and Engels's (1976 [1848]) conception of the early stage of 'primitive communism'.

7 The term 'tightly coupled' (or 'tight-coupled') is borrowed from Charles Perrow's (1984) discussion of the nature of organisations and the problem of accidents.

8 Althusser (1977b), for example, considered Marx's mature writings to have established an 'epistemological break' with the Hegelian and unscientific formulations of his youth. From a radically different perspective, Elster (1985) regards the Hegelian formulations in Marx's early writings literally as 'nonsense', superseded in later writings.

9 We shall see that Weber (1930 [1904/5]) makes a distinction between capitalism in general and modern capitalism that is similar to Marx's. However, Weber is more concerned with differences in the orientation

      to profit than with the conditions that make the different orientations possible.

10   For a particularly strong statement directed at the Marxian issue of 'class' from a neoclassical perspective, see Robbins (1939). Significantly, the collection that contains this essay also contains another, titled 'The Economics of Territorial Sovereignty', which purports to criticise empire in the name of free trade, but in effect relies upon empire to create the circumstances for the very possibility of that trade.

11   Marx sardonically told the story of Mr Peel, who brought the means of production – £50,000 in capital and a labour force of 3,000 working class men, women, and children – to set up an enterprise at Swan River in Western Australia, only for the 3,000 people to disappear. 'Unhappy Mr Peel', remarked Marx (1976 [1867]: 933), 'provided for everything except the export of English relations of production to Swan River!'

12   The section was called 'Results of the immediate process of production' and was drafted between June 1863 and December 1866, as part of Marx's reflections on primitive accumulation.

13   Others have distinguished between mode of production and social formation, with 'The Eighteenth Brumaire' furnishing an exemplary analysis of the 'conjunctural' features of a historically given social formation. The problem arises when those conjunctural features begin to be accounted for not with the help of pre-existing historical contingencies, but by resorting to factors inconsistent with the mode of production and continuous with the development of capitalism. For example, it is one thing to refer to feudal elements as conjunctural, but quite another to assign conjunctural status to an emerging welfare state. This is the point made by Abram Harris (1939) when he argued that the middle class that should disappear was in fact taking on new forms.

Notes to Chapter 4

1   Abraham (1992) is an exception to this view, which, he argues, is owed mostly to Marianne Weber's (2017 [1926]), biography, which he believes to be used uncritically.

2   Parsons's translation of Weber's *Protestant Ethic* study appeared in 1930, and his translation of the first part of Weber's massive *Economy and Society* was published as *The Theory of Social and Economic Organisation* in 1947. In 1949 Edward Shils and Henry Finch translated a selection of Weber's essays on the methodology of the social sciences. See Scaff (2011) for a discussion of the competitive element in the translation of Weber's texts.

3   The essay was published in English at the time and was included in proceedings of the Exposition. It is also reproduced in Gerth and Mills (1948 [1918]).

4 There were restrictions on the internal movement of ethnic Germans too; they were related to the requirement that those who moved be self-supporting in their new places of residence. These internal restrictions meant that for many people emigration from Germany was easier than movement within Germany.

5 For a discussion of this argument, see Poggi (1985).

6 On the basis of later philosophy of science, Weber appears to be what Lakatos (1970) called a 'naïve falsificationist'. What is at issue here is not, however, captured by Lakatos's distinction between 'naïve' and 'sophisticated' falsification and the evident superiority of the latter. The issue is that Weber is any kind of falsificationist in his approach to natural science while being no kind of falsificationist in the area of social inquiry.

Notes to Chapter 5

1 Curiously, Lehmann (1993: 9) states: 'Durkheim calls himself a socialist. In reality he stands for the reform of capitalism; he is a neo-liberal.'

2 The lecture series was eventually published in 1950, in French, under the title *Professional Ethics and Civic Morals* (Durkheim 1957 [1890–1900]; the dates in brackets indicate the period when the lectures were delivered). The fact that the first publication took place in Turkey indicates that local scholars there – for instance the sociologist Hüseyin Nail Kubali, who published the work – thought that this series would be a constructive contribution to debates on how a positive role for Islam might be found within modern civil society (Strenski 2006b).

3 The details of Durkheim's life are taken from Steven Lukes (1973) and the recent biography by Marcel Fournier (2013).

4 In fact, the connection was more closely to Hegelian dialectics (see Strenski 2006a). Jaurés had himself written a thesis on the Hegelian aspects of socialism.

5 It is perhaps worth mentioning that in 1893, the year of the first publication of *Division of Labour*, Durkheim delivered some lectures on the history of socialism. Those lectures were published in 1928 by his nephew, the anthropologist Marcel Mauss. See Durkheim (1959 [1928]).

6 Engels (1989 [1880]) had written an essay asserting the opposite. The idea of sociology as a 'science of reform' was also being developed within pragmatist sociology in the United States, with a similar critical focus on liberal individualist and Marxist accounts. For example, George Herbert Mead outlined a working hypothesis in social reform that distinguished 'opportunistic' reforms (i.e. reforms with good prospects of realisation) from utopian blueprints. He wrote: 'a conception of a different world comes to us always as the result of some specific problem which involves readjustment of the world as it is, not to meet a detailed ideal of a perfect

universe, but to obviate the present difficulty; and the test of the effort lies in the possibility of this readjustment fitting into the world as it is' (Mead 1899: 371). Durkheim was aware of pragmatism and delivered lectures on this topic in 1913–14; these were subsequently published as *Pragmatism and Sociology* (Durkheim 1983 [1955]). He regarded pragmatism as a form of philosophical utilitarianism. See Holmwood (2011).

7 Therborn (1976), for example, discusses 'classical sociology' as a bourgeois response to Marxism, but does not pay heed to the socio-logical conditions that make that response possible.

8 This also indicated Durkheim's interest in pedagogy. His thoughts on reform embraced social policies for industry and for political organis-ations, but also the education system and the practice of education itself. These were topics of lecture series that he offered. His first teaching post was at the University of Bordeaux in 1887; it preceded his appointment to a professorship in education at the Sorbonne in 1902.

9 Durkheim did experience the hostility to sociology that was especially associated with his appointment at the University of Bordeaux (Fournier 2013).

10 As we saw in the discussion of Weber, this is a methodologically contested point. Nonetheless, it remains true that, in the area of social inquiry, Weber was not a fallibilist, whereas Durkheim was.

11 The same suicide rate can be associated with different causes, so according to Pope the argument risks circularity or the fallacy of question begging, *petitio principii* (see Lukes 1973: 31).

12 This is partly an argument about the recording of suicides and is often cited in criticism of Durkheim's strictures against interpretivism. There is a stronger injunction against suicide among Catholics than Protestants; therefore fewer suicides will be recorded in mortality statistics in Catholic areas than in Protestant areas. As Parkin (1992) comments, this is relatively easily resolved by amalgamating 'unassigned causes of death', or 'deaths by misadventure', with those recorded as suicide, since the former will be correspondingly higher where there are scruples against recording suicide.

13 Instead he attributed it to the different natures of women and men and, in particular, to the greater sensitivity of men!

14 Significantly, in a later chapter where Durkheim discussed the phenomenon of the anomic division of labour, he devoted considerable attention to the division of labour within the sciences.

15 Allen and O'Boyle (2017: 35) go on to comment that Durkheim, in distinguishing between mechanical and organic solidarity, 'argues as if the entirety of human history can be understood in terms of these two mutually exclusive social categories. When one thinks of the different societies that have actually existed (city states, caste systems, slave economies, capitalist nation states, etc) this claim seems completely

outlandish.' However, *Division* is full of examples from the very societies that, according to them, Durkheim ignored.

16 In fairness to Poggi, the distance between his reconstruction and Durkheim's own concerns is implicitly registered in the decision to label the two societies as 'Type A' and 'Type B'. Nonetheless, Poggi is imposing a Weberian sensibility upon Durkheim's sociological concerns, which are very different methodologically and substantively.

17 It is in this chapter that he first discussed suicide and its predominance in modern societies – 'the decreasing happiness that the progression in the number of suicides demonstrates is the average happiness' (Durkheim 2013 [1893: 195]).

18 This is proposed in a discussion of Comte, who did not sufficiently appreciate that the solidarity deriving from likeness was specific to particular social conditions and was substituted by the interdependence of the division of labour itself. The general 'enfeeblement' of the *conscience collective* is normal, and the solution to the abnormal phenomena under discussion lies in regulating those functions both in their specific activities and in their mutual operation (Durkheim 2013 [1893, 1902]: 285).

19 The contrast between Durkheim and Weber is stark. Where Weber perceived national greatness as the obligation of the nation in its external relations, Durkheim saw greatness in the nation's care for its members. Roslyn Bologh (1990) represents these themes in Weber in terms of a 'masculine' choice of 'greatness' over 'love'. The 'patriarchal' theorist, Durkheim, chose love (Lehmann 1994).

20 For a discussion of the selection and use of ethnographies by Durkheim, see Watts-Miller (2012).

21 Durkheim objected to his contemporary Lévy-Bruhl's (1910 [1985]) idea of a separate and specific 'primitive' mode of thought.

22 Given that Durkheim invoked Kant in his essay on the Dreyfus affair, we might contrast his sensibility with Hannah Arendt's adoption of the Kantian requirement to understand the perspective of others. As Kathryn Gines has argued, Arendt showed herself able to adopt the perspective of colonising Europeans, but not the perspective of those they encountered: 'to Arendt, it is obvious that the Africans lacked civilization, reason, culture, history and political institutions. Race and racial oppression were understandable emergency explanations and rational responses by Europeans to their encounters with frightening and uncivilized African tribes' (Gines 2014: 128). Durkheim, however, sees 'us' in the 'other'.

23 One of his few published references to colonialism occurs in the lectures on moral education, where Durkheim condemned the use of violence in punishments and suggested that it was the 'civilised' who were 'savages'. This was a consequence of their failure to include non-European 'others' in their moral realm: 'the superiority that he arrogates tends, as though independently, to assert itself brutally, without object or reason, for the

mere pleasure of asserting itself. It produces a veritable intoxication, a sort of megalomania, which goes to the worst extremes' (Durkheim 1961 [1902–3]: 193).

Notes to Chapter 6

1 Tocqueville (2004 [1835]: 414–15) discounted the option of continuous oppression in favour of reflecting more on the possibilities of realising this alternative option. One such possibility was the establishment of a community in Liberia formed through white Americans' repatriation of African Americans to Africa. Tocqueville's collaborator, Gustave de Beaumont, mentions yet another possibility: Jefferson 'wanted a portion of American territory assigned to the Negroes, after the abolition of slavery, where they would live apart from the whites' (Beaumont 1999 [1835]: 208).

2 In his biography of Du Bois, Lewis (1993: 212) outlines the 'raw racism' faced by the Du Bois family in Jim Crow Atlanta. While Atlanta University had been set up as an integrated institution, by the time Du Bois arrived it 'had been subjected for several years to an almost total boycott by white Atlanta, its faculty treated as pariahs'; the Georgia legislature had deprived the university of 'its thirteen year old annual land-grant appropriation of eight thousand dollars in 1887, essentially for refusing to abandon race mixing in the dining hall' (214). The 'stinging apartheid' that characterised those years was evident in the segregated transit system, in the system of waiting in shops until all white customers had been served, and in there being 'not a single water fountain or park bench lawfully permitted to Negroes' (212, 346). It was further evidenced in the horrific 'lynching and burning' of the African American Sam Hose, which culminated in a mob of 2,000 white men, women, and children fighting over 'pieces of his flesh for souvenirs' (226). In Du Bois's own life, this horrific event was followed by the death of his firstborn, in 'a city where white physicians refused to treat even desperately sick black children' (228). He and his wife refused to bury their son in the red earth of Georgia and took his body north, to Barrington. As they walked behind the horse-drawn cart carrying their son's coffin to Atlanta train station, Du Bois recounted, 'the busy city dinned about us; they did not say much, those pale-faced hurrying men and women; they did not say much, – they only glanced and said "N-----s!"' (Du Bois 1997 [1903]: 162).

3 Although Merton discusses the issue of race, he does not cite Du Bois's arguments and declares the matter difficult: 'The role of the Negro in this connection raises almost as many theoretical as practical questions. It has been reported that large segments of the Negro population have assimilated the dominant caste's values of pecuniary success and social

advancement, but have "realistically" adjusted themselves to the "fact" that social ascent is presently confined almost entirely to movement within the caste' (Merton 1968 [1949]: 200). Merton's reference is to John Dollard's *Caste and Class in a Southern Town* and to Robert Warner's *New Haven Negroes*, of which Du Bois (1942) wrote a scathing review in the *American Historical Review*.

4 In part, the disregard for *The Philadelphia Negro* followed from the animus of Robert E. Park, W. I. Thomas's colleague at the University of Chicago. Park had been secretary and press agent to Booker T. Washington and, as a consequence of the latter's hostility to Du Bois (discussed further down), was responsible for the active marginalisation of Du Bois in public activities. For example, Du Bois's presence on public panels would be countered by individuals nominated by Park (Wilson 2006; Morris 2015). In addition, Park was hostile to the social survey methodology used so expertly by Du Bois because of its association with what he called 'do-gooder' social reformers active in the settlement movement (Lannoy 2004).

5 In his introduction to a reprint of the first edition of Du Bois's *Philadelphia Negro*, Digby Baltzell refers to a later tradition in American sociology that incorporates the *Polish Peasant* as well as the Chicago School of Urban Sociology and Lloyd Warner's community studies, stating that 'the origins, in both method and theoretical point of view, of all these studies are to be found in the *Philadelphia Negro*' (Baltzell 1967: xxvi).

6 The idea of standpoint epistemology would be developed further within feminism – for example by Nancy Hartsock (1983). In fact, Anna Julia Cooper's *A Voice from the South* had set out the intersecting oppressions of race and gender endured by African American women in the United States much earlier. She was insistent that the problems of the nation also required dealing with the specific conditions of poor African American women, and she stated that 'the race cannot be effectually lifted up till its women are truly elevated' (Cooper 1892: 42).

7 Frederick Douglass was a self-emancipated African American, leader of the abolitionist movement in the North, and a key spokesperson in the struggle against slavery in the mid-nineteenth century (Kohn 2005).

8 The successes of the civil rights movement would in turn be undermined by what Michelle Alexander (2010) calls 'the new Jim Crow' and Smith and King (2020) call 'white reconstruction'.

9 But Du Bois does not talk about the original dispossession of indigenous peoples that colonial settlement had caused.

10 The United States is widely thought to have a laggard welfare state because of its weak development of social rights of citizenship. The Civil Rights movement of the 1960s and the associated 'war on poverty' seemed to some sociologists to be able in principle to rectify this situation. Significantly, Talcott Parsons (1965) raised the question

of full citizenship for the Negro American and declared that African Americans would lead this movement for social and economic rights for all Americans. See Holmwood (forthcoming) for discussion.

11 The Congress was organised with a view to enhancing understandings between the East and the West and was promoted by the *Sociological Review*. There was an advertisement for the 'proposed congress' at p. 50 of issue 4 in that journal's volume for 1911, vol. a4, and it stated: 'Nothing is clearer to the instructed observer of the world movement than that the problems of race are destined in the near future to play a decisive part in international relations, and that, generally speaking, there is no department of public affairs in which politicians, administrators, and permanent officials are more urgently in need of scientific guidance.' In the congress report published in the same issue, A. Caldecott said that Du Bois gave a powerful paper 'and himself stood out as one of the most effective members of the Congress' (Caldecott 1911: 317).

12 For an examination of the institutional relationship between race, dispossession, enslavement, and the establishment of US universities, see Craig Steven Wilder (2013); see also Wilson (2006), Allen et al. (2007), and Smith (2016).

13 'Anti-Caste' was the name of a network 'devoted to the interests of coloured races' in the United States and in the British empire. It was organised in the late 1880s by an English Quaker feminist, Catherine Impey, had an eponymous newsletter, and campaigned against racialised difference (Bressey 2013).

14 Notwithstanding the superb nature of Cox's treatment of caste, class, and race, and his criticisms of mainstream sociology, he failed to understand the context of Du Bois's argument in *Black Reconstruction*. Equally, he failed to acknowledge Du Bois's pragmatic concern about the need to ameliorate the immediate conditions of those living the circumstances otherwise deplored in arguments about principles.

Notes to Conclusion

1 As Peo Hansen and Stefan Jonsson (2014) have argued, the European Union began as an organisation of states that brought their colonies as a 'dowry' to the political project of rebuilding after the Second World War; and this project included the consolidation of colonial interests in Africa.

2 Put simply, in modern social theory, 'race' has shifted from first being an issue of culture (i.e. reflecting different stages of society and their moral codes) to being an issue of biology (i.e. reflecting the scientific racism of the late nineteenth century) and back to being an issue of culture in the late twentieth century, reflecting cultural differences where 'our' traditions are presented as merely different from those of 'others'. But by

looking at race in the theoretical framework of colonialism we can better appreciate it as an issue of social structure and see how it is aligned with other social structures. In this way we become aware that our traditions are a consequence of processes of active domination through which others are constructed as different.

Bibliography

Abraham, Gary A. 1992. *Max Weber and the Jewish Question*. Chicago: University of Illinois Press.

Alexander, Jeffrey C. 1987. 'The Centrality of the Classics', in Anthony Giddens and Jonathan H. Turner (eds), *Social Theory Today*. Cambridge: Polity.

Alexander, Michelle 2010. *The New Jim Crow: Mass Incarceration in the Age of Colorblindness*. New York: New Press.

Allen, Danielle 2014. *Our Declaration: A Reading of the Declaration of Independence: In Defense of Equality*. New York: Liveright Publishing Corporation.

Allen, Kieran and Brian O'Boyle 2017. *Durkheim: A Critical Analysis*. London: Pluto Press.

Allen, Richard B. 2010. 'Satisfying the "Want for Labouring People": European Slave Trading in the Indian Ocean, 1500–1850', *Journal of World History* 21 (1): 45–73.

Allen, Richard B. 2017. 'Asian Indentured Labor in the 19th and Early 20th Century Colonial Plantation World', in *Oxford Research Encyclopedia of Asian History*, edited by David Ludden. New York: Oxford University Press.

Allen, Walter R., Joseph O. Jewell, Kimberly A. Griffin, and De'Sha S. Wolf 2007. 'Historically Black Colleges and Universities: Honoring the Past, Engaging the Present, Touching the Future', *Journal of Negro Education* 76 (3): 263–80.

Althusser, Louis 1977a. 'Contradiction and Over-Determination', in Louis Althusser, *For Marx*. London: New Left Books.

Althusser, Louis 1977b. 'On the Young Marx', in Louis Althusser, *For Marx*. London: New Left Books.

Anderson, Elijah 1996. 'Introduction to the 1996 Edition of *The Philadelphia Negro*', in W. E. B. Du Bois, *The Philadelphia Negro: A Social Study*. Philadelphia: University of Pennsylvania Press.

Anderson, Elijah and Douglas S. Massey 2001. 'The Sociology of Race in the United States', in Elijah Anderson and Douglas S. Massey (eds),

Problem of the Century: Racial Stratification in the United States. New York: Russell Sage.

Anghie, Antony 2006. 'The Evolution of International Law: Colonial and Postcolonial Realities', *Third World Quarterly* 27 (5): 739–53.

Antonio, Robert and Ronald J. Glassman 1986. *A Weber–Marx Dialogue*. Lawrence: University Press of Kansas.

Aravamudan, Srinivas 2009. 'Hobbes and America', in Daniel Carey and Lynn Festa (eds), *The Postcolonial Enlightenment: Eighteenth-Century Colonialism and Postcolonial Theory*. Oxford: Oxford University Press.

Arjomand, Saïd 2014. 'Introduction: The Challenge of Integrating Social Theory and Regional Studies', in Saïd Arjomand (ed.), *Social Theory and Regional Studies in a Global Age*. New York: SUNY Press.

Aron, Raymond 1965. *Main Currents in Sociological Thought*, vol. 1: *Montesquieu, Comte, Marx, Tocqueville: The Sociologists and the Revolution of 1848*. London: Weidenfeld & Nicolson.

Bade, Klaus J. 1995. 'From Emigration to Immigration: The German Experience in the Nineteenth and Twentieth Centuries', *Central European History* 28 (4): 507–35.

Baltzell, E. Digby 1967. 'Introduction', in W. E. B. Du Bois, *The Philadelphia Negro: A Social Study*. New York: Schocken Books.

Beaumont, Gustave 1999 [1835, 1958 (trans.)]. *Marie: Or Slavery in the United States*, translated by Barbara Chapman. Baltimore, MD: Johns Hopkins University Press.

Beauvois, Frédérique 2009. 'L'indemnité de Saint-Domingue: "Dette d'indépendance" ou "rançon de l'esclavage"?' *French Colonial History* 10: 109–24.

Beauvois, Frédérique 2010. 'Monnayer l'incalculable? L'indemnité de Saint-Domingue, entre approximations et bricolage', *Revue historique* 655 (3): 609–36.

Beauvois, Frédérique 2017. *Between Blood and Gold: The Debates over Compensation for Slavery in the Americas*, translated by Andrene Everson. Oxford: Berghahn Books.

Belmessous, Saliha (ed.) 2015. *Empire by Treaty: Negotiating European Expansion, 1600–1900*. Oxford: Oxford University Press.

Bendix, Reinhard 1980. *Kings or People: Power and the Mandate to Rule*. Berkeley: University of California Press.

Bernasconi, Robert 2000. 'With What Must the Philosophy of World History Begin? On the Racial Basis of Hegel's Eurocentrism', *Nineteenth Century Contexts* 22 (2): 171–201.

Berry, Christopher J. 1997. *Social Theory of the Scottish Enlightenment*. Edinburgh: Edinburgh University Press.

Bhabha, Homi K. 1994. *The Location of Culture*. London: Routledge.

Bhambra, Gurminder K. 2007. *Rethinking Modernity: Postcolonialism and the Sociological Imagination*. Basingstoke: Palgrave.

Bhambra, Gurminder K. 2009. 'Postcolonial Europe: Or, Understanding

Europe in Times of the Postcolonial', in Chris Rumford (ed.), *Sage Handbook of European Studies*. London: Sage.

Bhambra, Gurminder K. 2014. *Connected Sociologies*. London: Bloomsbury.

Bhambra, Gurminder K. and John Holmwood 2018. 'Colonialism, Post-Colonialism and the Liberal Welfare State', *New Political Economy* 23 (5): 574–87.

Bhambra, Gurminder K. and Victoria Margree 2010. 'Tocqueville, Beaumont and the Silences in Histories of the United States: An Interdisciplinary Endeavour across Literature and Sociology', *Journal of Historical Sociology* 24 (1): 116–31.

Bhambra, Gurminder K., Kerem Nişancioğlu, and Dalia Gebrial (eds) 2018. *Decolonising the University*. London: Pluto Press.

Bhaskar, Roy 1979. *The Possibility of Naturalism: A Philosophical Critique of the Contemporary Human Sciences*. Brighton: Harvester Press.

Blauner, Robert 2001 [1971]. 'Colonized and Immigrant Minorities', in *Still the Big News: Racial Oppression in America*. Philadelphia, PA: Temple University Press.

Bloor, David 1982. 'Durkheim and Mauss Revisited: Classification and the Sociology of Knowledge', *Studies in the History and Philosophy of Science* 13 (4): 267–97.

Boatcă, Manuela 2013. '"From the Standpoint of Germanism": A Postcolonial Critique of Weber's Theory of Race and Ethnicity', in Julian Go (ed.), *Postcolonial Sociology*. Bingley: Emerald.

Bologh, Roslyn 1990. *Love or Greatness: Max Weber and Masculinist Thinking: A Feminist Inquiry*. London: Allen & Unwin.

Bousquet, G. H. 1953. 'How the Natives of Algeria Became French Citizens', *The International and Comparative Law Quarterly* 2 (4): 596–605.

Bracey, John, August Meier, and Elliott Rudwick 1973. 'The Black Sociologists: The First Half Century', in Joyce A. Ladner (ed.), *The Death of White Sociology*. New York: Vintage Books.

Braverman, Harry 1974. *Labor and Monopoly Capitalism*. New York: Monthly Review Press.

Bressey, Caroline 2013. *Empire, Race and the Politics of Anti-Caste*. London: Bloomsbury.

Brooke-Smith, Robin 1987. *The Scramble for Africa. Documents and Debates*. London: Palgrave.

Brower, Benjamin Claude 2009. 'Rethinking Abolition in Algeria: Slavery and the "Indigenous Question"', *Cahiers d'études africaines* 195: 805–28.

Bruun, Hans H. 2007. *Science, Values, and Politics in Max Weber's Methodology*. Aldershot: Ashgate.

Buck-Morss, Susan 2000. 'Hegel and Haiti', *Critical Inquiry* 26 (4): 821–65.

Burger, Thomas 1976. *Max Weber's Theory of Concept Formation*. Durham, NC: Duke University Press.

Byrd, Jodi A. 2011. *The Transit of Empire: Indigenous Critiques of Colonialism*. Minneapolis: University of Minnesota Press.

Caldecott, A. 1911. 'Inter-Racial Problems', *Sociological Review* a4 (4): 314–18.

Campbell, David 1996. *The Failure of Marxism: The Concept of Inversion in Marx's Critique of Capitalism*. Aldershot: Dartmouth Publishing Company.

Canny, Nicholas P. 1976. *The Elizabethan Conquest of Ireland: A Pattern Established, 1565–76*. Hassocks: Harvester Press.

Canny, Nicholas P. 2001. *Making Ireland British, 1580–1650*. Oxford: Oxford University Press.

Carmichael, Stokely and Charles V. Hamilton 1967. *Black Power: The Politics of Liberation in America*. Middlesex: Penguin Books.

Cattelino, Jessica 2018. 'From Locke to Slots: Money and the Politics of Indigeneity', *Comparative Studies in Society and History* 60 (2): 274–307.

Césaire, Aimé 2000 [1955]. *Discourse on Colonialism*, translated by Joan Pinkham. New York: Monthly Review Press.

Chakrabarty, Dipesh 2000. *Provincializing Europe: Postcolonial Thought and Historical Difference*. Princeton, NJ: Princeton University Press.

Chandra, Rajshree 2013. 'Tocqueville for Our Times', *Economic and Political Weekly* 48 (10): 32–5.

Clark, Terry N. 1968. 'Émile Durkheim and the Institutionalization of Sociology in the French University System', *European Journal of Sociology* 9 (1): 36–71.

Clemens, Elisabeth S. 2016. *What is Political Sociology?* Cambridge: Polity.

Cohn, Bernard and Nicholas Dirks 1988. 'Beyond the Fringe: The Nation-State, Colonialism, and the Technologies of Power', *Journal of Historical Sociology* 1 (2): 224–9.

Cohen, G. A. 1978. *Karl Marx's Theory of History: A Defence*. Oxford: Oxford University Press.

Collins, Randall 1997. 'A Sociological Guilt Trip: Comment on Connell', *American Journal of Sociology* 102 (6): 1558–64.

Colwell, James L. 1967. '"The Calamities Which They Apprehend": Tocqueville on Race in America', *Western Humanities Review* 21: 93–100.

Connell, R. W. 1997. 'Why Is Classical Theory Classical?' *American Journal of Sociology* 102 (6): 1511–57.

Conrad, Sebastian 2013. 'Rethinking German Colonialism in a Global Age', *Journal of Imperial and Commonwealth History* 41 (4): 543–66.

Cooper, Anna Julia 1892. *A Voice from the South*. Xenia: Aldine Printing Company.

Cooper, Anna Julia 2006 [1925]. *Slavery and the French and Haitian Revolutionists: L'attitude de la France à l'égard de l'esclavage pendant la révolution*, edited and translated by Frances Richardson Keller. New York: Rowman & Littlefield.

Cormack, Patricia 1996. 'The Paradox of Durkheim's Manifesto: Reconsidering "The Rules of Sociological Method"', *Theory and Society* 25 (1): 85–104.

Cotesta, Vittorio 2017. 'Classical Sociology and the First World War: Weber, Durkheim, Simmel and Scheler in the Trenches', *History* 102 (351): 432–49.

Cox, Oliver Cromwell 1959 [1948]. *Caste, Class and Race: A Study in Social Dynamics*. New York: Monthly Review Press.

Deegan, Mary Jo 1988. 'W. E. B. Du Bois and the Women of Hull-House, 1895–1899', *American Sociologist* 19 (4): 301–11.

Delaney, Enda 2000. *Demography, State and Society: Irish Migration to Britain, 1921–1971*. Liverpool: Liverpool University Press.

Delnore, Allyson Jaye 2015. "Empire by Example? Deportees in France and Algeria and the Re-Making of a Modern Empire, 1846–1854." *French Politics, Culture & Society* 33 (1): 33–54.

Drescher, Seymour 1964. *Tocqueville and England*. Cambridge, MA: Harvard University Press.

Dross, Fritz 2008. 'The Price of Unification: The Emergence of Health and Welfare in Pre-Bismarckian Prussia', in Laurinda Abreua and Pierre Bourdelais (eds), *The Price of Life: Welfare Systems, Social Nets and Economic Growth*. Lisbon: Colibri.

Du Bois, W. E. B. 1910. 'Reconstruction and Its Benefits', *American Historical Review* 15 (4): 781–99.

Du Bois, W. E. B. 1911. 'The Economics of Negro Emancipation in the United States', *Sociological Review* a4 (4): 303–13.

Du Bois, W. E. B. 1935. *Black Reconstruction: An Essay toward a History of the Part which Black Folk Played in the Attempt to Reconstruct Democracy in America, 1860–1880*. Philadelphia, PA: Albert Saifer Publisher.

Du Bois, W. E. B. 1942. '*New Haven Negroes: A Social History* by Robert Austin Warner', *American Historical Review* 47 (2): 376–7.

Du Bois, W. E. B. 1944. 'Prospect of a World Without Race Conflict', *American Journal of Sociology* 49 (5): 450–6.

Du Bois, W. E. B. 1967 [1899]. *The Philadelphia Negro: A Social Study*. New York: Schocken Books.

Du Bois, W. E. B. 1995 [1911]. 'The First Universal Races Congress', in David Levering Lewis (ed.), *W. E. B. Du Bois: A Reader*. New York: Henry Holt.

Du Bois, W. E. B. 1995 [1929]. 'The American Federation of Labor and the Negro', in David Levering Lewis (ed.), *W. E. B. Du Bois: A Reader*. New York: Henry Holt.

Du Bois, W. E. B. 1995 [1940]. 'Propaganda and World War', in David Levering Lewis (ed.), *W. E. B. Du Bois: A Reader*. New York: Henry Holt.

Du Bois, W. E. B. 1995 [1957]. 'Gandhi and the American Negroes', in David Levering Lewis (ed.), *W. E. B. Du Bois: A Reader*. New York: Henry Holt.

Du Bois, W. E. B. 1997 [1903]. *The Souls of Black Folk*, edited by David W. Blight and Robert Gooding-Williams, with Introduction. Boston, MA: Bedford Books.

Du Bois, W. E. B. 2007 [1940]. *Dusk of Dawn: An Essay Toward an Autobiography of a Race Concept*, with Introduction by K. Anthony Appiah. Oxford: Oxford University Press.

Du Bois, W. E. B. 2007 [1945]. *Color and Democracy*, with Introduction by Gerald Horne. Oxford: Oxford University Press.

Dunbar-Ortiz, Roxanne 2014. *An Indigenous Peoples' History of the United States*. Boston, MA: Beacon Press.

Durkheim, Émile 1952 [1897]. *Suicide: A Study in Sociology*, translated by John A. Spaulding and George Simpson. London: Routledge & Kegan Paul.

Durkheim, Émile 1957 [1890–1900]. *Professional Ethics and Civic Morals*, translated by Cornelia Brookfield. London: Routledge.

Durkheim, Emile 1959 [1928]. *Socialism and Saint-Simon*, translated by Charlotte Sattler, edited by Alvin W. Gouldner, with Introduction. London: Routledge & Kegan Paul.

Durkheim, Émile 1961 [1902–3]. *Moral Education: A Study in the Theory and Application of the Sociology of Education*, translated by Everett K. Wilson and Herman Schnurer. New York: Free Press.

Durkheim, Émile 1969 [1898]. 'Individualism and the Intellectuals', in Steven Lukes 'Durkheim's "Individualism and the Intellectuals"', *Political Studies* 17 (1): 14–30.

Durkheim, Émile 1974 [1906]. 'The Determination of Moral Facts', in Émile Durkheim, *Sociology and Philosophy*, translated by D. F. Pocock. New York: Free Press.

Durkheim, Émile 1983 [1955]. *Pragmatism and Sociology*, translated by J. C. Whitehouse. Cambridge: Cambridge University Press.

Durkheim, Émile 1995 [1912]. *The Elementary Forms of Religious Life*, translated by Karen E. Fields. New York: Free Press.

Durkheim, Émile 2013 [1893, 1902]. *The Division of Labour in Society*, translated by W. D. Halls, edited by Steven Lukes (2nd edn). London: Palgrave Macmillan.

Durkheim, Émile 2013 [1895]. *The Rules of Sociological Method, and Selected Texts on Sociology and Its Method*, translated by W. D. Halls, edited by Steven Lukes (2nd edn). New York: Free Press.

Edwards, Jason 2007. *The Radical Attitude and Modern Political Theory*. Basingstoke: Palgrave.

Eisenstadt, Shmuel N. 1963. *The Political Systems of Empires: The Rise and Fall of the Historical Bureaucratic Societies*. London: Free Press of Glencoe.

Eisenstadt, Shmuel N. 2000. 'Multiple Modernities', *Daedalus* 129 (1): 1–29.

Ekirch, A. Roger 1987. *Bound for America: The Transportation of British Convicts to the Colonies, 1718–1775*. Oxford: Clarendon.

Ellison, Ralph 1973 [1944]. 'An American Dilemma: A Review', in Joyce A. Ladner (ed.), *The Death of White Sociology*. New York: Vintage Books.

Elster, Jon 1985. *Making Sense of Marx*. Cambridge: Cambridge University Press.

Engels, Frederick 1989 [1880]. 'Socialism: Utopian and Scientific', in *Karl Marx and Frederick Engels Collected Works*, vol. 24. London: Lawrence & Wishart.

Esping-Andersen, Gösta 1991. *The Three Worlds of Welfare Capitalism*. London: Polity.

Evans, Kasey 2012. 'Temperate Revenge: Religion, Profit, and Retaliation in 1622 Jamestown', *Texas Studies in Literature and Language* 54 (1): 155–88.

Evans, Martin and John Philips 2007. *Algeria: Anger of the Dispossessed*. New Haven, CT: Yale University Press.

Farr, James 1986. 'So Vile and Miserable an Estate: The Problem of Slavery in Locke's Political Thought', *Political Theory* 14 (2): 263–89.

Federici, Silvia 2004. *Caliban and the Witch: Women, the Body and Primitive Accumulation*. Brooklyn: Automedia.

Fedorowich, Kent and Andrew S. Thompson 2013. 'Mapping the Contours of the British World: Empire, Migration and Identity', in Kent Fedorowich and Andrew S. Thompson (eds), *Empire, Migration and Identity in the British World*. Manchester: Manchester University Press.

Ferguson, Adam 1966 [1767]. *An Essay on the History of Civil Society*, edited by Duncan Forbes, with Introduction. Edinburgh: Edinburgh University Press.

Fields, Karen E. 1995. 'Translator's Introduction: Religion as an Eminently Social Thing', in Émile Durkheim, *The Elementary Forms of Religious Life* [1912], translated by Karen E. Fields. New York: Free Press.

Fields, Karen E. 2012. 'Individuality and the Intellectuals: An Imaginary Conversation between Emile Durkheim and W. E. B. Du Bois', in Karen E Fields and Barbara J. Fields, *Racecraft: The Soul of Inequality in American Life*. London: Verso.

Fischer, Sibylle 2004. *Modernity Disavowed: Haiti and the Cultures of Slavery in the Age of Revolution*. Durham, NC: Duke University Press.

Fitzhugh, George 1854. *Sociology for the South, or, The Failure of Free Society*. Richmond: A. Morris.

Foner, Eric 2005. *Forever Free: The Story of Emancipation and Reconstruction*. New York: Vintage Books.

Fournier, Marcel 2013. *Émile Durkheim: A Biography*, translated by David Macey. Cambridge: Polity.

Fox, Christopher 1995. 'Introduction: How to Prepare a Noble Savage: The Spectacle of Human Science', in Christopher Fox, Roy Porter and Robert Wokler (eds), *Inventing Human Science: Eighteenth Century Domains*. Berkeley: University of California Press.

Franklin, John Hope 1980. 'Mirror for Americans: A Century of Reconstruction History', *American Historical Review* 85 (1): 1–14.

Fröbel, Folker, Jürgen Heinrichs, and Otto Kreye 1980. *The New International*

Division of Labour: Structural Unemployment in Industrialised Countries and Industrialisation in Developing Countries. Cambridge: Cambridge University Press.

Frymer, Paul 2017. *Building an American Empire: The Era of Territorial and Political Expansion.* Princeton, NJ: Princeton University Press.

Furniss, Edgar S. 1965 [1923]. *The Position of the Laborer in a System of Nationalism: A Study in the Labor Theory of the Later English Mercantilists.* New York: Augustus M. Kelley.

Gane, Mike 1999. *On Durkheim's Rules of Sociological Method.* London: Routledge.

Geggus, David P. 2002. *Haitian Revolutionary Studies.* Bloomington: Indiana University Press.

Gelderblom, Oscar, Abe de Jong, and Joost Jonker 2013. 'The Formative Years of the Modern Corporation: The Dutch East India Company VOC, 1602–1623', *The Journal of Economic History* 73 (4): 1050–76.

Gerbner, Katherine 2019. *Christian Slavery: Conversion and Race in the Protestant Atlantic World.* Philadelphia: University of Pennsylvania Press.

Gerth, Hans H. and C. Wright Mills 1948 [1918]. *From Max Weber: Essays in Sociology.* London: Routledge & Kegan Paul.

Giddens, Anthony 1971. *Capitalism and Modern Social Theory: An Analysis of the Writings of Marx, Durkheim and Max Weber.* Cambridge: Cambridge University Press.

Giddens, Anthony 1976. *New Rules of Sociological Method.* London: Hutchinson.

Giddens, Anthony 1984. *The Constitution of Society.* Cambridge: Polity.

Gilroy, Paul 1993. *The Black Atlantic: Modernity and Double Consciousness.* London: Verso.

Gines, Kathryn 2014. *Hannah Arendt and the Negro Question.* Bloomington: Indiana University Press.

Greer, Allan 2012. 'Commons and Enclosure in the Colonization of North America', *American Historical Review* 117 (2): 365–86.

Habermas, Jürgen 1984. *The Theory of Communicative Action*, vol. 1: *Reason and the Rationalization of Society*, translated by Thomas McCarthy. London: Heinemann.

Habermas, Jürgen 1987. *The Theory of Communicative Action*, vol. 2: *The Critique of Functionalist Reason*, translated by Thomas McCarthy. Cambridge: Polity.

Habermas, Jürgen 1996. 'Modernity: An Unfinished Project', in M. P. d'Entrèves and Seyla Benhabib (eds), *Habermas and the Unfinished Project of Modernity: Critical Essays on The Philosophical Discourse of Modernity.* Cambridge: Polity.

Häämäläinen, Pekka 2008. *The Comanche Empire.* New Haven, CT: Yale University Press.

Hahn, Steven 2016. *A Nation without Borders: The United States and its World in an Age of Civil Wars, 1830–1910.* New York: Penguin.

Hall, Stuart 1992. 'The West and the Rest: Discourse and Power', in Stuart Hall and Bram Gieben (eds), *Formations of Modernity*. Cambridge: Polity and Open University.

Hampsher-Monk, Iain 1992. *A History of Modern Political Thought: Major Political Thinkers from Hobbes to Marx*. Oxford: Blackwell Publishers.

Hansen, Peo 2002. 'European Integration, European Identity and the Colonial Connection', *European Journal of Social Theory* 5 (4): 483–98.

Hansen, Peo and Stefan Jonsson 2014. *Eurafrica: The Untold History of European Integration and Colonialism*. London: Bloomsbury Academic.

Harlan, Louis 1988. 'Booker T Washington in Biographical Perspective', in Raymond Smock (ed.), *Booker T. Washington in Perspective: Essays of Louis R. Harlan*. Mississippi: University Press of Mississippi.

Harris, Abram 1939. 'Pure Capitalism and the Disappearance of the Middle Class', *Journal of Political Economy* 47 (3): 328–56.

Hart, David 2018. 'Herbert Spencer, "The Militant Type of Society"', in David M. Hart, Gary Chartier, Ross Miller Kenyon, and Roderick T. Long (eds), *Social Class and State Power: Exploring an Alternative Radical Tradition*. Basingstoke: Palgrave.

Hartshorne, Edward Y. 1937. *The German Universities and National Socialism*. Cambridge, MA: Harvard University Press.

Hartsock, Nancy C. M. 1983. 'The Feminist Standpoint: Developing the Ground for a Specifically Feminist Historical Materialism', in Sandra Harding and Merrill B. Hintikka (eds), *Discovering Reality*. Dordrecht: Springer.

Hegel, G. W. F. 1952 [1821]. *Hegel's Philosophy of Right*, translated by T. M. Knox, with Commentary. Oxford: Oxford University Press.

Hegel, G. W. F. 1975 [1830]. *Lectures on the Philosophy of World History. Introduction: Reason in History*, translated by H. B. Nisbet. Cambridge: Cambridge University Press.

Heilbron, Johan 1995. *The Rise of Social Theory*. Cambridge: Polity.

Hirst, Paul 1975. *Durkheim, Bernard and Epistemology*. London: Routledge & Kegan Paul.

Hobbes, Thomas 1991 [1651]. *Leviathan*, edited by Richard Tuck. Cambridge: Cambridge University Press.

Hobsbawm, Eric J. 1962. *The Age of Revolution, 1789–1848*. New York: Signet.

Hobsbawm, Eric J. 1964. 'Introduction', in *Karl Marx Pre-Capitalist Formations*, translated by Jack Cohen, edited by Eric J. Hobsbawm. London: Lawrence & Wishart.

Hobsbawm, Eric J. 1977. *The Age of Capital, 1848–1875*. London: Weidenfeld & Nicolson.

Holmwood, John 1996. *Founding Sociology? Talcott Parsons and the Idea of General Theory*. Harlow: Longman.

Holmwood, John 2011. 'Pragmatism and the Prospects of Sociological Theory', *Journal of Classical Sociology* 11 (1): 15–30.

Holmwood, John 2016. 'Moral Economy versus Political Economy: Provincializing Polanyi', in C. Karner and B. Weicht (eds), *The Commonalities of Global Crises: Markets, Communities and Nostalgia*. London: Palgrave Macmillan.

Holmwood, John forthcoming. 'The Problem of Race in Parsons' Account of the Citizenship Complex', in Javier Trevino and Helmut Staubmann (eds), *Routledge International Handbook of Talcott Parsons Studies*. London: Routledge.

Holmwood, John and Alexander Stewart 1991. *Explanation and Social Theory*. London: Macmillan.

Hume, David 1898 [1752]. *Essays, Moral, Political, and Literary: An Enquiry Concerning the Principles of Morals*, edited by T. H. Green and T. H. Grose. London: Longmans, Green.

Itzigsohn, José and Karida L. Brown 2020. *The Sociology of W. E. B. du Bois: Racialized Modernity and the Global Color Line*. New York: NYU Press.

James, C. L. R. 1989 [1963, 1938]. *The Black Jacobins: Toussaint L'Ouverture and the San Domingo Revolution* (2nd edn). New York: Vintage Books.

Jardin, André 1988. *Tocqueville, A Biography*, translated by Lydia Davis and Robin Hemenway. Baltimore, MD: Johns Hopkins University Press.

Jennings, Francis 1971. 'Virgin Land and Savage People', *American Quarterly* 23 (4): 519–41.

Joas, Hans and Wolfgang Knöbl 2013. *War in Social Thought: Hobbes to the Present*, translated by Alex Skinner. Princeton, NJ: Princeton University Press.

Johnson, Kimberley S. 2008. 'Jim Crow Reform and the South', in Joseph Lowndes, Julie Novkov, and Dorian T. Warren (eds), *Race and American Political Development*. New York: Routledge.

Jones, Robert Alun 1999. *The Development of Durkheim's Social Realism*. Cambridge: Cambridge University Press.

Käsler, Dirk 1988. *Max Weber: An Introduction to his Life and Work*. Cambridge: Polity.

Kalberg, Stephen 1994. *Max Weber's Comparative–Historical Sociology*. Cambridge: Polity.

Katznelson, Ira 1999. 'Du Bois's Century', *Social Science History* 23 (4): 459–74.

Keita, Maghan 2002. 'Africa and the Construction of a Grand Narrative in World History', in Eckhardt Fuchs and Benedikt Stuchtey (eds), *Across Cultural Borders: Historiography in Global Perspective*. New York: Rowman & Littlefield.

Kelsey, Sean 2004. 'Politics and Procedure in the Trial of Charles I', *Law and History Review* 22 (1): 1–25.

Kermode, Frank 1985. *Forms of Attention*. Chicago, IL: University of Chicago Press.

King, Desmond S. 1995. *Separate and Unequal: Black Americans and the US Federal Government*. Oxford: Oxford University Press.

Kohn, Margaret 2005. 'Frederick Douglass's Master–Slave Dialectic', *Journal of Politics* 67 (2): 497–514.

Kojève, Alexander 1969. *Introduction to the Reading of Hegel*, translated by J. H. Nicholls Jr, edited by Allan Bloom. New York: Basic Books.

Kolchin, Peter 1987. *Unfree Labor: American Slavery and Russian Serfdom*. Cambridge, MA: Harvard University Press.

Kurasawa, Fuyuki 2013. 'The Durkheimian School and Colonialism: Exploring the Constitutive Paradox', in George Steinmetz (ed.), *Sociology and Empire: The Imperial Entanglements of a Discipline*. Durham, NC: Duke University Press.

La Capra, Dominick 1972. *Émile Durkheim: Sociologist and Philosopher*. Chicago, IL: University of Chicago Press.

Ladner, Joyce A. (ed.) 1973. *The Death of White Sociology*. New York: Vintage Books.

Lakatos, Imre 1970. 'Falsification and the Methodology of Scientific Research Programmes', in Imre Lakatos and Alan Musgrave (eds), *Criticism and the Growth of Knowledge*. Cambridge: Cambridge University Press.

Lannoy, Pierre 2004. 'When Robert E. Park Was (Re)Writing "The City": Biography, the Social Survey, and the Science of Sociology', *American Sociologist* 35 (1): 34–62.

Lebovics, Herman 1986. 'The Uses of America in Locke's Second Treatise of Government', *Journal of the History of Ideas* 47 (4): 567–81.

Lehmann, Jennifer M. 1993. *Deconstructing Durkheim: A Post-Post-Structuralist Critique*. London: Routledge.

Lehmann, Jennifer M. 1994. *Durkheim and Women*. Lincoln: University of Nebraska Press.

Lemert, Charles 1994. 'A Classic from the Other Side of the Veil: Du Bois's Souls of Black Folk', *Sociological Quarterly* 35 (3): 383–96.

Lengermann, Patricia and Gillian Niebrugge 2007. 'Thrice Told: Narratives of Sociology's Relation to Social Work', in Craig Calhoun (ed.), *Sociology in America: A History*. Chicago, IL: University of Chicago Press.

Lévy-Bruhl, Lucien 1910 [1985]. *How Natives Think*. Princeton, NJ: Princeton University Press.

Lewis, David Levering 1993. *W. E. B. Du Bois: Biography of a Race, 1868–1919*. New York: Henry Holt.

Lewis, David Levering 2000. *W. E. B. Du Bois: The Fight for Equality and the American Century, 1919–1963*. New York: Henry Holt.

Lewis, Simon L. and Mark A. Maslin 2015. 'Perspective: Defining the Anthropocene', *Nature* 519: 171–80.

Lipset, Seymour Martin 1963. *The First New Nation: The United States in Historical and Comparative Perspective*. New York: Basic Books.

Locke, John 1960 [1698]. *Two Treatises of Government*, edited by Peter

Laslett, with Introduction and Commentary. Cambridge: Cambridge University Press.

Lubasz, Heinz 1976. 'Marx's Initial Problematic: The Problem of Poverty', *Political Studies* 24 (1): 24–42.

Lukács, Georg 1968. 'The Standpoint of the Proletariat', in Georg Lukács, *History and Class Consciousness: Studies in Marxist Dialectics*. London: Merlin Press.

Lukes, Steven 1973. *Émile Durkheim: His Life and Work: A Historical and Critical Study*. London: Allen Lane.

Macaulay, Thomas Babington 1848. *The History of England from the Accession of James II*, vol. 4. Philadelphia, PA: Porter & Coates.

McAuley, Christopher A. 2019. *The Spirit vs the Souls: Max Weber, W. E. B. Du Bois, and the Politics of Scholarship*. Notre Dame, IN: University of Notre Dame Press.

McLellan, David 1973. *Karl Marx: His Life and Thought*. London: Macmillan.

Macpherson, C. B. 1962. *The Political Theory of Possessive Individualism: Hobbes to Locke*. Oxford: Oxford University Press.

Malthus, T. R. 2018 [1803]. *An Essay on the Principle of Population*, edited by Shannon C. Stimson, with Introduction. New Haven, CT: Yale University Press.

Mamdani, Mahmood 2019. 'Decolonising Universities', in Jonathan D. Jansen and Grant Parker (eds), *Decolonisation in Universities: The Politics of Knowledge*. Johannesburg: Wits University Press.

Mandel, Ernest 1971. *Formation of the Economic Thought of Karl Marx, 1843 to Capital*. New York: Monthly Review Press.

Marshall, T. H. 1950. *Citizenship and Social Class and Other Essays*. Cambridge: Cambridge University Press.

Marx, Karl 1973 [1852]. 'The Eighteenth Brumaire', in Karl Marx, *Political Writings*, vol. 2: *Surveys from Exile*, edited by David Fernbach, with Introduction. Harmondsworth: Penguin.

Marx, Karl 1973 [1853]. 'The Future Results of British Rule in India', in Karl Marx and Frederick Engels, *Collected Works*, vol. 12. London: Lawrence & Wishart.

Marx, Karl 1973 [1857/8]. *Grundrisse: Foundations of the Critique of Political Economy (Rough Draft)*, translated with Martin Nicolaus, with Foreword. Harmondsworth: Penguin.

Marx, Karl 1974 [1865]. 'Letter to Schweitzer', in Karl Marx, *Political Writings*, vol. 3: *The First International and After*, edited by David Fernbach, with Introduction. Harmondsworth: Penguin.

Marx, Karl 1974 [1875]. 'Critique of the Gotha Programme', in Karl Marx, *Political Writings*, vol. 3: *The First International and After*, edited by David Fernbach, with Introduction. Harmondsworth: Penguin.

Marx Karl 1975 [1842a]. 'On the Jewish Question', in Karl Marx, *Early Writings*, translated by Rodney Livingstone and Gregory Benton. Harmondsworth: Penguin.

Marx, Karl 1975 [1842b]. 'Proceedings of the Sixth Rhine Province Assembly: Third Article: Debates on the Law on Thefts of Wood', in Karl Marx and Frederick Engels, *Collected Works*, vol. 1. London: Lawrence & Wishart.

Marx, Karl 1975 [1843a]. 'Critique of Hegel's Doctrine of the State', in Karl Marx, *Early Writings*, translated by Rodney Livingstone and Gregory Benton. Harmondsworth: Penguin.

Marx, Karl 1975 [1843b]. 'Justification of the Correspondent from the Mosel', in Karl Marx and Frederick Engels, *Collected Works*, vol. 1. London: Lawrence & Wishart.

Marx, Karl 1975 [1844]. 'Economic and Philosophical Manuscripts', in Karl Marx, *Early Writings*, translated by Rodney Livingstone and Gregory Benton. Harmondsworth: Penguin.

Marx, Karl 1975 [1845]. 'Concerning Feuerbach', in Karl Marx, *Early Writings*, translated by Rodney Livingstone and Gregory Benton. London: Penguin.

Marx, Karl 1976 [1848]. *The German Ideology*, in Karl Marx and Frederick Engels, *Collected Works*, vol. 6. London: Lawrence & Wishart.

Marx, Karl 1976 [1867]. *Capital: A Critique of Political Economy*, vol. 1. Harmondsworth: Penguin.

Marx, Karl 1981 [1894]. *Capital*, vol. 3, translated by David Fernbach. London: Penguin.

Marx, Karl 1983 [1852]. 'Marx to Joseph Weydemeyer, 5th March', in Karl Marx and Frederick Engels, *Collected Works*, vol. 39. London: Lawrence & Wishart.

Marx, Karl and Friedrich Engels 1956 [1844]. *The Holy Family, or Critique of Critical Critique*. Moscow: Foreign Languages Publishing House.

Marx, Karl and Friedrich Engels 1973 [1850]. 'Review: May–October 1850 (from *Neue Rheinische Zeitung Revue*)', in Karl Marx, *Political Writings*, vol. 1: *The Revolutions of 1848*, edited by David Fernbach, with Introduction. Harmondsworth: Penguin.

Marx, Karl and Friedrich Engels 1976 [1848]. 'The Communist Manifesto', in Karl Marx, *Political Writings*, vol. 1: *The Revolutions of 1848*, edited by David Fernbach, with Introduction. Harmondsworth: Penguin.

Marx, Karl and Friedrich Engels 2016. *The Civil War in the United States*, edited by Andrew Zimmerman, with Introduction. New York: International Publishers.

Mayblin, Lucy 2017. *Asylum after Empire: Colonial Legacies in the Politics of Asylum Seeking*. London: Rowman & Littlefield.

Mead, George Herbert 1899. 'The Working Hypothesis in Social Reform', *American Journal of Sociology* 5 (3): 367–71.

Mead, George Herbert 1934. *Mind, Self and Society: From the Standpoint of a Social Behaviourist*. Chicago, IL: University of Chicago Press.

Meek, Ronald 1976. *Social Science and the Ignoble Savage*. Cambridge: Cambridge University Press.

Meer, Nasar 2019. 'W. E. B. Du Bois, Double Consciousness and the "Spirit" of Recognition', *Sociological Review* 67 (1): 47–62.

Mehta, Uday Singh 1999. *Liberalism and Empire: A Study in Nineteenth Century Liberal Thought*. Chicago, IL: University of Chicago Press.

Memmi, Albert 1965 [1957]. *The Coloniser and the Colonised*, translated by Howard Greenfeld. New York: Orion Press.

Merton, Robert 1968 [1949]. 'Social Structure and Anomie', in Robert Merton, *Social Theory and Social Structure*. New York: The Free Press.

Miège, J. L. 1993. 'Migration and Decolonization', *European Review* 1 (1): 81–6.

Mignolo, Walter D. 2007. 'Delinking: The Rhetoric of Modernity, the Logic of Coloniality and the Grammar of De-coloniality', *Cultural Studies* 21 (2): 449–514.

Millar, John 1990 [1779]. *The Origin of the Distinction of Ranks*. Bristol: Thoemmes Antiquarian Books.

Mills, Charles 1997. *The Racial Contract*. Ithaca, NY: Duke University Press.

Mommsen, Wolfgang J. 1974. *The Age of Bureaucracy: Perspectives on the Political Sociology of Max Weber*. Oxford: Basil Blackwell.

Mommsen, Wolfgang J. 1984 [1959]. *Max Weber and German Politics 1890–1920*, translated by Michael S. Steinberg. Chicago, IL: University of Chicago Press.

Montesquieu, Baron de 1965 [1748]. *The Spirit of the Laws*, vols 1–2, translated by Thomas Nugent. New York: Hafner Publishing Company.

Montesquieu, Baron de 2008 [1721]. *Persian Letters*, translated by Margaret Mauldon and edited by Andrew Kahn. Oxford: Oxford University Press.

Morris, Aldon 2015. *A Scholar Denied: W. E. B. Du Bois and the Birth of Modern Sociology*. Oakland: University of California Press.

Morrison, Toni 1989. 'Unspeakable Things Unspoken: The Afro-American Presence in American Literature', *Michigan Quarterly Review* 28 (1): 1–34.

Munholland, Kim 1978. 'The French Army and the Imperial Frontier in Tonkin, 1885–1897', *Proceedings of the Meeting of the French Colonial Historical Society* 3: 82–107.

Myrdal, Gunnar 1962 [1944]. *An American Dilemma: The Negro Problem and Modern Democracy*. New York: Harper & Brothers.

Ndlovu-Gatsheni, Sabelo J. 2015. 'Decoloniality as the Future of Africa', *History Compass* 13 (10): 485–96.

Nelson, Lynn Hankinson 1990. *Who Knows: From Quine to Feminist Empiricism*. Philadelphia, PA: Temple University Press.

Nesbitt, Nick 2013. *Caribbean Critique: Antillean Critical Theory from Toussaint to Glissant*. Liverpool: Liverpool University Press.

Nichols, Robert 2018. 'Theft Is Property! The Recursive Logic of Dispossession', *Political Theory* 46 (1): 3–28.

Nielsen, Jens Kaalhauge 1991. 'The Political Orientation of Talcott Parsons:

The Second World War and Its Aftermath', in Roland Robertson and Bryan S. Turner (eds), *Talcott Parsons: Theorist of Modernity*. London: Sage.

Nisbet, Robert A. 1966. *The Sociological Tradition*. New York: Basic Books.

Noakes, Jeremy 1993. 'The Ivory Tower under Siege: German Universities in the Third Reich', *Journal of European Studies* 23 (4): 371–407.

Nzongola-Ntalaja, Georges 2002. The Congo from Leopold to Kabila: A People's History. London: Zed Books.

Oakeshott, Michael 1975. *Hobbes on Civil Association*. Oxford: Basil Blackwell.

Obama, Barack 2009. 'A More Perfect Union', in T. Denean Sharpley-Whiting (ed.), *The Speech: Race and Barack Obama's 'A More Perfect Union'*. New York: Bloomsbury.

Outhwaite, William 1987. *New Philosophies of Social Science: Realism, Hermeneutics and Critical Theory*. London: Palgrave.

Parkin, Frank 1992. *Durkheim*. Oxford: Oxford University Press.

Parsons, Talcott 1937. *The Structure of Social Action: A Study in Social Theory with Special Reference to a Group of Recent European Writers*. New York: Free Press of Glencoe.

Parsons, Talcott 1951. *The Social System*. London: Routledge & Kegan Paul.

Parsons, Talcott 1965. 'Full Citizenship for the Negro American? A Sociological Problem', *Daedalus* 94 (4): 1009–54.

Parsons, Talcott 1971. *The System of Modern Societies*. Englewood Cliffs, NJ: Prentice Hall.

Pateman, Carole 1988. *The Sexual Contract*. Cambridge: Polity.

Pearce, Frank 1989. *The Radical Durkheim*. London: Routledge.

Pedersen, Jean Elisabeth 2014. 'Alsace-Lorraine and Africa: French Discussions of French and German Politics, Culture, and Colonialism in the Deliberations of the Union for Truth, 1905–1913', *Historical Reflections / Réflexions Historiques* 40 (1): 9–28.

Perez-Diaz, Victor 1978. *State, Bureaucracy and Civil Society*. London: Macmillan.

Perrow, Charles 1984. *Normal Accidents: Normal Accidents: Living with High Risk Technologies*. New York: Basic Books.

Peyre, Henri 1960. 'Durkheim: The Man, his Time and his Intellectual Background', in Kurt H. Wolff (ed.), *Émile Durkheim, 1858–1917*. Columbus: Ohio State University Press.

Phillips, Andrew and J. C. Sharman 2020. *Outsourcing Empire: How Company-States made the Modern World*. Princeton, NJ: Princeton University Press.

Pickering, William S. F. 1990. 'The Eternality of the Sacred: Durkheim's Error?', *Archives des sciences sociales des religions* 69: 91–108.

Pitts, Jennifer 2000. 'Empire and Democracy: Tocqueville and the Algeria Question', *Journal of Political Philosophy* 8 (3): 295–318.

Pitts, Jennifer (ed.) 2001. *Writing on Empire and Slavery: Alexis de Tocqueville*, translated and edited by Jennifer Pitts. Baltimore, MD: Johns Hopkins University Press.

Plummer, Brenda Gayle 1988. *Haiti and the Great Powers, 1902–1915*. Baton Rouge: Louisiana State University Press.

Pocock, John G. A. 1977. 'Gibbon's Decline and Fall and the World View of the Late Enlightenment', *Eighteenth-Century Studies* 10 (3): 287–303.

Poggi, Gianfranco 1972. *Images of Society: Essays on the Sociological Theories of Tocqueville, Marx and Durkheim*. Stanford, CA: Stanford University Press.

Poggi, Gianfranco 1978. *The Development of the Modern State: A Sociological Introduction*. Stanford, CA: Stanford University Press.

Poggi, Gianfranco 1985. *Calvinism and the Capitalist Spirit: Max Weber's Protestant Ethic*. London: Macmillan.

Pope, Whitney 1976. *Durkheim's 'Suicide': A Classic Analyzed*. Chicago, IL: Chicago University Press.

Pradella, Lucia 2013. 'Imperialism and Capitalist Development in Marx's *Capital*', *Historical Materialism* 21 (2): 117–47.

Quijano, Aníbal 2007. 'Coloniality and Modernity/Rationality', *Cultural Studies* 21 (2): 168–78.

Quinn, David Beers 1966. *The Elizabethans and the Irish*. Ithaca: Cornell University Press.

Rabaka, Reiland 2010. *Against Epistemic Apartheid: W. E. B. Du Bois and the Disciplinary Decadence of Sociology*. New York: Lexington Books.

Radkau, Joachim 2011. *Max Weber: A Biography*, translated by Patrick Camiller. Cambridge: Polity.

Reed Jr, Adolph L. 1997. *W. E. B. Du Bois and American Political Thought: Fabianism and the Color Line*. Oxford: Oxford University Press.

Richter, Melvin 1963. 'Tocqueville on Algeria', *Review of Politics* 25 (3): 362–98.

Robbins, Lionel 1939. 'The Economic Basis of Class Conflict', in Lionel Robbins, *The Economic Basis of Class Conflict and Other Essays in Political Economy*. London: Macmillan.

Robertson, William 1818 [1777]. *The History of America*, vol. 2. Edinburgh: Peter Hill.

Robinson, Cedric 1983. *Black Marxism: The Making of the Black Radical Tradition*. London: Zed Books.

Rose, Gillian 1981. *Hegel: Contra Sociology*. London: Athlone Press.

Rozental, Alek A. 1956. 'The Enclosure Movement in France', *American Journal of Economics and Sociology* 16 (1): 55–71.

Saada, Emmanuelle 2011. 'The Republic and the Indigènes', in Edward Berenson, Vincent Duclert, and Christophe Prochasson (eds), *The French Republic: History, Values, Debates*. Cornell: Cornell University Press.

Sahay, Arun 1972. *Sociological Analysis*. London: Routledge.

Said, Edward W. 1995 [1978]. *Orientalism: Western Conceptions of the Orient*. London: Penguin.

Saint-Arnaud, Pierre 2009. *African American Pioneers of Sociology: A Critical History*, translated by Peter Feldstein. Toronto: University of Toronto Press.

Sala-Molins, Louis 2006. *Dark Side of the Light: Slavery and the French Enlightenment*, translated by John Conteh-Morgan, with Introduction. Minneapolis: University of Minnesota Press.

Scaff, Lawrence A. 1992. *Fleeing the Iron Cage: Culture, Politics, and Modernity in the Thought of Max Weber*. Berkeley: University of California Press.

Scaff, Lawrence A. 2011. *Max Weber in America*. Princeton, NJ: Princeton University Press.

Schutz, Alfred 1972 [1932]. *The Phenomenology of the Social World*. Evanston, IL: Northwestern University Press.

Seidman, Steven 1983. *Liberalism and the Origins of European Social Theory*. Berkeley: University of California Press.

Seidman, Steven 1996. 'Empire and Knowledge: More Troubles, New Opportunities for Sociology', *Contemporary Sociology* 25 (3): 313–16.

Sessions, Jennifer E. 2015. 'Colonizing Revolutionary Politics: Algeria and the French Revolution of 1848', *French Politics, Culture & Society* 33 (1): 75–100.

Sheehan, James J. 1981. 'What is German History? Reflections on the Role of the Nation in German History and Historiography', *Journal of Modern History* 53 (1): 1–23.

Shilliam, Robbie 2019. *Race and the Undeserving Poor*. Newcastle: Agenda Publishing.

Shilliam, Robbie 2020. 'The Past and Present of Abolition: Reassessing Adam Smith's "Liberal Reward of Labor"', *Review of International Political Economy*. https://doi.org/10.1080/09692290.2020.1741425.

Silver, Allan 1990. 'Friendship in Commercial Society: Eighteenth-Century Social Theory and Modern Sociology', *American Journal of Sociology* 95 (6): 1474–504.

Singh, Nikhil Pal 2004. *Black Is a Country: Race and the Unfinished Struggle for Democracy*. Cambridge, MA: Harvard University Press.

Smith, Adam 1970 [1776]. *The Wealth of Nations: Books I–III*, edited by Andrew Skinner, with Introduction and Commentary. London: Penguin.

Smith, Christi M. 2016. *Reparation and Reconciliation: The Rise and Fall of Integrated Higher Education*. Chapel Hill: University of North Carolina Press.

Smith, Rogers M. 1993. 'Beyond Tocqueville, Myrdal, and Hartz: The Multiple Traditions in America', *American Political Science Review* 87 (3): 549–66.

Smith, Rogers M. and Desmond King 2020. 'White Protectionism in America', *Perspectives on* Politics. https://doi.org/10.1017/S1537592720001152.

Smith, Woodruff D. 1980. 'Friedrich Ratzel and the Origins of Lebensraum', *German Studies Review* 3 (1): 51–68.

Smithers, Gregory D. 2015. *The Cherokee Diaspora: An Indigenous History of Migration, Resettlement, and Identity*. New Haven, CT: Yale University Press.

Spivak, Gayatri Chakravorty 1988. 'Can the Subaltern Speak?', in Cary Nelson and Lawrence Grossberg, *Marxism and the Interpretation of Culture*. Chicago: University of Illinois Press.

Spring, David 1980. 'An Outsider's View: Alexis de Tocqueville on Aristocratic Society and Politics in 19th-Century England', *Albion* 12 (2): 122–31.

Steiner, Philippe 2011. *Durkheim and the Birth of Modern Sociology*, translated by Keith Tribe. Princeton, NJ: Princeton University Press.

Steinmetz, George 2007. *The Devil's Handwriting: Precoloniality and the German Colonial State in Qingdao, Samoa, and Southwest Africa*. Chicago, IL: University of Chicago Press.

Stokes, Curtis 1990. 'Tocqueville and the Problem of Racial Inequality', *Journal of Negro History* 75 (1/2): 1–15.

Stone, Alison 2017. 'Hegel and Colonialism', *Hegel Bulletin* 41 (2): 247–70.

Stone, John and Stephen Mennell 1980. 'Introduction', in *Alexis de Tocqueville on Democracy, Revolution and Society: Selected Writings*, edited by John Stone and Stephen Mennell. Chicago, IL: University of Chicago Press.

Strenski, Ivan 1997. *Durkheim and the Jews of France*. Chicago, IL: University of Chicago Press.

Strenski, Ivan 2006a. 'Durkheim, Hamelin and the "French Hegel"', in Ivan Strenski, *The New Durkheim*, New Brunswick: Rutgers University Press.

Strenski, Ivan 2006b. 'A Durkheimean Text in Turkey: Zia Gökalp Hüseyin Nail Kubali and Muslim Civil Society', in Ivan Strenski, *The New Durkheim*. New Brunswick: Rutgers University Press.

Strong, Robert A. 1987. 'Alexis de Tocqueville and the Abolition of Slavery', *Slavery and Abolition* 8 (2): 204–15.

Tageldin, Shaden M. 2014. 'The Place of Africa, in Theory: Pan-Africanism, Postcolonialism, Beyond', *Journal of Historical Sociology* 26 (3): 302–23.

Tawney, R. H. 1930. 'Foreword', in Max Weber, *The Protestant Ethic and the Spirit of Capitalism* [1904/5]. London: Allen & Unwin.

Taylor, Charles 1975. *Hegel*. Cambridge: Cambridge University Press.

Therborn, Göran 1976. *Science, Class and Society: On the Formation of Sociology and Historical Materialism*. London: New Left Books.

Therborn, Göran 1980. *The Ideology of Power, the Power of Ideology*. London: Verso.

Thiara, Ravinder K. 1995. 'Indian Indentured Workers in Mauritius, Natal and Fiji', in Robin Cohen (ed.), *The Cambridge Survey of World Migration*. Cambridge: Cambridge University Press.

Thomas, William I. and Florian Znaniecki 1996 [1918–21]. *The Polish

Peasant in Europe and America, edited by Eli Zaretsky. Chicago, IL: University of Chicago Press.

Thompson, Edgar 2010 [1932]. *The Plantation*, edited by Sidney W. Mintz and George Baca, with Introduction. Columbia: University of South Carolina Press.

Tocqueville, Alexis de 2001 [1841]. 'Essay on Algeria', in Jennifer Pitts (ed.), *Writing on Empire and Slavery: Alexis de Tocqueville*, translated and edited by Jennifer Pitts. Baltimore, MD: Johns Hopkins University Press.

Tocqueville, Alexis de 2001 [1843]. 'The Emancipation of Slaves', in Jennifer Pitts (ed.), *Writing on Empire and Slavery: Alexis de Tocqueville*, translated and edited by Jennifer Pitts. Baltimore, MD: Johns Hopkins University Press.

Tocqueville, Alexis de 2001 [1847]. 'First Report on Algeria', in Jennifer Pitts (ed.), *Writing on Empire and Slavery: Alexis de Tocqueville*, translated and edited by Jennifer Pitts. Baltimore, MD: Johns Hopkins University Press.

Tocqueville, Alexis de 2004 [1835]. *Democracy in America*, translated by Arthur Goldhammer, edited by Olivier Zunz. New York: Penguin Random House.

Tocqueville, Alexis de 2008 [1856]. *The Ancien Régime and the Revolution*, translated and edited by Gerald Bevan. London: Penguin.

Traugott, Mark 1985. *Armies of the Poor: Determinants of Working-Class Participation in the Parisian Insurrection of June 1848*. Princeton, NJ: Princeton University Press.

Treves, Tullio 2015. 'Historical Development of the Law of the Sea', in Donald R. Rothwell, Alex G. Oude Elferink, Karen N. Scott, and Tim Stephens (eds), *The Oxford Handbook of the Law of the Sea*. Oxford: Oxford University Press.

Tully, James 1980. *A Discourse on Property: John Locke and His Adversaries*. Cambridge: Cambridge University Press.

Turgot, Anne Robert Jacques 1973 [1766]. 'Reflections on the Formation and the Distribution of Wealth', in Ronald Meek (ed.), *Turgot on Progress, Sociology and Economics*, translated and edited by Ronald Meek. Cambridge: Cambridge University Press.

Veracini, Lorenzo 2010. *Settler Colonialism: A Theoretical Overview*. Basingstoke: Palgrave.

Vitalis, Robert 2015. *White World Order, Black Power Politics: The Birth of American International Relations*. Cornell: Cornell University Press.

Viveros-Vigoya, Mara 2020. 'The Political Vitality and Vital Politics of Césaire's Discourse on Colonialism: A Reading in Light of Contemporary Racism', *Sociological Review* 68 (3): 476–91.

Wagner, Peter 2001. *Theorizing Modernity: Inescapability and Attainability in Social Theory*. London: Sage.

Wallwork, Eugene 1972. *Durkheim: Morality and Milieu*. Cambridge, MA: Harvard University Press.

Washington, Booker T. 1895. Atlanta Exposition Speech (18 September

1895). Library of Congress' African American Odyssey database. http://memory.loc.gov/ammem/aaohtml/exhibit/aopart6.html#0605.

Washington, Booker T. 1945 [1901]. *Up from Slavery: An Autobiography*. London: Oxford University Press.

Washington, Booker T. 2007 [1909]. *The Story of the Negro: The Rise of the Race from Slavery*. Stroud: Nonsuch Publishing.

Watts-Miller, William 2012. 'Durkheim's Re-imagination of Australia: A Case Study of the Relation between Theory and "Facts"', *L'Année sociologique* 62 (2): 329–49.

Weber, Eugene 1976. *Peasants into Frenchmen: The Modernization of Rural France, 1870–1914*. Stanford, CA: Stanford University Press.

Weber, Marianne 2017 [1926]. *Max Weber: A Biography*, translated and edited by Harry Zohn. London: Routledge.

Weber, Max 1930 [1904/5]. *The Protestant Ethic and the Spirit of Capitalism*, translated by Talcott Parsons. London: Allen & Unwin.

Weber, Max 1947 [1922]. *The Theory of Social and Economic Action*, translated by A. R. Henderson and Talcott Parsons. London: William Hodge.

Weber, Max 1948 [1906]. 'Capitalism and Rural Society in Germany', in Max Weber, *Essays in Sociology*, translated and edited by H. H. Gerth and C. Wright Mills. London: Routledge & Kegan Paul.

Weber, Max 1948 [1918]. 'Science as Vocation', in Max Weber, *Essays in Sociology*, translated and edited by H. H. Gerth and C. Wright Mills. London: Routledge & Kegan Paul.

Weber, Max 1949 [1904]. '"Objectivity" in Social Science and Social Policy', in Max Weber, *The Methodology of the Social Sciences*, translated by E. A. Shils and H. A. Finch. New York: Free Press.

Weber, Max 1968. *Economy and Society: An Outline of Interpretive Sociology*, vols 1–3, edited by Guenther Roth and Calus Wittich. New York: Bedminster Press.

Weber, Max 1975 [1903]. *Roscher and Knies: The Logical Problems of Historical Economics*, translated by Guy Oakes, with Introduction. New York: Free Press.

Weber, Max 1980 [1895]. 'The National State and Economic Policy, Freiburg address', translated by Ben Fowkes, *Economy and Society* 9 (4): 428–49.

Welch, Cheryl B. 2003. 'Colonial Violence and the Rhetoric of Evasion: Tocqueville on Algeria', *Political Theory* 31 (2): 235–64.

Welch, Cheryl B. 2011. 'Out of Africa: Tocqueville's Imperial Voyages', *Review of Middle East Studies* 45 (1): 53–61.

Welchman, Jennifer 1995. 'Locke on Slavery and Inalienable Rights', *Canadian Journal of Philosophy* 25 (1): 67–81.

Wilder, Craig Steven 2013. *Ebony and Ivy: Race, Slavery, and the Troubled History of America's Universities*. New York: Bloomsbury Press.

Williams, Robert R. 1997. *Hegel's Ethics of Recognition*. Berkeley: University of California Press.

Williamson, T. 1987. 'Common Land', in J. Eatwell, M. Milgate, and P. Newman (eds), *The New Palgrave Dictionary of Economics*. Palgrave Macmillan: London.

Wilson, Francille Rusan 2006. *The Segregated Scholars: Black Social Scientists and the Creation of Black Labor Studies, 1890–1950*. Charlottesville: University of Virginia Press.

Wolf, Eric 1997 [1982]. *Europe and the People Without History*. Berkeley: University of California Press.

Wolin, Sheldon S. 1985. 'Postmodern Politics and the Absence of Myth', *Social Research* 52 (2): 217–39.

Wright, Earl, II 2002a. 'The Atlanta Sociological Laboratory, 1896–1924: A Historical Account of the First American School of Sociology', *Western Journal of Black Studies* 26 (3): 165–74.

Wright, Earl, II 2002b. 'Using the Master's Tools: Atlanta University and American Sociology, 1896–1924', *Sociological Spectrum* 22 (1): 15–39.

Wright, Erik Olin 1985. *Classes*. London: Verso.

Zahra, Tara 2016. *The Great Departure: Mass Migration from Eastern Europe and the Making of the Free World*. New York: Norton.

Zimmerman, Andrew 2006. 'Decolonizing Weber', *Postcolonial Studies* 9 (1): 53–79.

Zimmerman, Andrew 2010. *Alabama in Africa: Booker T. Washington, the German Empire, and the Globalization of the New South*. Princeton, NJ: Princeton University Press.

Zubrzycki, Jerzy 1953. 'Emigration from Poland in the Nineteenth and Twentieth Centuries', *Population Studies* 6 (3): 248–72.

Index

Abraham, Gary, 117, 127, 168,
    222n.1
Africa, 125–7, 145, 169, 174, 180,
    220n.14, 225n.22, 228n.1
  Congo, Belgian, 9
  slavery and forced labour, 9, 14,
    17, 35–6, 45, 49, 57, 61, 65–8,
    92, 94, 113, 118, 176, 189,
    193, 204, 221n.15
  see also Berlin Conference
Algeria
  French colonialism and, 53, 55, 78,
    86, 208
  Durkheim on, 144, 164, 169,
    174–5
  Marx on, 86
  Tocqueville on, 56–7, 75, 78–80
American Declaration of
    Independence, 14, 22, 52–3,
    121, 187, 196, 219n.7, 220n.9
Australia, 16, 34, 199, 222n.11
  Durkheim on, 157, 171–2, 176
  Marx on, 94, 101, 221n.11
Anghie, Antony, 7
antiquity/ancient world, 8, 44, 68,
    92
Aravamudan, Srinivas, 11, 15, 30, 38
aristocratic order, 52, 57–61
  caste in, 58–9
  commerce, rise of, 57, 59–61
  localism in, 57, 59–61, 63
    compared with democracy, 63

nobility in, 58–60, 62, 73
centralisation of political power,
    52–3, 60, 64, 71
see also feudalism; Hegel, estate
    society in

Beauvois, Frédérique, 73–4, 76
Berlin Conference, 18, 126, 145, 169,
    180
Berry, Christopher, 39, 42–3
Beaumont, Gustave de, 55–6, 67,
    219n.8, 226n.1
Burke, Edmund, 218n.15

canon, construction of, 15–21
  classical sociology and, 18–20
  Du Bois excluded from, 20–1
  Karl Marx and, 18–20
  social movements and, 19–21
capitalism
  social theory and, 19, 25
  see also Marx; Weber
Catholicism, 11–12, 56, 64, 116,
    122, 146, 154, 170, 173,
    224n.12
China, 7, 9, 80, 125, 139, 169, 193,
    199, 208
civil society, 36, 39, 48, 88, 95–6,
    107, 109, 164–5, 167, 173,
    223n.2
civil war: see wars
climate, 39–40, 94

colonialism
  colour line and, 178–9, 198–201,
    206
  dispossession, 9–11, 13, 24, 31,
    38, 44, 46, 52, 57, 65–7, 79,
    86, 92, 101, 110, 118, 178,
    216n.2, 216n.6, 218n.14,
    218n.14, 221n.15, 227n.9,
    228n.12
  empire distinguished from, 5–6, 25
  enclosure and, 34–5, 38, 92, 101
  migration role of, 10, 13, 69, 79,
    116–17, 181, 223n.4, 220n.9
  settler, 4, 9, 13–14, 16, 35–6, 56–7,
    61, 64, 65–71, 73, 78–9,
    117–18, 121, 125–6, 216n.2,
    217n.3, 220n.10, 220n.14,
    221n.15
  see also labour, forced; plantations;
    slavery
colour line, 22–4, 182–3, 185, 187,
  196, 202, 205
  colonialism and, 178–9, 198–201,
    206
commerce, 4
  enslavement and, 34, 36, 44, 99,
    102, 204
  fur trade, 11, 44, 218n.14
  Royal Charters, 11, 38, 59, 61, 71
  share ownership, 11
  see also East India Company
commercial society
  Durkheim on, 154, 162–5, 167,
    169
  Hegel on, 46, 85–6
  Marx on, 86, 91–3, 102
  stadial theory and, 38, 40–2, 45–6,
    219n.15
  Tocqueville on, 57, 59
commons, 28, 32–4
  see also colonialism; enclosure (of
    land)
commonwealth, 28, 31, 35, 204, 212
Connell, Raewyn, 16–18, 21
contract
  Hobbes on, 28, 30–1
  Locke on, 32–5, 37
  market exchange and, 15, 42–4,
    51, 85, 90–1, 95–100, 121,
    221n.3

Cotesta, Vittorio, 146, 174
Cox, Oliver Cromwell, 204–5,
  228n.14

decolonisation, 21–2, 143
  see also universities, decolonising
Douglass, Frederick, 189–90, 227n.7
Du Bois, W. E. B.
  Atlanta Compromise, 185, 188
  Atlanta Sociological Laboratory,
    184–5, 202
  caste, 181, 190, 202, 204–6
  class, 181, 186–7
    citizenship and, 197, 205
    colonialism and, 194, 200
  colour line, 182–3, 185, 187, 196,
    202, 205
  colonialism and, 178–9,
    198–201, 206
  double consciousness, 176, 185–8
    master–slave relation, 185–6
    social self, 186
    standpoint epistemology, 186–7
    veil, 187
  Dumbarton Oaks Conference,
    199–200
  Freedmen's Bureau, 187, 197
  Jim Crow, 180, 188, 192–3, 196,
    198, 226n.2, 227n.8
  life, 178–80, 226n.2
  Marx, and 186, 194, 205
  NAACP, 179, 191, 198–9, 201
  Philadelphia Negro
    crime, 182–3
    history of African Americans,
      181–2
    segregation, 202
    status in sociology, 183–4,
      227n.4, 227n.5
  reconstruction
    gains of, 187, 192–3
    historiography challenged,
      191–3, 195
    white racial prejudice towards,
      178, 188, 195
  segregation, 23, 178, 180, 183,
    185, 188–90, 192, 201–2,
    216n.5
    universities and, 180, 184, 198,
      202, 216n.5

working within, 198–9, 204
see also Jim Crow
slavery
  abolition of, 178, 180–1,
    188–91, 194–5, 196, 227n.1
  double consciousness and, 185–6
  legacy of, 181, 183, 187–9,
    192–3, 196–8
  Tocqueville and, 178, 183, 193,
    196, 226n.1
  Universal Races Congress, 197,
    198, 200
  Washington and, 188–90, 227n.4
  Weber and, 177, 179, 189
Durkheim, Émile
  Algeria and, 144, 164, 169, 174–5
  Australia and, 157, 171–2, 176
  conservatism, alleged, 141–2,
    223n.1
  Du Bois and, 144, 175–6
  dialectical method in, 147, 150,
    158, 164, 223n.4
  division of labour, 143–4, 154–66,
    173, 224n.14, 225n.18
    anomic, 154, 162–5, 167, 169,
      224n.14
    forced, 163–5
  Dreyfus affair, 146, 170–1,
    225n.22
  family, 155, 159, 162–3, 165, 167
  happiness, 149, 161, 225n.17
  integration, 154, 160, 164, 169
  Jewish question and, 144, 168,
    170, 172–3, 176
  life, 145–7
  moral individualism, 144, 146–9,
    152, 165, 167
  morals, civic and professional
    ethics, 143, 148, 156, 160–2,
    165–7, 225n.23
  normal and pathological, 148–50,
    156, 158, 163–4, 225n.18
  Parsons's interpretation of, 141–2
  patriotism, 145–6, 167–8, 175
  religion
    collective belonging and, 143,
      167, 171, 173
    reality of, 150, 157, 171–2
    secularism and, 143–4, 146, 167,
      171–2, 175

  regulation, 154, 156, 160–1,
    163–6, 225n.18
  rights, 143–4, 165, 167, 169–70,
    172
  secularism, see religion
  socialism, 146–8, 165, 170, 173–4,
    233n.4, 233n.5
  social facts, 151–4, 172
  solidarity, 143–4, 147, 150, 156,
    161, 167, 170–2, 224n.15,
    225n.18
    mechanical, 157, 159–60,
      161–3
    organic, 159–60, 162–3
  stadial, theory, disavowed, 156–7,
    171, 224n.15
  state, 164–70, 173–5
  suicide, 149, 153–4, 160, 163,
    224n.11, 224n.12, 225n.17
  Union for Truth, 174
  war
    Franco-Prussian, 145, 174–5
    First World War, 145–6, 174–6
    Tonkin War, 169

East India Company, 11, 38, 71, 76,
    218n.9
Eisenstadt, Shmuel, 8, 12, 124, 127
empire
  colonialism, distinguished from
    5–6, 25
  nation distinguished from, 7–9, 13,
    126–9, 135–6
  European domination and,
    109–11, 115, 117, 126,
    129–30, 145, 199–200, 206,
    207, 210, 213
  extraction, 8
  premodern, 8
  United States as, 14, 53, 219n.2
enclosure (of land), 33–5, 38, 60, 92,
    101
Engels, Frederick, 93–4, 107, 221n.1,
    221n.6., 223n.6
enlightenment, 4–5, 14, 28, 35, 49,
    170–1, 196, 215
  Scottish, 26, 38–42
Esping-Andersen, Gösta, 106
Eurocentrism, 4, 47, 87, 93, 96, 110,
    137–8, 216n.6

feminism, 1, 19, 217n.1, 227n.6, 228n.13
feudalism, 6–7, 52, 56, 60, 73, 85, 89–90, 92, 101, 167, 207, 211, 219n.6, 222n.13
  see also aristocratic order
Ferguson, Adam, 39–41
Fields, Karen E., 144, 150, 175–6, 207, 214
Filmer, Sir Robert, 27, 32, 217n.7
Frankfurt School, 47, 87, 142, 212
Franklin, Benjamin, 121, 125
Frymer, Paul, 14, 53, 219n.2

Giddens, Anthony, 19–20, 141, 217n.6

Hahn, Steven, 14
Haiti, 50, 54, 71–7, 83, 184, 220n.13
  abolition of slavery in, 72
  reparations paid to France, 73–5
Hansen, Peo, 22, 228n.1
Harris, Abram, 103, 105, 222n.13
Hegel, Georg Friedrich Wilhelm,
  Africa and, 49–50
  critique in, 47
  estate society in, 85, 87–9
  history, philosophy of, 47–8
  master–slave relation, 46–50
  recognition, 48–9
  slavery justified, 49–50
Heilbron, Johan, 4, 39
historiography, 1, 23
Hobbes, Thomas, 26–33, 38, 211, 216n.3, 217n.4
Hume, David, 38, 42–3, 92

ideal types, 15, 56
  see also Weber
India, 9–11, 80, 92–4, 125, 164, 169, 191, 193, 200, 208, 216n.6, 218n.15
  see also East India Company
indenture, 9, 12, 14, 35, 92–4, 214
individualism
  moral, 144, 146–9, 152, 165, 167
  possessive, 28
  utilitarian, 31, 87–8, 144, 147, 149, 160, 170, 223n.6

indigenous people
  colonialism and dispossession of, 9, 11, 14, 216n.2
  Durkheim and, 157, 171–2, 176
  Hegel and, 48–50
  Hobbes and, 24, 29–31, 217n.3
  Locke and, 34–6, 218n.8
  Tocqueville and, 54, 66–8, 220n.9
industry (moral), 29, 40, 42–3, 76, 118, 188
industrial, 4–5, 15, 17, 43, 45, 85, 101, 104, 128, 155, 164, 166, 182, 193, 204, 206
Ireland, 29, 216n.1, 217n.2

James, C. L. R, 71–2, 220n.13
Jones, Robert A., 23, 146, 150

King, Desmond S., 193, 227n.8
knowledge
  historical construction of, 1–2
  intellectual history, approaches to, 23
  reconstruction and, 2, 24
  social movements and, 2, 19–21
Kojève, Alexander, 48–9
Kolchin, Peter, 45, 61, 218n.13

labour
  forced, 5, 9, 12, 24, 34–5, 37–8, 51, 55, 61, 65, 83, 93–4, 101, 118, 164, 216n.2, 221n.5
    see also indenture; slavery
  free, 37, 44, 65, 69, 83, 90, 92–4, 99, 101–2, 104, 106, 110, 213–14
  waged, 33, 37, 43, 45, 94–5, 99, 101, 105, 118, 120
Lebovics, Herman, 34, 37, 125, 218n.8
Lehmann, Jennifer, 142, 162, 223n.1, 225n.19
Lewis, David Levering, 180, 191, 193, 198, 201, 203, 205, 226n.2
Locke, John
  property and labour, 32–4, 37–8
  spoilage, 34–5
  slavery, 35–6
  transportation of convicts, 34–5

Louis Napoleon, 55, 75, 128, 219n.4
Lubasz, Heinz, 85, 89

McAuley, Christopher A., 115,
  118–9, 177, 189
Macpherson, C. B., 28–31, 34, 37–8,
  217n.1
Marx, Karl
  capital–labour relation, 83, 86,
    93–95, 102–3, 110, 118
    accumulation and, 100–1, 103
    dialectical criticism and, 47,
      82–3, 87, 110, 147, 186
  classical political economy and, 96–8
  commodity production and market
    exchange, 95–9
  Eighteenth Brumaire coup, 86
    razzia, in 86
  estate society, 85, 89–92
  Gotha programme, 110
  Hegel, critique of, 85–6, 88–90
  ideology, role of, 106–8
  imperialism, 83, 98, 100, 102
  Jewish question, 173, 221n.1
  life, 84–5
  modes of production,
    capitalist, 95–101
    precapitalist, 40–1, 44, 92, 221n.6
  polarisation of classes in, 83, 99,
    102–3
  poverty, 91–2, 95, 105
  primitive accumulation, 89, 92–3,
    101–2, 222n.12
  proletariat, 83, 85–7, 89, 93, 95,
    100, 104–5, 107–8
  slavery, 83, 92–4, 101–2
  stadial theory in, 92–4
  wage labour
    alienation and, 90–1, 94
    poverty and, 91–2, 95, 104
  welfare state
    colonial patrimony and, 83, 95,
      106, 110
    decommodification and, 106,
      222n.13
  master–slave relation, 26, 37,
    46–50, 83, 135, 195
Meek, Ronald, 40, 44
Mead, George Herbert, 148, 186,
  223n.6

Mehta, Uday Singh, 31, 47, 81,
  218n.15
Millar, James, 38, 43, 45
Mommsen, Wolfgang, 113, 115,
  127–30
Montesquieu, Baron de, 38–40
Morris, Aldon, 23, 177, 185, 189,
  198, 227n.4
Muslims, 144, 173–6, 223n.2
Myrdal, Gunnar,
  American Dilemma, 20, 203–4

nation states
  empires distinguished from, 7–9,
    13, 126–6, 135–6
  nationalism and, 114, 129, 148,
    174, 204
nature, state of
  Hegel on, 45, 48–9
  liberal theory on, 29–31, 33, 36, 38
  state of society and, 29–30, 38, 48,
    211
Nelson, Lynn Hankinson, 1–2
Nisbet, Robert, 4, 17–19

Parsons, Talcott, 18–22, 216n.3
  action theory and, 134–6, 141–2
  Du Bois and, 177, 227n.10
  Durkheim, interpretation of, 141–2
  Marx, interpretation of, 18, 82
  Weber, interpretation of, 113–14,
    120
patriarchal theory, 27, 30
Pedersen, Jean, 174
Pitts, Jennifer, 75, 78–9
plantations, 5, 9, 11–12, 14, 38, 45,
  61–2, 69, 71, 79–80, 83, 94,
  116–17, 164, 189, 194, 196
  see also labour, forced; slavery
Poggi, Gianfranco, 56–7, 126, 150,
  157, 223n.5, 225n.16
postcolonial theory, 3, 14–15, 84, 86,
  131–2, 137, 139, 156, 171
Pradella, Lucia, 102
Protestantism, 4, 11–12, 27, 212,
  220n.12
  Durkheim and, 146, 154, 173,
    224n.12
  Weber and, 115–16, 119–20,
    122–3, 125, 132–3, 135

revolutions
    American, 14, 52, 65, 219n.7
    French, 22, 52, 54, 56, 59, 61,
        72, 77, 84, 145, 170, 195,
        218n.15, 219n.7
    Haitian, 50, 54, 71–5, 77, 83, 181,
        220n.13
    1848, 12, 84, 86
Richter, Melvin, 78–80
Robinson, Cedric, 20, 46, 83, 86

Saint Domingue, see Haiti
Scaff, Lawrence A., 114–15, 118,
    222n.2
Seidman, Steven, 5, 24
settler colonialism, see colonialism
slavery
    social theory and,
        Du Bois on its legacy, 181, 183,
            187–9, 192–3, 196–8
        Hegel, 48–51
        Locke, 34–7
        Marx, 83, 92–4, 101–2
        stadial theory, 43–6
        Tocqueville, 65–70, 74–8
    serfdom compared with, 43–6, 61,
        218n.13
    trade, 9, 15, 34–36, 44–5, 50, 71,
        204, 218n.14
    abolition of, 69, 73–7, 79, 93,
        102, 178, 181, 190, 197, 214,
        226n.1
    wage slavery, 30, 37, 44, 90, 94,
        206
    see also indenture
Smith, Adam, 38, 41–3, 96, 155
Spencer, Herbert
    militant vs industrial society, 15
stadial theory, 10, 26,
    commercial society in, 38, 40–2,
        45–6, 219n.15
    Durkheim, disavowed by, 156–7,
        171
    Enlightenment thought, 38–46,
        217n.2
    Hegel and, 50–1
    Marx and, 92–4
    mode of subsistence in, 41–2, 44, 46
    savages, representations of, 30–1,
        34, 43, 45–6, 49–51

    sociability and, 42–2
    Tocqueville and, 65, 68, 220n.10,
        220n.11, 220n.14
stages of history: see stadial theory
Strenski, Ivan, 146, 155, 164–5, 172,
    223n.2, 223n.4

Tocqueville, Alexis de
    Algeria and, 56–7, 75, 78–80
    aristocratic order, 52, 57–61
        caste in, 58–9
        commerce, rise of, 57, 59–61
        localism in, 57, 59–61, 63
        nobility in, 58–60, 62, 73
        political power, centralised in,
            52–3, 60, 64, 71
    Britain and, 56–7, 60, 71, 75–6
    Haiti and, 54, 71–7
    Choctaw people, removal of, 55,
        56–8
    democratic order
    education in, 63–4
        inheritance, 62
        localism, 63–4
        religion and liberty in, 64
        race prejudice in, 69–71
        social mobility in, 62–3
        spirit of equality in, 57–8, 61, 64
        see also tyranny
    life, 54–6
    slavery
        abolition and reparations, 69,
            71–7, 79
        Algeria, 74–8
        USA, 65–70
    stadial theory and, 65, 68,
        220n.10, 220n.11, 220n.14
    tyranny
        African Americans as a threat to
            democracy, 70, 75
        majority of, 52, 64, 178
        white race over others, 66–7,
            69–71
Turgot, Anne Robert Jacques, 38,
    43–4

universities
    decolonising, 21–2, 131, 137, 209
    segregation and, 23, 180, 184, 198,
        202, 216n.5

Washington, Booker T., 23, 185, 186, 196
    Du Bois and, 188–90, 227n.4
    Weber and, 118
wars
    Civil War
        English, 12, 27, 217n.4
        US, 65, 69, 117, 178, 180, 187, 191–2, 194, 197, 221n.1
    Cold War, 22, 201
    Eighty Years' War, 11
    Franco-Prussian War, 14, 113, 145, 175
    First World War, 113, 117, 145–6, 175–6, 179
    Second World War, 18, 95, 113, 145, 197
    Thirty Years' War, 7, 11
    Tonkin War, 169
Weber, Max
    Africa, 113–18, 120, 122–5
    capitalism
        economic traditionalism and, 116–18, 120, 124
        Franklin Benjamin and, 121, 125
        Protestantism, 122–4
        specificity of, 120–2
        spirit of, 121–2, 124–5
    Catholicism, 116, 112
    China, Chinese, 125, 127, 138–9
    Du Bois and, 115–6
    empire, 113, 115–17, 126, 129–30
    First World War, 113, 117
    Freiburg address, 116, 119, 124
    ideal types
        heuristic role, 56, 131–3
        one-sidedness, 136–7

    perspectivalism and, 131, 136
    pure types and, 134–6
    science, distinguished from theories in, 223n.6
    value relevance and, 119, 134, 138–9
    Jews, 117, 119, 125, 127, 168, 173
    Junkers, 116–17, 128
    life, 113, 115–16
    nationalism, 114, 129
    peasant economy, 116–17, 119, 127
    Poles, 116–20, 125–7
    Protestantism, 115–16, 119–20, 122–4, 125, 132–3, 135
    Prussia, 116–8, 121, 128
    reputation of, 112–5
    state, modern
        empire and, 113, 115, 126–9
        legitimacy of, 115, 125, 127–8, 130
        territorial definition of, 117, 125
    universities, 113–4, 134
    value free social science, 112–13, 129
    Verein für Sozialpolitik, 94, 116, 118–19, 139
        Tuskegee Institute and, 118
Welch, Cheryl, 78–80
Welchman, Jennifer, 36, 218n.10
Westphalia, Treaty of, 7, 12
Wright II, Earl, 184
Wright, Erik Olin, 103

Zimmerman, Andrew, 94, 115, 118, 126–7